Financial Theory and Corporate Policy

FOURTH EDITION

STUDENT SOLUTIONS MANUAL

Thomas E. Copeland   *Managing Director of Corporate Finance*
Monitor Group, Cambridge, Massachusetts

J. Fred Weston   *Professor of Finance Recalled, The Anderson School*
University of California at Los Angeles

Kuldeep Shastri   *Roger S. Ahlbrandt, Sr. Endowed Chair in Finance*
and Professor of Business Administration
Joseph M. Katz Graduate School of Business
University of Pittsburgh

PEARSON
Addison
Wesley

Boston   San Francisco   New York
London   Toronto   Sydney   Tokyo   Singapore   Madrid
Mexico City   Munich   Paris   Cape Town   Hong Kong   Montreal

Contents

Preface

The last forty years have seen a revolution in thought in the field of Finance. The basic questions remain the same. How are real and financial assets valued? Does the market place provide the best price signals for the allocation of scarce resources? What is meant by risk and how can it be incorporated into the decision-making process? Does financing affect value? These will probably always be the central questions. However, the answers to them have changed dramatically in the recent history of Finance. Forty years ago the field was largely descriptive in nature. Students learned about the way things were rather than why they came to be that way. Today the emphasis is on answering the question — why have things come to be the way we observe them? If we understand why then we can hope to understand whether or not it is advisable to change things.

The usual approach to the question of "why" is to build simple mathematical models. Needless to say, mathematics cannot solve every problem, but it does force us to use more precise language and to understand the relationship between assumptions and conclusions. In their efforts to gain better understanding of complex natural phenomena, academicians have adopted more and more complex mathematics. A serious student of Finance must seek prerequisite knowledge in matrix algebra, ordinary calculus, differential equations, stochastic calculus, mathematical programming, probability theory, statistics and econometrics. This bewildering set of applied mathematics makes the best academic journals in Finance practically incomprehensible to the layman. In most articles, he can usually understand the introduction and conclusions, but little more. This has the effect of widening the gap between theory and application. The more scientific and more mathematical Finance becomes the more magical it appears to the layman who would like to understand and use it. We remember a quote from an old Japanese science fiction movie where a monster is about to destroy the world. From the crowd on screen an individual is heard to shout, "Go get a scientist. He'll know what to do!" It was almost as if the scientist was being equated with a magician or witchdoctor. By the way — the movie scientist did know what to do. Unfortunately, this is infrequently the case in the real world.

In order to narrow the gap between the rigorous language in academic Finance journals and the practical business world it is necessary for the academician to translate his logic from mathematics into English. But it is also necessary for the layman to learn a little mathematics. This is already happening. Technical words in English can be found unchanged in almost every language throughout the world. In fact, technical terms are becoming a world language. The words computer, transistor, and car are familiar throughout the globe. In Finance, variance is a precise measure of risk and yet almost everyone has an intuitive grasp for its meaning.

This solutions manual and the textbook which it accompanies represent an effort to bridge the gap between the academic and the layman. The mathematics employed here is at a much lower level than in most academic journals. On the other hand it is at a higher level than that which the layman usually sees. We assume a basic understanding of algebra and simple calculus. We are hoping that the reader will meet us halfway.

Most theory texts in Finance do not have end-of-chapter questions and problems. Notable exceptions were Fama's *Foundations of Finance* and Levy and Sarnat's *Capital Investment and Financial Decisions*. Problem sets are useful because they help the reader to solidify his knowledge with a hands-on approach to learning. Additionally, problems can be used to stretch the reader's understanding of the textbook material by asking a question whose answer cannot be found in the text. Such extrapolative questions ask the student to go beyond simple feedback of something he has just read. The student is asked to combine the elements of what he has learned into something slightly different — a new result. He must think for himself instead of just regurgitating earlier material.

The objective of education is for each student to become his own teacher. This is also the objective of the end-of-chapter problems in our text. Consequently, we highly recommend that the solutions manual be made available to the students as an additional learning aid. Students can order it from the publisher without any restrictions whatsoever. It cannot be effectively employed if kept behind locked doors as an instructor's manual.

We wish to express our thanks to the following for their assistance in the preparation of this solutions manual: Betly Saybolt, and the MBA students at UCLA.

We think the users will agree that we have broken some new ground in our book and in the end-of-chapter problems whose solutions are provided in this manual. If our efforts stimulate you, the user, to other new ideas, we will welcome your suggestions, comments, criticisms and corrections. Any kinds of communications will be welcome.

Thomas E. Copeland
Monitor Groups
Cambridge, MA 02141

Kuldeep Shastri
University of Pittsburgh
Pittsburgh, PA

J. Fred Weston
Anderson Graduate School
of Management
University of California
Los Angeles, CA 90024

Chapter 1
Introduction: Capital Markets, Consumption, and Investment

1. Assume the individual is initially endowed, at point A, with current income of y_0 and end-of-period income of y_1. Using the market rate, the present value of his endowment is his current wealth, W_0:

$$W_0 = y_0 + \frac{y_1}{1 + r_f}$$

The individual will take on investment up to the point where the marginal rate of return on investment

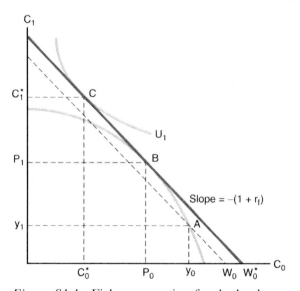

Figure S1.1 Fisher separation for the lender case

equals the market rate of interest at point B. This determines the optimal investment in production (P_0, P_1). Finally, in order to achieve his maximum utility (on indifference curve U_1) the individual will lend (i.e., consume less than P_0) along the capital market line until he reaches point C. At this point his optimal consumption is C_0^*, C_1^* which has a present value of

$$W_0^* = C_0^* + \frac{C_1^*}{1 + r_f}$$

2.

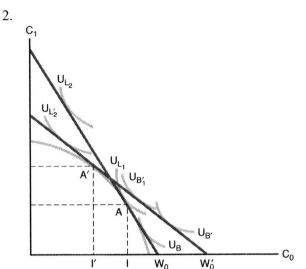

Figure S1.2   An exogenous decline in the interest rate

(a) An exogenous decrease in the interest rate shifts the capital market line from the line through AW_0 to the line through $A'W_0'$. Borrowers originally chose levels of current consumption to the right of A. After the decrease in interest rate, their utility has increased unambiguously from U_B to U_B'. The case for those who were originally lenders is ambiguous. Some individuals who were lenders become borrowers under the new, lower, rate, and experience an increase in utility from U_{L_1} to $U_{B_1'}$. The remaining lenders experience a decrease in utility, from U_{L_2} to $U_{L_2'}$.

(b) Because borrowers and lenders face the same investment opportunity set and choose the same optimal investment (at A before the interest rate decreases and at A' afterward), current wealth is the intercept of the capital market line with the C_0 axis. Originally it is at W_0; then it *increases* to W_0'.

(c) The amount of investment increases from I to I'.

3. Assuming that there are no opportunity costs or spoilage costs associated with storage, then the rate of return from storage is zero. This implies a capital market line with a 45° slope (a slope of minus 1) as shown in Figure S1.3.

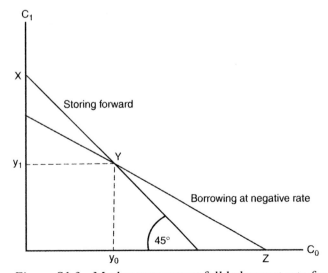

Figure S1.3   Market rate cannot fall below net rate from storage

Also shown is a line with lower absolute slope, which represents a negative borrowing and lending rate. Any rational investor would choose to store forward from his initial endowment (at y_0, y_1) rather than lending (to the left of y_0). He would also prefer to borrow at a negative rate rather than storing backward (i.e., consuming tomorrow's endowment today). These dominant alternatives are represented by the heavy lines in Figure S1.3. However, one of them is not feasible. In order to borrow at a negative rate it is necessary that someone lend at a negative rate. Clearly, no one will be willing to do so because storage at a zero rate of interest is better than lending at a negative rate. Consequently, points along line segment YZ in Figure S1.3 are infeasible. The conclusion is that the market rate of interest cannot fall below the storage rate.

4. Assume that Robinson Crusoe has an endowment of y_0 coconuts now and y_1 coconuts which will mature at the end of the time period. If his time preference is such that he desires to save some of his current consumption and store it, he will do so and move to point A in Figure S1.4. In this case he is storing forward.

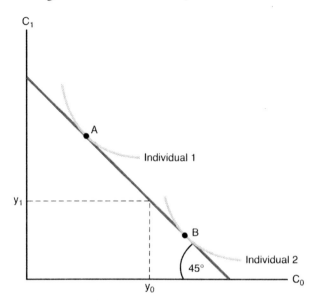

Figure S1.4   Storage as the only investment

On the other hand, if the individual wishes to consume more than his current supply of coconuts in order to move to point B, it may not be possible. If next year's coconut supply does not mature until then, it may be impossible to store coconuts backward. If we were not assuming a Robinson Crusoe economy, then exchange would make it possible to attain point B. An individual who wished to consume more than his current allocation of wealth could contract with other individuals for some of their wealth today in return for some of his future wealth.

5. Figure S1.5 shows a schedule of investments, all of which have the same rate of return, R^*.

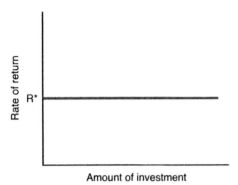

Figure S1.5   All investment projects have the same rate of return

The resultant investment opportunity set is a straight line with slope $-(1 + R^*)$ as shown in Figure S1.6. The marginal rate of substitution between C_0 and C_1 is a constant.

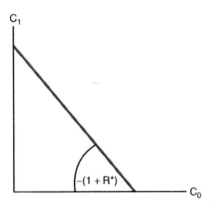

Figure S1.6   Investment opportunity set

6. In order to graph the production opportunity set, first order the investments by their rate of return and sum the total investment required to undertake the first through the ith project. This is done below.

Project	One Plus the Rate of Return	Outlay for the ith Project	Sum of Outlays
D	1.30	$3,000,000	$3,000,000
B	1.20	1,000,000	4,000,000
A	1.08	1,000,000	5,000,000
C	1.04	2,000,000	7,000,000

The production opportunity set plots the relationship between resources utilized today (i.e., consumption foregone along the C_0 axis) and the extra consumption provided at the end of the investment period. For example, if only project D were undertaken then $3 million in current consumption would be foregone in order to receive $1.3 \times$ ($3 million) = $3.9 million in end-of-period consumption. This is graphed below in Figure S1.7.

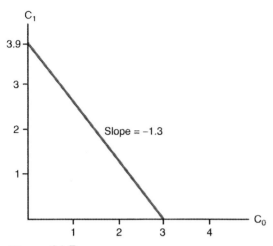

Figure S1.7

If we aggregate all investment opportunities then $7 million in consumption could be foregone and the production opportunity set looks like Figure S1.8. The answer to part b of the question is found by drawing in a line with a slope of -1.1 and finding that it is tangent to point B. Hence the optimal production decision is to undertake projects D and B. The present value of this decision is

$$W_0 = \frac{C_1}{1+r} + C_0$$

$$= \frac{5.1}{1.1} + 3 = \$7.6364 \text{ million}$$

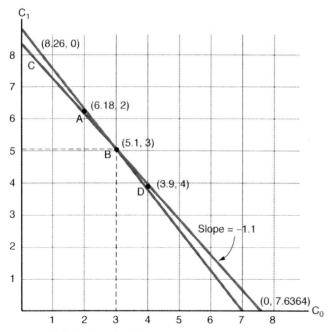

Figure S1.8 Production opportunity set

Chapter 2
Investment Decisions: The Certainty Case

1. (a) Cash flows adjusted for the depreciation tax shelter

Sales = cash inflows	$140,000
Operating costs = cash outflows	100,000
Earnings before depreciation, interest and taxes	40,000
Depreciation (Dep)	10,000
EBIT	30,000
Taxes @ 40%	12,000
Net income	$18,000

Using equation 2-13:

$$CF = (\Delta Rev - \Delta VC)(1 - \tau_c) + \tau_c \Delta dep$$
$$= (140,000 - 100,000)(1 - .4) + .4(10,000) = 28,000$$

Alternatively, equation 2-13a can be used:

$$CF = \Delta NI + \Delta dep + (1 - \tau_c)\Delta\, k_d D$$
$$= 18,000 + 10,000 + (1 - .4)(0) = 28,000$$

(b) Net present value using straight-line depreciation

$$NPV = \sum_{t=1}^{N} \frac{(Rev_t - VC_t)(1 - \tau_c) + \tau_c (dep_t)}{(1 + WACC)^t} - I_0$$

$$= (\text{annual cash inflow})(\text{present value annuity factor} @ 12\%, 10 \text{ years}) - I_0$$

$$= (5.650)(28,000) - 100,000$$

$$= 158,200 - 100,000$$

$$= 58,200$$

2. (a)

Earnings before depreciation, interest and taxes	$22,000
Depreciation (straight-line)	10,000
EBIT	12,000
Taxes @ 40%	4,800
Net income	$7,200

Net present value using straight-line depreciation

$$CF = (\Delta Rev - \Delta VC)(1 - \tau_c) + \tau_c \Delta dep$$
$$= (22,000)(1 - .4) + .4(10,000) = 17,200$$
$$NPV = \sum_{t=1}^{N} \frac{CF_t}{(1 + WACC)^t} - I_0$$
$$= \text{(annual cash flow) (present value annuity factor @ 12\%, 10 years)} - I_0$$
$$= 17,200(5.650) - 100,000$$
$$= 97,180 - 100,000 = -2,820$$

(b) NPV using sum-of-years digits accelerated depreciation

In each year the depreciation allowance is:

$$Dep_t = \frac{T+1-t}{\sum_{i=1}^{T} i} = \frac{T+1-t}{55}, \text{ where } T = 10$$

In each year the cash flows are as given in the table below:

(1) Year	(2) $Rev_t - VC_t$	(3) Dep_t	(4) $(Rev_t - VC_t)(1 - \tau_c) + \tau_c dep$	(5) PV Factor	(6) PV
1	22,000	(10/55)100,000	13,200 + 7,272.72	.893	18,282.14
2	22,000	(9/55)100,000	13,200 + 6,545.45	.797	15,737.12
3	22,000	(8/55)100,000	13,200 + 5,818.18	.712	13,540.94
4	22,000	(7/55)100,000	13,200 + 5,090.91	.636	11,633.02
5	22,000	(6/55)100,000	13,200 + 4,363.64	.567	9,958.58
6	22,000	(5/55)100,000	13,200 + 3,636.36	.507	8,536.03
7	22,000	(4/55)100,000	13,200 + 2,909.09	.452	7,281.31
8	22,000	(3/55)100,000	13,200 + 2,181.82	.404	6,214.26
9	22,000	(2/55)100,000	13,200 + 1,454.54	.361	5,290.29
10	22,000	(1/55)100,000	13,200 + 727.27	.322	4,484.58
					100,958.27

$$NPV = PV \text{ of inflows} - I_0$$
$$NPV = 100,958.27 - 100,000 = 958.27$$

Notice that using accelerated depreciation increases the depreciation tax shield enough to make the project acceptable.

3. Replacement

	Amount before Tax	Amount after Tax	Year	PVIF @ 12%	Present Value
Outflows at t = 0					
Cost of new equipment	$100,000	$100,000	0	1.0	$100,000
Inflows, years 1–8					
Savings from new investment	31,000	18,600	1–8	4.968	92,405
Tax savings on depreciation	12,500	5,000	1–8	4.968	24,840
				Present value of inflows =	$117,245
		Net present value = $117,245 − 100,000 = $17,245			

If the criterion of a positive NPV is used, buy the new machine.

4. Replacement with salvage value

	Amount before Tax	Amount after Tax	Year	PVIF @ 12%	Present Value
Outflows at t = 0					
Investment in new machine	$100,000	$100,000	0	1.00	$100,000
Salvage value of old	−15,000	−15,000	0	1.00	−15,000
Tax loss on sale	−25,000	−10,000	0	1.00	−10,000
				Net cash outlay =	$75,000
Inflows, years 1–8					
Savings from new machine	$31,000	$18,600	1–8	4.968	$92,405
Depreciation saving on new	11,000	4,400	1–8	4.968	21,859
Depreciation lost on old	−5,000	−2,000	1–8	4.968	−9,936
Salvage value of new	12,000	12,000	8	.404	4,848
				Net cash inflows =	$109,176
		Net present value = $109,176 − 75,000 = $34,176			

Using the NPV rule the machine should be replaced.

5. The correct definition of cash flows for capital budgeting purposes (equation 2-13) is:

$$CF = (\Delta Rev - \Delta VC)(1 - \tau_c) + \tau_c \Delta dep$$

In this problem

Rev = revenues. There is no change in revenues.

VC = cash savings from operations = −3,000

τ_c = the tax rate = .4

dep = depreciation = 2,000

Therefore, the annual net cash flows for years one through five are

$$CF = 3,000(1 - .4) + .4(2,000) = 2,600$$

The net present value of the project is

$$NPV = -10,000 + 2,600(2.991) = -2,223.40$$

Therefore, the project should be rejected.

6. The NPV at different positive rates of return is[1]

Discounted Cash Flows				
@ 0%	@ 10%	@ 15%	@ 16%	@ 20%
400	363.64	347.83	344.83	333.33
400	330.58	302.46	297.27	277.78
−1,000	−751.32	−657.52	−640.66	−578.70
−200	−57.10	−7.23	1.44	32.41

Figure S2.1 graphs NPV versus the discount rate. The IRR on this project is approximately 15.8 percent.

At an opportunity cost of capital of 10 percent, the project has a negative NPV; therefore, it should be rejected (even though the IRR is greater than the cost of capital).

This is an interesting example which demonstrates another difficulty with the IRR technique; namely, that it does not consider the order of cash flows.

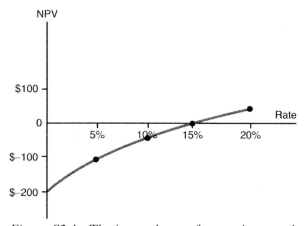

Figure S2.1   The internal rate of return ignores the order of cash flows

---

[1]There is a second IRR at −315.75%, but it has no economic meaning. Note also that the function is undefined at IRR = −1.

7. These are the cash flows for project A which was used as an example in section E of the chapter. We are told that the IRR for these cash flows is −200%. But how is this determined? One way is to graph the NPV for a wide range of interest rates and observe which rates give NPV = 0. These rates are the

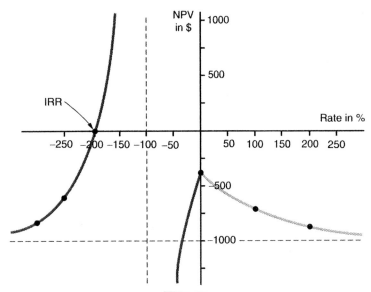

Figure S2.2   An IRR calculation

internal rates of return for the project. Figure S2.2 plots NPV against various discount rates for this particular set of cash flows. By inspection, we see that the IRR is −200%.

8. All of the information about the financing of the project is irrelevant for computation of the correct cash flows for capital budgeting. Sources of financing, as well as their costs, are included in the computation of the cost of capital. Therefore, it would be "double counting" to include financing costs (or the tax changes which they create) in cash flows for capital budgeting purposes.

    The cash flows are:

$$(\Delta \text{Rev} - \Delta \text{VC} - \Delta \text{FCC} - \Delta \text{dep})(1 - \tau_c) + \tau_c \Delta \text{dep} = (200 - (-360) - 0 - 0)(1 - .4) + .4(400)$$
$$= 336 + 160$$
$$= 496$$
$$\text{NPV} = 496 \ (\text{PVIF}_a: 10\%, 3 \text{ years})^* - 1{,}200$$
$$= 496 \ (2.487) - 1{,}200 = 33.55$$

The project should be accepted.

9. First calculate cash flows for capital budgeting purposes:

$$\text{CF}_t = (\Delta \text{Rev}_t - \Delta \text{VC}_t)(1 - \tau_c) + \tau_c \Delta \text{dep}$$
$$= (0 - (-290))(1 - .5) + .5(180)$$
$$= 145 + 90 = 235$$

---

* Note: PVIF$_a$: 10%, 3 years, the discount factor for a three year annuity paid in arrears (at 10%).

Next, calculate the NPV:

$$NPV = \sum_{t=1}^{5} \frac{CF_t}{(1+WACC)^t} - I_0$$

$$= (CF_t) \text{ (present value annuity factor @ 10\%, 5 years)} - I_0$$

$$= 235(3.791) - 900.00$$

$$= 890.89 - 900.00 = -9.12$$

The project should be rejected because it has negative net present value.

10. The net present values are calculated below:

Year	PVIF	A	PV (A)	B	PV (B)	C	PV (C)	A + C	B + C
0	1.000	−1	−1.00	−1	−1.00	−1	−1.00	−2	−2
1	.909	0	0	1	.91	0	0	0	1
2	.826	2	1.65	0	0	0	0	2	0
3	.751	−1	−.75	1	.75	3	2.25	2	4
			−.10		.66		1.25		

$$NPV(A + C) = 1.15$$

$$NPV(B + C) = 1.91$$

Project A has a two-year payback.

Project B has a one-year payback.

Project C has a three-year payback.

Therefore, if projects A and B are mutually exclusive, project B would be preferable according to both capital budgeting techniques.

Project (A + C) has a two-year payback, NPV = $1.15.

Project (B + C) has a three-year payback, NPV = $1.91.

Once Project C is combined with A or B, the results change if we use the payback criterion. Now A + C is preferred. Previously, B was preferred. Because C is an independent choice, it should be irrelevant when considering a choice between A and B. However, with payback, this is not true. Payback violates value additivity. On the other hand, NPV does not. B + C is preferred. Its NPV is simply the sum of the NPV's of B and C separately. Therefore, NPV does obey the value additivity principle.

11. Using the method discussed in section F.3 of this chapter, in the first year the firm invests $5,000 and expects to earn IRR. Therefore, at the end of the first time period, we have

$$5,000(1 + IRR)$$

During the second period the firm borrows from the project at the opportunity cost of capital, k. The amount borrowed is

$$(10,000 - 5,000(1 + IRR))$$

By the end of the second time period this is worth

$$(10,000 - 5,000(1 + \text{IRR}))(1 + k)$$

The firm then lends 3,000 at the end of the second time period:

$$3,000 = (10,000 - 5,000(1 + \text{IRR}))(1.10)$$

Solving for IRR, we have

$$\frac{\frac{3,000}{1.10} - 10,000}{-5,000} - 1 = \text{IRR} = 45.45\%$$

Chapter 3
The Theory of Choice: Utility Theory Given Uncertainty

1. The minimum set of conditions includes

    (a) The five axioms of cardinal utility
    - complete ordering and comparability
    - transitivity
    - strong independence
    - measurability
    - ranking

    (b) Individuals have positive marginal utility of wealth (greed).

    (c) The total utility of wealth increases at a decreasing rate (risk aversion); i.e., $E[U(W)] < U[E(W)]$.

    (d) The probability density function must be a normal (or two parameter) distribution.

2. As shown in Figure 3.6, a risk lover has positive marginal utility of wealth, $MU(W) > 0$, which increases with increasing wealth, $dMU(W)/dW > 0$. In order to know the shape of a risk-lover's indifference curve, we need to know the marginal rate of substitution between return and risk. To do so, look at equation 3.19:

$$\frac{dE}{d\sigma} = \frac{-\int U'(E + \sigma\tilde{Z})Zf(Z)dZ}{\int U'(E + \sigma\tilde{Z})f(Z)dZ} \tag{3.19}$$

The denominator must be positive because marginal utility, $U'(E + \sigma Z)$, is positive and because the frequency, $f(Z)$, of any level of wealth is positive. In order to see that the integral in the numerator is positive, look at Figure S3.1 on the following page.

The marginal utility of positive returns, $+Z$, is always higher than the marginal utility of equally likely (i.e., the same $f(Z)$) negative returns, $-Z$. Therefore, when all equally likely returns are multiplied by their marginal utilities, matched, and summed, the result must be positive. Since the integral in the numerator is preceded by a minus sign, the entire numerator is negative and the marginal rate of substitution between risk and return for a risk lover is negative. This leads to indifference curves like those shown in Figure S3.2.

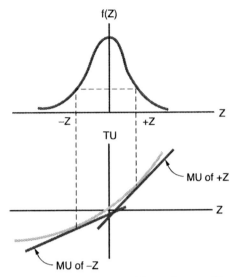

Figure S3.1   Total utility of normally distributed returns for a risk lover

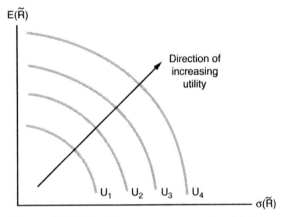

Figure S3.2   Indifference curves of a risk lover

3. (a)

$$E[U(W)] = .5\ln(4,000) + .5\ln(6,000)$$
$$= .5(8.29405) + .5(8.699515)$$
$$= 8.4967825$$
$$e^{\ln W} = W$$
$$e^{8.4967825} = \$4,898.98 = W$$

Therefore, the individual would be indifferent between the gamble and \$4,898.98 for sure. This amounts to a risk premium of \$101.02. Therefore, he would not buy insurance for \$125.

(b) The second gamble, given his first loss, is \$4,000 plus or minus \$1,000. Its expected utility is

$$E[U(W)] = .5\ln(3,000) + .5\ln(5,000)$$
$$= .5(8.006368) + .5(8.517193) = 8.26178$$
$$e^{\ln W} = e^{8.26178} = \$3,872.98 = W$$

Now the individual would be willing to pay up to \$127.02 for insurance. Since insurance costs only \$125, he will buy it.

4. Because $1,000 is a large change in wealth relative to $10,000, we can use the concept of risk aversion in the large (Markowitz). The expected utility of the gamble is

$$E(U(9,000,11,000;\ .5)) = .5\,U(9,000) + .5\,U(11,000)$$
$$= .5\ \ln 9,000 + .5\ \ln 11,000$$
$$= .5(9.10498) + .5(9.30565)$$
$$= 4.55249 + 4.652825$$
$$= 9.205315$$

The level of wealth which has the same utility is

$$\ln W = 9.205315$$
$$W = e^{9.205315} = \$9,949.87$$

Therefore, the individual would be willing to pay up to

$$\$10,000 - 9,949.87 = \$50.13$$

in order to avoid the risk involved in a fifty-fifty chance of winning or losing $1,000.
If current wealth is $1,000,000, the expected utility of the gamble is

$$E(U(999,000,\ 1,001,000;\ .5))$$
$$= .5\ln\ 999,000 + .5\ln 1,001,000$$
$$= .5(13.81451) + .5(13.81651)$$
$$= 13.81551$$

The level of wealth with the same utility is

$$\ln W = 13.81551$$
$$W = e^{13.81551} = \$999,999.47$$

Therefore, the individual would be willing to pay $1,000,000.00 - 999,999.47 = \$0.53$ to avoid the gamble.

5. (a) The utility function is graphed in Figure S3.3.

$$U(W) = -e^{-aW}$$

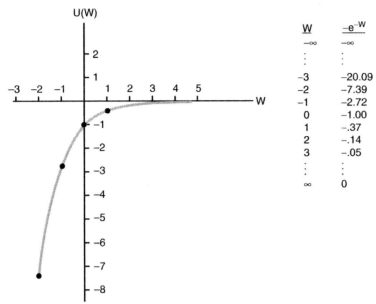

W	$-e^{-W}$
$-\infty$	$-\infty$
$\vdots$	$\vdots$
-3	-20.09
-2	-7.39
-1	-2.72
0	-1.00
1	$-.37$
2	$-.14$
3	$-.05$
$\vdots$	$\vdots$
∞	0

Figure S3.3   Negative exponential utility function

The graph above assumes a = 1. For any other value of a > 0, the utility function will be a monotonic transformation of the above curve.

(b) Marginal utility is the first derivative with respect to W.

$$U'(W) = \frac{dU(W)}{dW} = -(-a)e^{-aW} > 0$$

Therefore, marginal utility is positive. This can also be seen in Figure S3.3 because the slope of a line tangent to the utility function is always positive, regardless of the level of wealth.

Risk aversion is the rate of change in marginal utility.

$$U''(W) = \frac{dMU(W)}{dW} = a(-a)e^{-aW} = -a^2 e^{-aW} < 0$$

Therefore, the utility function is concave and it exhibits risk aversion.

(c) Absolute risk aversion, as defined by Pratt-Arrow, is

$$ARA = -\frac{U''(W)}{U'(W)}$$

$$ARA = -\frac{-a^2 e^{-aW}}{ae^{-aW}} = a$$

Therefore, the function does not exhibit decreasing absolute risk aversion. Instead it has constant absolute risk aversion.

(d) Relative risk aversion is equal to

$$RRA = W(ARA) = -W\frac{U''(W)}{U'(W)}$$

$$= Wa$$

Therefore, in this case relative risk aversion is not constant. It increases with wealth.

6. Friedman and Savage [1948] show that it is possible to explain both gambling and insurance if an individual has a utility function such as that shown in Figure S3.4. The individual is risk averse to decreases in wealth because his utility function is concave below his current wealth. Therefore, he will be willing to buy insurance against losses. At the same time he will be willing to buy a lottery ticket which offers him a (small) probability of enormous gains in wealth because his utility function is convex above his current wealth.

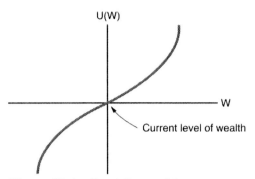

Figure S3.4   Gambling and insurance

7.   We are given that $A > B > C > D$

Also, we know that $U(A) + U(D) = U(B) + U(C)$

Transposing, we have $U(A) - U(B) = U(C) - U(D)$ (3.1)

Assuming the individual is risk-averse, then

$$\frac{\partial U}{\partial W} > 0 \quad \text{and} \quad \frac{\partial^2 U}{\partial W^2} < 0 \tag{3.2}$$

Therefore, from (1) and (2) we know that

$$\frac{U(A) - U(B)}{A - B} < \frac{U(C) - U(D)}{C - D} \tag{3.3}$$

Using equation (3.1), equation (3.3) becomes

$$\frac{1}{A - B} < \frac{1}{C - D}$$

$$A - B > C - D$$

$$A + D > C + B$$

$$\frac{1}{2}A + \frac{1}{2}D > \frac{1}{2}C + \frac{1}{2}B$$

$$U\left[\frac{1}{2}(A) + \frac{1}{2}(D)\right] > U\left[\frac{1}{2}(C) + \frac{1}{2}(B)\right]$$

In general, risk averse individuals will experience decreasing utility as the variance of outcomes increases, but the utility of (1/2)B + (1/2)C is the utility of an expected outcome, an average.

8. First, we have to compute the expected utility of the individual's risk.

$$E(U(W)) = \sum p_i U(W_i)$$
$$= .1U(1) + .1U(50,000) + .8U(100,000)$$
$$= .1(0) + .1(10.81978) + .8(11.51293)$$
$$= 10.292322$$

Next, what level of wealth would make him indifferent to the risk?

$$\ln W = 10.292322$$
$$W = e^{10.292322}$$
$$W = 29,505$$

The maximum insurance premium is

$$\text{Risk premium} = E(W) - \text{certainty equivalent}$$
$$= \$85,000.1 - \$29,505$$
$$= \$55,495.1$$

9. The utility function is

$$U(W) = -W^{-1}$$

Therefore, the level of wealth corresponding to any utility is

$$W = -(U(W))^{-1}$$

Therefore, the certainty equivalent wealth for a gamble of $\pm 1,000$ is $\overline{W}$.

$$\overline{W} = -[.5(-(W+1,000)^{-1}) + .5(-(W-1,000)^{-1})]^{-1}$$

The point of indifference will occur where your current level of wealth, W, minus the certainty equivalent level of wealth for the gamble is just equal to the cost of the insurance, $500.

Thus, we have the condition

$$W - \overline{W} = 500$$

$$W - \left[-\cfrac{1}{.5\cfrac{-1}{W+1,000} + .5\cfrac{-1}{W-1,000}} \right] = 500$$

$$W - \left[\cfrac{-1}{\cfrac{-W}{W^2 = 1,000,000}} \right] = 500$$

$$W + \left[\cfrac{-W^2 - 1,000,000}{-W} \right] = 500$$

$$W^2 - W^2 + 1,000,000 = 500W$$

$$W = 2,000$$

Therefore, if your current level of wealth is $2,000, you will be indifferent. Below that level of wealth you will pay for the insurance while for higher levels of wealth you will not.

10. Table S3.1 shows the payoffs, expected payoffs, and utility of payoffs for n consecutive heads.

Table S3.1

Number of Consecutive Heads = N	Probability $= (1/2)^{n+1}$	Payoff $= 2^N$	E(Payoff)	U(Payoff)	E U(Payoff)
0	1/2	1	$.50	ln 1 = .000	.000
1	1/4	2	.50	ln 2 = .693	.173
2	1/8	4	.50	ln 4 = 1.386	.173
3	1/16	8	.50	ln 8 = 2.079	.130
⋮	⋮	⋮	⋮	⋮	⋮
N	$(1/2)^{N+1}$	2^N	.50	$\ln 2^N = N \ln 2$	$\dfrac{N \ln 2}{2^{N+1}} = 0$

The gamble has a .5 probability of ending after the first coin flip (i.e., no heads), a $(.5)^2$ probability of ending after the second flip (one head and one tail), and so on. The expected payoff of the gamble is the sum of the expected payoffs (column four), which is infinite. However, no one has ever paid an infinite amount to accept the gamble. The reason is that people are usually risk averse. Consequently, they would be willing to pay an amount whose utility is equal to the expected utility of the gamble. The expected utility of the gamble is

$$E(U) = \sum_{i=0}^{N} (\tfrac{1}{2})^{i+1} \ln 2^i$$

$$E(U) = \tfrac{1}{2} \sum_{i=0}^{N} (\tfrac{1}{2})^i \, i \ln 2$$

$$E(U) = \tfrac{1}{2} \ln 2 \sum_{i=0}^{N} \frac{i}{2^i}$$

Proof that $\displaystyle\sum_{i=0}^{\infty} \frac{i}{2^i} = 2$ follows:

First, note that the infinite series can be partitioned as follows:

$$\sum_{i=0}^{\infty} \frac{i}{2^i} = \sum_{i=0}^{\infty} \frac{1+i-1}{2^i} = \sum_{i=0}^{\infty} \frac{1}{2^i} + \sum_{i=0}^{\infty} \frac{i-1}{2^i}$$

Evaluating the first of the two terms in the above expression, we have

$$\sum_{i=0}^{\infty} \frac{1}{2^i} = 1 + \tfrac{1}{2} + \tfrac{1}{4} + \frac{1}{8} + \cdots$$

$$= 1 + \frac{1/2}{1 - 1/2} = 2$$

Evaluating the second term, we have

$$\sum_{i=0}^{\infty}\frac{i-1}{2^i}=-1+0+\frac{1}{4}+\frac{2}{8}+\frac{3}{16}+\frac{4}{32}+\cdots$$

The above series can be expanded as

$$-1 \qquad\qquad\qquad\qquad =-1$$

$$\frac{1}{4}+\frac{1}{8}+\frac{1}{16}+\frac{1}{32}+\cdots=\frac{1}{2}$$

$$\frac{1}{8}+\frac{1}{16}+\frac{1}{32}+\cdots=\frac{1}{4}$$

$$\frac{1}{16}+\frac{1}{32}+\cdots=\frac{1}{8}$$

$$\frac{1}{32}+\cdots=\frac{1}{16}$$

$$\vdots$$

Therefore, we have

$$\sum_{i=0}^{\infty}\frac{i-1}{2^i}=-1+\frac{1}{2}+\frac{1}{4}+\frac{1}{8}+\frac{1}{16}+\cdots$$

$$\sum_{i=0}^{\infty}\frac{i-1}{2^i}=-1+1=0$$

Adding the two terms, we have the desired proof that

$$\sum_{i=0}^{\infty}\frac{i}{2^i}=\sum_{i=0}^{\infty}\frac{1}{2^i}+\sum_{i=0}^{\infty}\frac{i-1}{2^i}=2+0=2$$

Consequently, we have

$$E(U)\ =\ 1/2\ \ln 2\sum_{i=0}^{N}\frac{i}{2^i}\ =\ \ln 2,\ \text{since}\ \sum_{i=0}^{N}\frac{i}{2^i}\ =\ 2$$

If the expected utility of wealth is ln2, the corresponding level of wealth is

$$U(W)=\ln 2$$

$$e^{\ln 2}=W=\$2$$

Therefore, an individual with a logarithmic utility function will pay \$2 for the gamble.

11. (a) First calculate AVL from the *insurer's* viewpoint, since the insurer sets the premiums.

$$AVL_1\ (\$30{,}000\ \text{insurance})=0(.98)+5{,}000(.01)+10{,}000(.005)+30{,}000(.005)$$

$$=\$250$$

$$AVL_2\ (\$40{,}000\ \text{insurance})=0(.98)+5{,}000(.01)+10{,}000(.005)+40{,}000(.005)$$

$$=\$300$$

$$AVL_3\ (\$50{,}000\ \text{insurance})=0(.98)+5{,}000(.01)+10{,}000(.005)+50{,}000(.005)$$

$$=\$350$$

We can now calculate the premium for each amount of coverage:

Amount of Insurance	Premium
$30,000	30 + 250 = $280
$40,000	27 + 300 = $327
$50,000	24 + 350 = $374

Next, calculate the insuree's ending wealth and utility of wealth in all contingencies (states). Assume he earns 7 percent on savings and that premiums are paid at the beginning of the year. The utility of each ending wealth can be found from the utility function $U(W) = \ln W$. (See Table S3.2a.)

Finally, find the expected utility of wealth for each amount of insurance,

$$E(U(W)) = \sum_i P_i\ U(W_i)$$

and choose the amount of insurance which yields the highest expected utility.

Table S3.2a   Contingency Values Of Wealth And Utility of Wealth (Savings = $20,000)

	End-of-Period Wealth (in $10,000's)	Utility of Wealth $U(W) = \ln W$
With no insurance		
No loss (P = .98)	5 + 2(1.07) = 7.14	1.9657
$5,000 loss (P = .01)	5 + 2.14 − .5 = 6.64	1.8931
$10,000 loss (P = .005)	5 + 2.14 − 1.0 = 6.14	1.8148
$50,000 loss (P = .005)	5 + 2.14 − 5.0 = 2.14	0.7608
With $30,000 insurance		
No loss (P = .995)	5 + 2.14 − .0280(1.07) ≅ 7.11	1.9615
$20,000 loss (P = .005)	5 + 2.14 − .03 − 2 ≅ 5.11	1.6312
With $40,000 insurance		
No loss (P = .995)	5 + 2.14 − .0327(1.07) ≅ 7.105	1.9608
$10,000 loss (P = .005)	5 + 2.14 − .035 − 1.0 ≅ 6.105	1.8091
With $50,000 insurance		
No loss (P = 1.0)	5 + 2.14 − .0374(1.07) ≅ 7.10	1.9601

With no Insurance: $E(U(W)) = 1.9657(.98) + 1.8931(.01) + 1.8148(.005)$
$+ 0.7608(.005)$

$= 1.9582$

With $30,000 insurance: $E(U(W)) = 1.9615(.995) + 1.6312(.005)$

$= 1.9598$

With $40,000 insurance: $E(U(W)) = 1.9608(.995) + 1.8091(.005)$

$= 1.9600$

With $50,000 insurance: $E(U(W)) = 1.9601$

Therefore, the optimal insurance for Mr. Casadesus is $50,000, given his utility function.

Table S3.2b   Contingency Values of Wealth and Utility of Wealth(Savings = $320,000)

	End-of-Period Wealth (in $10,000's)	Utility of Wealth U(W) = ln W (Wealth in $100,000's)
With no insurance		
No loss (P = .98)	5 + 32.00(1.07) = 39.24	1.3671
$5,000 loss (P = .01)	5 + 34.24 − .5 = 38.74	1.3543
$10,000 loss (P = .005)	5 + 34.24 − 1.0 = 38.24	1.3413
$50,000 loss (P = .005)	5 + 34.24 − 5.0 = 34.24	1.2308
With $30,000 insurance		
No loss (P = .995)	5 + 34.24 − .028(1.07) ≅ 39.21	1.3663
$20,000 loss (P = .005)	5 + 34.24 − .03 − 2 ≅ 37.21	1.3140
With $40,000 insurance		
No loss (P = .995)	5 + 34.24 − .0327(1.07) ≅ 39.205	1.3662
$10,000 loss (P = .005)	5 + 34.24 − .035 − 1.0 ≅ 38.205	1.3404
With $50,000 insurance		
No loss (P = 1.0)	5 + 34.24 − .0374(1.07) ≅ 39.20	1.3661

(b) Follow the same procedure as in part a), only with $320,000 in savings instead of $20,000. (See Table S3.2b above for these calculations.)

With no Insurance: $E(U(W)) = .98(1.3671) + .01(1.3543)$
$$+ .005(1.3413) + .005(1.2308)$$
$$= 1.366162$$

With $30,000 insurance: $E(U(W)) = .995(1.3663) + .005\,(1.3140)$
$$= 1.366038$$

With $40,000 insurance: $E(U(W)) = .995(1.3662) + .005(1.3404)$
$$= 1.366071$$

With $50,000 insurance: $E(U(W)) = (1)1.366092 = 1.366092$

The optimal amount of insurance in this case is no insurance at all. Although the numbers are close with logarithmic utility, the analysis illustrates that a relatively wealthy individual may choose no insurance, while a less wealthy individual may choose maximum coverage.

(c) The end-of-period wealth for all contingencies has been calculated in part a), so we can calculate the expected utilities for each amount of insurance directly.

With no insurance:

$$E\,(U(W)) = .98(U(71.4)) + .01(U(66.4)) + .005(U(61.4)) + .005U(21.4)$$
$$= -.98(200/71.4) - .01(200/66.4) - .005(200/61.4) - .005(200/21.4)$$
$$= -2.745 - .030 - .016 - .047$$
$$= -2.838$$

With $30,000 insurance:

$$E(U(W)) = .995(U(71.1)) + .005(U(51.1))$$
$$= -.995\,(200/71.1) - .005(200/51.1)$$
$$= -2.799 - .020$$
$$= -2.819$$

With $40,000 insurance:

$$E(U(W)) = .995(U(71.05) + .005(U(61.05))$$
$$= -.995(200/71.05) - .005(200/61.05)$$
$$= -2.8008 - .0164$$
$$= -2.8172$$

With $50,000 insurance:

$$E(U(W)) = (1)(-200/71) = -2.8169$$

Hence, with this utility function, Mr. Casadesus would renew his policy for $50,000.

Properties of this utility function, $U(W) = -200,000W^{-1}$:

$$MU_W = 200,000W^{-2} > 0 \qquad \text{nonsatiation}$$

$$MU'_W = -400,000W^{-3} < 0 \qquad \text{risk aversion}$$

$$ARA = \frac{-MU'_W}{MU_W} = 2W^{-1} > 0$$

$$\frac{\partial ARA}{\partial W} = -2W^{-2} < 0 \qquad \text{decreasing absolute risk aversion}$$

$$RRA = W(ARA) = 2 > 0$$

$$\frac{\partial RRA}{\partial W} = 0 \qquad \text{constant relative risk aversion}$$

Since the individual has decreasing absolute risk aversion, as his savings account is increased he prefers to bear greater and greater amounts of risk. Eventually, once his wealth is large enough, he would prefer not to take out any insurance. To see this, make his savings account = $400,000.

12. Because returns are normally distributed, the mean and variance are the only relevant parameters.

Case 1

(a) Second order dominance—B dominates A because it has lower variance and the same mean.

(b) First order dominance—There is no dominance because the cumulative probability functions cross.

Case 2

(a) Second order dominance—A dominates B because it has a higher mean while they both have the same variance.

(b) First order dominance—A dominates B because its cumulative probability is less than that of B. It lies to the right of B.

Case 3

(a) Second order dominance—There is no dominance because although A has a lower variance it also has a lower mean.

(b) First order dominance—Given normal distributions, it is not possible for B to dominate A according to the first order criterion. Figure S3.5 shows an example.

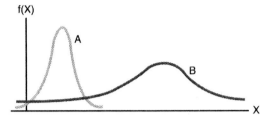

Figure S3.5   First order dominance not possible

13. (a)

Prob X	X	$p_i X_i$	$X_i - E(X)$	$p_i(X_i - E(X))^2$	
.1	−10	−1.0	−16.4	.1(268.96)	= 26.896
.4	5	2.0	−1.4	.4(1.96)	= .784
.3	10	3.0	3.6	.3(12.96)	= 3.888
.2	12	2.4	5.6	.2(31.36)	= 6.272
		E(X) = 6.4		var (X) = 37.840	

Prob Y	Y	$p_i Y_i$	$Y_i - E(Y)$	$p_i(Y_i - E(Y))^2$	
.2	2	.4	−3.7	.2(13.69)	= 2.738
.5	3	1.5	−2.7	.5(7.29)	= 3.645
.2	4	.8	−1.7	.2(2.89)	= .578
.1	30	3.0	24.3	.1(590.49)	= 59.049
		E(Y) = 5.7		var(Y) = 66.010	

X is clearly preferred by *any* risk averse individual whose utility function is based on mean and variance, because X has a higher mean and a lower variance than Y, as shown in Figure S3.6.

(b) Second order stochastic dominance may be tested as shown in Table S3.3 on the following page. Because $\Sigma(F - G)$ is not less than (or greater than) zero for all outcomes, there is no second order dominance.

Table S3.3

Outcome	Prob(X)	Prob(Y)	$\Sigma P_x = F$	$\Sigma P_y = G$	F − G	Σ (F − G)
−10	.1	0	.1	0	.1	.1
−9	0	0	.1	0	.1	.2
−8	0	0	.1	0	.1	.3
−7	0	0	.1	0	.1	.4
−6	0	0	.1	0	.1	.5
−5	0	0	.1	0	.1	.6
−4	0	0	.1	0	.1	.7
−3	0	0	.1	0	.1	.8
−2	0	0	.1	0	.1	.9
−1	0	0	.1	0	.1	1.0
0	0	0	.1	0	.1	1.1
1	0	0	.1	0	.1	1.2
2	0	.2	.1	.2	−.1	1.1
3	0	.5	.1	.7	−.6	.5
4	0	.2	.1	.9	−.8	−.3
5	.4	0	.5	.9	−.4	−.7
6	0	0	.5	.9	−.4	−1.1
7	0	0	.5	.9	−.4	−1.5
8	0	0	.5	.9	−.4	−1.9
9	0	0	.5	.9	−.4	−2.3
10	.3	0	.8	.9	−.1	−2.4
11	0	0	.8	.9	−.1	−2.5
12	.2	0	1.0	.9	.1	−2.4
13	0	0	1.0	.9	.1	−2.3
14	0	0	1.0	.9	.1	−2.2
15	0	0	1.0	.9	.1	−2.1
16	0	0	1.0	.9	.1	−1.9
17	0	0	1.0	.9	.1	−1.8
18	0	0	1.0	.9	.1	−1.7
19	0	0	1.0	.9	.1	−1.6
20	0	0	1.0	.9	.1	−1.5
21	0	0	1.0	.9	.1	−1.4
22	0	0	1.0	.9	.1	−1.3
23	0	0	1.0	.9	.1	−1.2
24	0	0	1.0	.9	.1	−1.1
25	0	0	1.0	.9	.1	−1.0
26	0	0	1.0	.9	.1	−.9
27	0	0	1.0	.9	.1	−.8
28	0	0	1.0	.9	.1	−.7
29	0	0	1.0	.9	.1	−.6
30	0	.1	1.0	1.0	0	−.6
	1.0	1.0				

Because Σ (F − G) is not less than (or greater than) zero for all outcomes, there is no second order dominance.

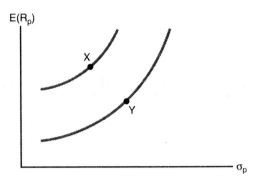

Figure S3.6   Asset X is preferred by mean-variance risk averters

14. (a) Table S3.4 shows the calculations.

Table S3.4

p_i	Co. A	Co. B	$p_i A_i$	$p_i[A - E(A)]^2$	$p_i B_i$	$p_i[B - E(B)]^2$
.1	0	−.50	0	.144	−.05	.4000
.2	.50	−.25	.10	.098	−.05	.6125
.4	1.00	1.50	.40	.016	.60	0
.2	2.00	3.00	.40	.128	.60	.4500
.1	3.00	4.00	.30	.324	.40	.6250
			1.20	.710	1.50	2.0875

$$E(A) = 1.20, \quad \sigma_A = .84$$
$$E(B) = 1.50, \quad \sigma_B = 1.44$$

(b) Figure S3.7 shows that a risk averse investor with indifference curves like #1 will prefer A, while a less risk averse investor (#2) will prefer B, which has higher return and higher variance.

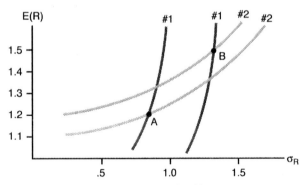

Figure S3.7   Risk-return tradeoffs

(c) The second order dominance criterion is calculated in Table S3.5 on the following page.

15. (a) False. Compare the normally distributed variables in Figure S3.8 below. Using second order stochastic dominance, A dominates B because they have the same mean, but A has lower variance. But there is no first order stochastic dominance because they have the same mean and hence the cumulative probability distributions cross.

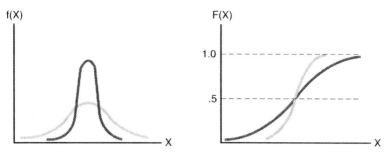

Figure S3.8   First order stochastic dominance does not obtain

(b) False. Consider the following counterexample.

Table S3.5   (Problem 3.14) Second Order Stochastic Dominance

Return	Prob(A)	Prob(B)	F(A)	G(B)	F − G	Σ (F − G)
−.50	0	.1	0	.1	−.1	−.1
−.25	0	.2	0	.3	−.3	−.4
0	.1	0	.1	.3	−.2	−.6
.25	0	0	.1	.3	−.2	−.8
.50	.2	0	.3	.3	0	−.8
.75	0	0	.3	.3	0	−.8
1.00	.4	0	.7	.3	.4	−.4
1.25	0	0	.7	.3	.4	0
1.50	0	.4	.7	.7	0	0
1.75	0	0	.7	.7	0	0
2.00	.2	0	.9	.7	.2	.2
2.25	0	0	.9	.7	.2	.4
2.50	0	0	.9	.7	.2	.6
2.75	0	0	.9	.7	.2	.8
3.00	.1	.2	1.0	.9	.1	.9
3.25	0	0	1.0	.9	.1	1.0
3.50	0	0	1.0	.9	.1	1.1
3.75	0	0	1.0	.9	.1	1.2
4.00	0	.1	1.0	1.0	0	1.2
	1.0	1.0				

Because Σ (F − G) is not always the same sign for every return, there is no second order stochastic dominance in this case.

Payoff	Prob (A)	Prob (B)	F (A)	G (B)	G (B) − F(A)
$1	0	.3	0	.3	.3
$2	.5	.1	.5	.4	−.1
$3	.5	.3	1.0	.7	−.3
$4	0	.3	1.0	1.0	0
	1.0	1.0			

E(A) = $2.50,   var(A) = $.25 squared

E(B) = $2.60,   var(B) = $1.44 squared

The cumulative probability distributions cross, and there is no first order dominance.

(c) False. A risk neutral investor has a linear utility function; hence he will always choose the set of returns which has the highest mean.

(d) True. Utility functions which have positive marginal utility and risk aversion are concave. Second order stochastic dominance is equivalent to maximizing expected utility for risk averse investors.

16. From the point of view of shareholders, their payoffs are

Project 1		Project 2	
Probability	**Payoff**	**Probability**	**Payoff**
.2	0	.4	0
.6	0	.2	0
.2	0	.4	2,000

Using either first order or second order stochastic dominance, Project 2 clearly dominates Project 1.

If there were not limited liability, shareholder payoffs would be the following:

Project 1		Project 2	
Probability	**Payoff**	**Probability**	**Payoff**
.2	−4000	.4	−8000
.6	−3000	.2	−3000
.2	−2000	.4	2,000

In this case shareholders would be obligated to make debt payments from their personal wealth when corporate funds are inadequate, and project 2 is no longer stochastically dominant.

17. (a) The first widow is assumed to maximize expected utility, but her tastes for risk are not clear. Hence, first order stochastic dominance is the appropriate selection criterion.

$$E(A) = 6.2 \qquad E(D) = 6.2$$
$$E(B) = 6.0 \qquad E(E) = 6.2$$
$$E(C) = 6.0 \qquad E(F) = 6.1$$

One property of FSD is that $E(X) > E(Y)$ if X is to dominate Y. Therefore, the only trusts which might be inferior by FSD are B, C, and F. The second property of FSD is a cumulative probability $F(X)$ that never crosses but is at least sometimes to the right of $G(Y)$. As Figure S3.9 shows, A > C and D > F, so the feasible set of trusts for investment is A, B, D, E.

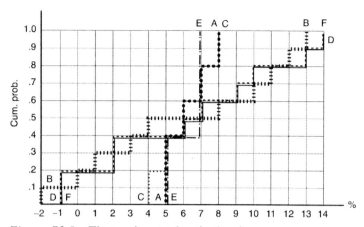

Figure S3.9   First order stochastic dominance

(b) The second widow is clearly risk averse, so second order stochastic dominance is the appropriate selection criterion. Since C and F are eliminated by FSD, they are also inferior by SSD. The pairwise comparisons of the remaining four funds, $\Sigma(F(X) - G(Y))$ are presented in Table S3.6 on the following page and graphed in Figure S3.10. If the sum of cumulative differences crosses the horizontal axis, as in the comparison of B and D, there is no second order stochastic dominance.

By SSD, E > A, E > B, and E > D, so the optimal investment is E.

Table S3.6   Second Order Stochastic Dominance

Ret.	P(A)*	P(B)	P(D)	P(E)	SSD** (BA)	SSD (DA)	SSD (EA)	SSD (DB)	SSD (EB)	SSD (ED)
−2	0	.1	0	0	.1	0	0	−.1	−.1	0
−1	0	.1	.2	0	.2	.2	0	0	−.2	−.2
0	0	.2	.2	0	.4	.4	0	0	−.4	−.4
1	0	.3	.2	0	.7	.6	0	−.1	−.7	−.6
2	0	.3	.4	0	1.0	1.0	0	0	−1.0	−1.0
3	0	.4	.4	0	1.4	1.4	0	0	−1.4	−1.4
4	0	.5	.4	0	1.9	1.8	0	−.1	−1.9	−1.8
5	.4	.5	.4	.4	2.0	1.8	0	−.2	−2.0	−1.8
6	.6	.5	.5	.4	1.9	1.7	−.2	−.2	−2.1	−1.9
7	.8	.5	.6	1.0	1.6	1.5	0	−.1	−1.6	−1.5
8	1.0	.6	.6	1.0	1.2	1.1	0	−.1	−1.2	−1.1
9	1.0	.6	.7	1.0	.8	.8	0	0	−.8	−.8
10	1.0	.7	.8	1.0	.5	.6	0	.1	−.5	−.6
11	1.0	.8	.8	1.0	.3	.4	0	.1	−.3	−.4
12	1.0	.9	.8	1.0	.2	.2	0	0	−.2	−.2
13	1.0	1.0	.8	1.0	.2	0	0	−.2	−.2	0
14	1.0	1.0	1.0	1.0	.2	0	0	−.2	−.2	0
					A > B	A > D	A < E	no 2nd order dominance	B < E	D < E

* cumulative probability

** SSD calculated according to $\Sigma (F(X) - G(Y))$ where $F(X)$ = cumulative probability of X and $G(Y)$ = cumulative probability of Y.

18. (a) Mean-variance ranking may not be appropriate because we do not know that the trust returns have a two-parameter distribution (e.g., normal).

To dominate Y, X must have higher or equal mean and lower variance than Y, or higher mean and lower or equal variance. Means and variances of the six portfolios are shown in Table S3.7. By mean-variance criteria, E > A, B, C, D, F and A > B, C, D, F. The next in rank cannot be determined. D has the highest mean of the four remaining trusts, but also the highest variance. The only other unambiguous dominance is C > B.

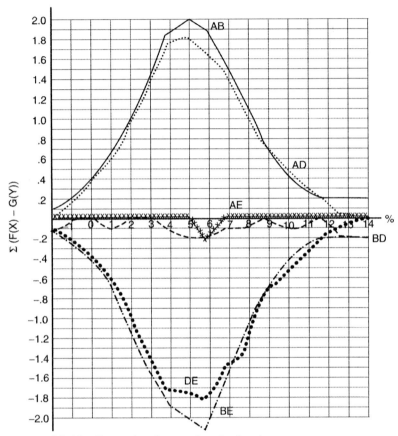

Figure S3.10   Second order stochastic dominance

Table S3.7

	E(X)	var(X)
A	6.2	1.36
B	6.0	26.80
C	6.0	2.00
D	6.2	28.36
E	6.2	0.96
F	6.1	26.89

(b) Mean-variance ranking and SSD both select trust E as optimal. However, the rankings of suboptimal portfolios are not consistent across the two selection procedures.

	Optimal	Dominance Relationships
FSD	A, B, D, E	$A > C$, $D > F$
SSD	E	$A > B$, $A > D$
M-V	E	$A > B, C, D, F$; $C > B$

Chapter 4
State Preference Theory

1. (a)

	Payoff		
	State 1	State 2	Price
Security A	$30	$10	$P_A = \$5$
Security B	$20	$40	$P_B = \$10$

(b) The prices of pure securities are given by the equations below:

$$P_1 Q_{A1} + P_2 Q_{A2} = P_A$$

$$P_1 Q_{B1} + P_2 Q_{B2} = P_B$$

Q_{ij} = dollar payoff of security i in state j

P_i = price of security i (i = A, B)

P_j = price of pure security j (j = 1, 2)

Substituting the correct numbers,

$$30P_1 + 10P_2 = 5$$

$$20P_1 + 40P_2 = 10$$

Multiplying the first equation by 4 and subtracting from the second equation,

$$20P_1 + 40P_2 = 10$$

$$\underline{-[120P_1 + 40P_2 = 20]}$$

$$100P_1 \qquad = 10$$

$$P_1 \qquad = .10$$

Substituting into the first equation,

$$20P_1 + 40P_2 = 10$$

$$2 + 40P_2 = 10$$

$$40P_2 = 8$$

$$P_2 = .20$$

$$P_1 = .10$$

$$P_2 = .20$$

2. (a) The equations to determine the prices of pure securities, P_1 and P_2, are given below:

$$P_1Q_{j1} + P_2Q_{j2} = P_j$$

$$P_1Q_{k1} + P_2Q_{k2} = P_k$$

where Q_{j1} is the payoff of security j in state 1; P_1 is the price of a pure security which pays \$1 if state 1 occurs; and P_j is the price of security j.

Substitution of payoffs and prices for securities j and k in the situation given yields

$$12P_1 + 20P_2 = 22$$

$$24P_1 + 10P_2 = 20$$

Multiplying the first equation by two, and subtracting the second equation from the first,

$$24P_1 + 40P_2 = 44$$

$$-[24P_1 + 10P_2 = 20]$$

$$30P_2 = 24$$

$$P_2 = 24/30 = .8$$

Substituting .8 for P_2 in the first equation,

$$12P_1 + 20(.8) = 22$$

$$12P_1 = 22 - 16$$

$$P_1 = 6/12 = .5$$

(b) The price of security i, P_i, can be determined by the payoff of i in states 1 and 2, and the prices of pure securities for states 1 and 2. From part a) we know the prices of pure securities, $P_1 = .5$ and $P_2 = .8$. Thus,

$$P_i = P_1Q_{i1} + P_2Q_{i2}$$

$$= .5(6) + .8(10)$$

$$= 3 + 8$$

$$= \$11.00$$

3. (a) The payoff table is:

	S_1 = Peace	S_2 = War
Nova Nutrients = j	St. 6	St. 6
Galactic Steel = k	St. 4	St. 36

To find the price of pure securities, P_1 and P_2, solve two equations with two unknowns:

$$6P_1 + 6P_2 = \text{St. } 10$$

$$4P_1 + 36P_2 = \text{St. } 20$$

Multiplying the first equation by six, and subtracting it from the second equation,

$$4P_1 + 36P_2 = St.\ 20$$

$$\underline{-[36P_1 + 36P_2 = St.\ 60]}$$

$$-32P_1 \qquad = -40$$

$$P_1 = St.\ 1.25$$

$$6(1.25) + 6P_2 = 10$$

$$P_2 = .4167$$

(b) Let n_j = number of Nova Nutrients shares and n_k = number of Galactic Steel shares. Then

$$n_j = W_0/P_j = 1{,}000/10 = 100$$

$$n_k = W_0/P_k = 1{,}000/20 = 50$$

If he buys only Nova Nutrients, he can buy 100 shares. If he buys only Galactic Steel, he can buy 50 shares.

Let W_1 = his final wealth if peace prevails, and W_2 = his final wealth if war prevails.

If he buys N.N.: $W_1 = n_j Q_{j1}$

$$= 100(6)$$

$$= 600\ St.$$

$$W_2 = n_j Q_{j2}$$

$$= 100(6)$$

$$= 600\ St.$$

If he buys G.S.: $W_1 = n_k Q_{k1}$

$$= 50(4)$$

$$= 200\ St.$$

$$W_2 = n_k Q_{k2}$$

$$= 50(36)$$

$$= 1{,}800\ St.$$

(c) For sales of j (N.N.) and purchases of k (G.S.): If he sells $-n_j$ shares of j, he receives $-n_j P_j$, and with his initial W_0 he will have $-n_j P_j + W_0$. With this he can buy at most $(-n_j P_j + W_0)/P_k$ shares of k, which will return at least $[(-n_j P_j + W_0)/P_k]Q_{k1}$; he must pay out at most $-n_j Q_{j1}$. Therefore, the minimum $-n_j$ is determined by

$$\frac{-n_j P_j + W_0}{P_k} Q_{k1} = -n_j Q_{j1}$$

$$\frac{(-10n_j + 1{,}000)}{20} 4 = -6n_j$$

$$-2n_j + 200 = -6n_j$$

$$n_j = -50 \text{ shares of j (N.N.)}$$

For sales of k and purchase of j: If he sells $-n_k$ shares of k, he receives $-n_k P_k$, and with his initial W_0 he will have $-n_k P_k + W_0$. With this he can buy at most $(-n_k P_k + W_0)/P_j$ shares of j, which will return at least $[(-n_k P_k + W_0)/P_j]Q_{j2}$; he must pay out at most $-n_k Q_{k2}$. Therefore, the minimum $-n_k$ is determined by

$$\frac{-n_k P_k + W_0}{P_j}Q_{j2} = -n_k Q_{k2}$$

$$\frac{(-20n_k + 1{,}000)}{10}6 = -36n_k$$

$$-12n_k + 600 = -36n_k$$

$$n_k = -25 \text{ shares of k (G.S.)}$$

(d) Let P_a = price of Astro Ammo. Then

$$P_a = P_1 Q_{a1} + P_2 Q_{a2}$$

$$= 1.25(28) + .4167(36)$$

$$= 35 + 15$$

$$= 50 \text{ St.}$$

(e) See Figure S4.1 on the following page.

(f) The slope of the budget line must equal the slope of the utility curve (marginal rate of substitution) at optimum, as given in the equation below:

$$-\partial W_2 / \partial W_1 = -[\partial U / \partial W_1 \div \partial U / \partial W_2]$$

With utility function $U = W_1^{.8} W_2^{.2}$, this equality results in

$$.8W_1^{-.2}W_2^{.2} \div .2W_1^{.8}W_2^{-.8} = 4W_1^{-1}W_2 = 4W_2 / W_1$$

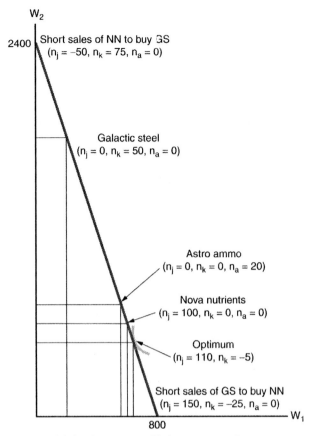

Figure S4.1   State payoffs in peace and war

In equilibrium,

$$\partial W_2 / \partial W_1 = P_1 / P_2$$
$$4W_2 / W_1 = P_1 / P_2$$
$$= (5/4)/(5/12) = (12/4) = 3$$

Therefore,

$$4W_2 = 3W_1$$
$$W_1 = (4/3)W_2$$

The wealth constraint is:

$$W_0 = P_1 W_1 + P_2 W_2$$

Substituting the correct numbers,

$$1,000 = (5/4)(4/3)W_2 + (5/12)W_2$$
$$= (20/12)W_2 + (5/12)W_2$$
$$= (25/12)W_2$$
$$W_2 = (1,000)(12/25)$$
$$= \$480$$
$$W_1 = (4/3)480$$
$$= \$640$$

To find optimal portfolio, solve the two simultaneous equations

$$W_1 = n_j Q_{j1} + n_k Q_{k1}$$

$$W_2 = n_j Q_{j2} + n_k Q_{k2}$$

Substituting the correct numbers,

$$640 = 6n_j + 4n_k$$

$$480 = 6n_j + 36n_k$$

Subtracting the second equation from the first yields

$$160 = -32n_k$$

$$n_k = -5$$

Substituting –5 for n_k in equation 2 gives a value for n_j:

$$480 = 6n_j - 36(5)$$

$$= 6n_j - 180$$

$$660 = 6n_j$$

$$n_j = 110$$

Hence ($n_j = 110$, $n_k = -5$) is the optimum portfolio; in this case the investor buys 110 shares of Nova Nutrients and issues five shares of Galactic Steel.

4. Let n_j = the number of shares the investor can buy if she buys only j, and n_k the number she can buy if she buys only k. Then

(a)
$$n_j = \frac{W_0}{P_j} = \frac{1,200}{10} = 120; \quad n_k = \frac{W_0}{P_k} = \frac{1,200}{12} = 100$$

If she buys j: $W_1 = n_j Q_{j1} = 120(10) = \$1,200$ final wealth in state 1

$W_2 = n_j Q_{j2} = 120(12) = \$1,440$ final wealth in state 2

If she buys k: $W_1 = n_k Q_{k1} = 100(20) = \$2,000$ final wealth in state 1

$W_2 = n_k Q_{k2} = 100(8) = \$800$ final wealth in state 2

(b) For sales of j and purchases of k: If she sells $-n_j$ shares of j, she receives $-n_j P_j$, and with her initial wealth W_0 she will have $-n_j P_j + W_0$; with this she can buy at most $(-n_j P_j + W_0)/P_k$ shares of k which will return *at least* $[(-n_j P_j + W_0)/P_k]Q_{k2}$; she must pay out *at most* $-n_j Q_{j2}$. Therefore, the minimum $-n_j$ is determined by:

$$\frac{-n_j P_j + W_0}{P_k}(Q_{k2}) = -n_j Q_{j2}$$

$$\frac{-10n_j + 1,200}{12}(8) = -12n_j$$

$$-20n_j + 2,400 = -36n_j$$

$$n_j = -150$$

For sales of k and purchases of j: If she sells $-n_k$ shares of k, she receives $-n_kP_k$, and with her initial wealth W_0 she will have $-n_kP_k + W_0$; with this she can buy at most $(-n_kP_k + W_0)/P_j$ shares of j, which will return at least $[(-n_kP_k + W_0)/P_j]Q_{j1}$; she must pay out at most $-n_kQ_{k1}$. Therefore, the minimum $-n_k$ is determined by:

$$\frac{-n_kP_k + W_0}{P_j}(Q_{j1}) = -n_kQ_{k1}$$

$$\frac{-12n_k + 1,200}{10}(10) = -20n_k$$

$$n_k = -150$$

Final wealth for sales of j and purchases of k:

State 1: $-150(10) + 225(20) = 3,000$

State 2: $-150(12) + 225(8) = 0$

Final wealth for sales of k and purchases of j:

State 1: $300(10) - 150(20) = 0$

State 2: $300(12) - 150(8) = 2,400$

(c) To find the price of pure securities, solve two equations for two unknowns as follows:

$$10P_1 + 12P_2 = 10$$

$$20P_1 + 8P_2 = 12$$

Multiplying the first equation by two, and subtracting the second equation from the first equation,

$$20P_1 + 24P_2 = 20$$
$$-[20P_1 + 8P_2 = 12]$$
$$16P_2 = 8$$
$$P_2 = .50$$

Substituting .50 for P_2 in equation 1,

$$10P_1 + 12(.5) = 10$$

$$P_1 = .40$$

(d) The price of security i is given by

$$P_i = P_1Q_{i1} + P_2Q_{i2}$$
$$= (.40)5 + (.50)12$$
$$= 2 + 6$$
$$= 8$$

(e) (The state contingent payoffs of a portfolio invested exclusively in security i are plotted in Figure S4.2.)

If the investor places all of her wealth in i, the number of shares she can buy is given by

$$n_i = \frac{W_0}{P_i} = \frac{1,200}{8} = 150$$

Her wealth in state one would be

$$n_i Q_{i1} = 150(5) = \$750$$

Her wealth in state two would be

$$n_i Q_{i2} = 150(12) = \$1,800$$

If the investor sells k to purchase j, her wealth in state one will be zero. This portfolio plots as the W_2 intercept in Figure S4.2 on the following page. The W_1 intercept is the portfolio of j shares sold to buy k, resulting in zero wealth in state two.

(f)   Set the slope of the budget line equal to the slope of the utility curve in accordance with the equation below:

$$\partial W_2 / \partial W_1 = (\partial U / \partial W_1) \div (\partial U / \partial W_2)$$

Given utility function

$$U = W_1^{.6} W_2^{.4}$$

and substituting the correct numbers,

$$\frac{\partial W_2}{\partial W_1} = (.6 W_1^{-.4} W_2^{.4}) \div (.4 W_2^{-.6} W_1^{.6})$$

$$= 1.5 W_2 / W_1$$

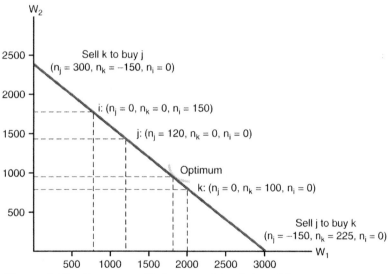

Figure S4.2   State payoffs for securities i, j, and k

In equilibrium:

$$dW_2/dW_1 = P_1/P_2$$

$$1.5 W_2/W_1 = .4/.5 = 0.8$$

$$1.5 W_2 = 0.8 W_1$$

$$W_1 = 1.875 W_2$$

Wealth constraint: $W_0 = P_1 W_1 + P_2 W_2$

$$1,200 = .4(1.875 W_2) + .5 W_2$$

$$W_2 = 1,200/1.25 = 960$$

$$W_1 = 1.875(960) = 1,800$$

Optimal portfolio: Solve the two simultaneous equations for the final wealth in each state:

$$W_1 = n_j Q_{j1} + n_k Q_{k1}$$

$$W_2 = n_j Q_{j2} + n_k Q_{k2}$$

Solve for n_k and n_j, the number of shares of each security to be purchased. Substituting the correct numbers,

$$W_1 = 1,800 = 10 n_j + 20 n_k$$

$$W_2 = 960 = 12 n_j + 8 n_k$$

Solving equation one for n_k in terms of n_j, and substituting this value into equation two:

$$20 n_k = 1,800 - 10 n_j$$

$$n_k = (1,800 - 10 n_j) \div 20$$

$$960 = 12 n_j + 8 \, [(1,800 - 10 n_j) \div 20]$$

$$4,800 = 60 n_j + 3,600 - 20 n_j$$

$$1,200 = 40 n_j$$

$$n_j = 30$$

$$n_k = (1,800 - 10 nj)/20$$

$$n_k = 75$$

The investor should buy 30 shares of j and 75 shares of k.

5. (a) If we know the maximum payout in each state, it will be possible to determine what an equal payout will be. If the individual uses 100 percent of his wealth to buy security j, he can buy

$$\frac{\$720}{\$8} = 90 \text{ shares with payout} \quad S_1 = \$900, \quad S_2 = \$1,800$$

If he spends \$720 on security k, he can obtain

$$\frac{\$720}{\$9} = 80 \text{ shares with payout} \quad S_1 = \$2,400, \quad S_2 = \$800$$

Since both of these payouts lie on the budget constraint (see Figure S4.3 on page 42), we can use them to determine its equation. The equation for the line is

$$W_2 = a + b W_1$$

Substituting in the values of the two points, which we have already determined, we obtain two equations with two unknowns, "a" and "b."

$$1,800 = a + b(900)$$

$$-[800 = a + b(2,400)]$$

$$1,000 = b(-1,500)$$

$$-\frac{1,000}{1,500} = b = \frac{2}{3}$$

Therefore, the slope is $-\frac{2}{3}$ and the intercept is

$$1,800 = a - \frac{2}{3}(900)$$

$$a = 2,400$$

The maximum wealth in state two is $2,400. The maximum wealth in state one is

$$0 = 2,400 - \frac{2}{3} W_1$$

$$3/2(2,400) = W_1 = \$3,600$$

A risk-free asset is one which has a constant payout, regardless of the state of nature which occurs. Therefore, we want to find the point along the budget line where $W_2 = W_1$. We now have two equations and two unknowns

$$W_2 = 2,400 - \frac{2}{3} W_1 \quad \text{(the budget constraint)}$$

$$W_2 = W_1 \qquad \text{(equal payout)}$$

Substituting the second equation into the first, the payout of the risk-free asset is

$$W_1 = 2,400 - \frac{2}{3} W_1$$

$$W_1 = \frac{2,400}{5/3} = \$1,440 = W_2$$

If you buy n_j shares of asset j and n_k shares of k, your payout in states one and two will be

State 1: $n_j 10 + n_k 30 = 1,440$

State 2: $n_j 20 + n_k 10 = 1,440$

Multiplying the first equation by 2 and subtracting, we have

$$n_j 20 + n_k 60 = 2,880$$

$$-[n_j 20 + n_k 10 = 1,440]$$

$$n_k 50 = 1,440$$

$$n_k = 28.8$$

and $\qquad\qquad n_j = 57.6$

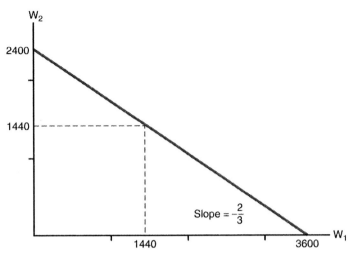

Figure S4.3   The budget constraint

(b) The risk-free portfolio contains 57.6 shares of asset j and 28.8 shares of asset k. It costs $720 and returns $1,440 for sure. Therefore, the risk-free rate of return is

$$720 = \frac{1,440}{1+r_f}$$

$$1+r_f = \frac{1,440}{720} = 2$$

$$r_f = 100\%$$

(c) It would be impossible to find a completely risk-free portfolio in a world with more states of nature than assets (if all assets are risky). Any attempt to solve the problem would require solving for three unknowns with only two equations. No feasible solution exists. In general, it is necessary to have at least as many assets as states of nature in order for complete capital markets to exist.

6. We to solve

$$\text{Max}[\log C + 2/3 \log Q_1 + 1/3 \log Q_2]   \qquad (4.1)$$

subject to

$$C + .6Q_1 + .4Q_2 = 50,000   \qquad (4.2)$$

We can solve for C in (4.2) and substitute for C in (4.1).

$$\text{Max}[\log (50,000 - .6Q_1 - .4Q_2) + 2/3 \log Q_1 + 1/3 \log Q_2]$$

Take the partial derivative with respect to Q_1 and set it equal to zero:

$$\frac{-.6}{50,000 - .6Q_1 - .4Q_2} + \frac{2}{3Q_1} = 0$$

$$\text{or}   \quad 1.8Q_1 = 100,000 - 1.2Q_1 - .8Q_2   \qquad (4.3)$$

Take the partial derivative with respect to Q_2 and set it equal to zero:

$$\frac{-.4}{50,000 - .6Q_1 - .4Q_2} + \frac{1}{3Q_2} = 0$$

$$\text{or}   \quad 1.2Q_2 = 50,000 - .6Q_1 - .4Q_2   \qquad (4.4)$$

Together, (4.3) and (4.4) imply

$$1.8Q_1 = 2.4Q_2, \quad \text{or} \quad Q_1 = 1.3333Q_2$$

Substituting into (4.3) yields

$$2.4Q_2 = 50,000$$

$$Q_2 = 20,833.33$$

$$\text{hence } Q_1 = 27,777.78$$

(a) The risk-averse individual will purchase 27,777.78 units of pure security 1 at $0.60 each for a total of $16,666.67; and 20,833.33 units of pure security 2 at $0.40 each for a total of $8,333.33.

(b) From (4.2) and (4.4),

$$C = 1.2Q2 = 25,000$$

$$\text{also from (4.2), } C = \$50,000 - \$16,666.67 - \$8,333.33$$

$$= \$25,000$$

Hence, the investor divides his wealth equally between current and future consumption (which we would expect since the risk-free rate is zero and there is no discounting in the utility functions), but he buys more of pure security 1 (because its price per probability is lower) than of pure security 2.

Chapter 5
Objects of Choice: Mean-Variance Portfolio Theory

1.

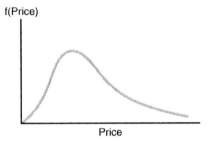

f(Price)

Price

Figure S5.1 Skewed distribution of stock prices

The reason stock prices are skewed right is because theoretically there is no upper bound to the price level a stock can attain, while, with limited liability, the probability distribution is bounded on the left by $P = 0$.

2. The equation for correlation between x and y,

$$r_{x,y} = \frac{\text{cov}(x, y)}{\sigma_x \sigma_y}$$

requires the calculation of var(x), var(y), and cov(x, y). Given $y = a - bx$,

$$\text{var}(y) = \text{var}(a - bx)$$

$$= E\{[a - bx - E(a - bx)]^2\}$$

$$= E\{[a - bx - a - E(-bx)]^2\}$$

$$= E\{[-bx + bE(x)]^2\}$$

$$= (-b)^2 E\{[x - E(x)]^2\}$$

$$= b^2 \, \text{var}(x)$$

Therefore, because the standard deviation must be positive

$$\sigma_y = b\sigma_x$$

$$\text{and} \quad \sigma_x \sigma_y = b\sigma_x^{\,2}$$

$$\text{cov}(x, y) = \text{cov}(x, a - bx)$$

$$= E[(x - E(x))(a - bx - E(a - bx))]$$

$$= E[x(a - bx) - xE(a - bx) - E(x)(a - bx) + E(x)E(a - bx)]$$

$$= E[ax - bx^2 - ax - x(-b)E(x) - E(x)a - (-b)xE(x) + aE(x) - b(E(x))^2]$$

$$= E[(-b)(x^2 - 2xE(x) + (E(x))^2]$$

$$= -b E(x - E(x))^2$$

$$= -b \, \text{var}(x)$$

Substitution into the correlation equation yields

$$r_{xy} = \frac{\text{cov}(x, y)}{\sigma_x \sigma_y} = \frac{-b \, \text{var}(x)}{b \, \text{var}(x)} = -1$$

Thus, x and y are perfectly negatively correlated.

3. (a) **Table S5.1**

Prob.	r_i	$p_i r_i$	$p_i(r_i - E(r))^2$
.15	−.30	−.045	.014
.10	−.16	−.016	.003
.30	0	0	.000
.20	.10	.020	.002
.25	.20	.050	.009
		$\Sigma = .009$	$\Sigma = .028$

where

$$r = \frac{P_1 - P_0}{P_0}, \quad P_0 = 50$$

$$E(r) = \sum p_i r_i = .009$$

$$\text{Var}(r) = \sum p_i (r_i - E(r))2 = .028$$

$$\text{Range } (r) = r_{max} - r_{min} = .20 - (-.30) = .50$$

$$\text{Semi-interquartile range} = 1/2(r_{.75} - r_{.25}) = 1/2(.10 - (-.16)) = .13$$

(b) **Table S5.2**

Prob.	r_i	$p_i r_i$	$p_i (r_i^- - E(r))^2$ (semivariance)
.01	−1.00	−.010	.010
.05	−.30	−.015	.005
.07	−.23	−.016	.004
.02	−.20	−.004	.001
.10	−.16	−.016	.003
.30	0	0	.000
.20	.10	.020	—
.15	.14	.021	—
.05	.20	.010	—
.05	.38	.019	—
		$\Sigma = .009$	$\Sigma = .023$

$$E(r) = \Sigma p_i r_i = .009$$

$$\text{Range} = r_{max} - r_{min} = .38 - (-1.0) = 1.38$$

$$\text{Semi-interquartile range} = 1/2(r_{.75} - r_{.25}) = 1/2(.10 - (-.16))$$

$$= 0.13$$

The expected return and semi-interquartile range are the same, because future possible prices are drawn from the same probability distribution as in part a). Only n, the number of observations, has increased. The range increases with n. Semi-variance is given by

$$E[(x_i^- - E(x))^2]$$

where

$$x_i^- = x_i \quad \text{if} \quad x_i < E(x); \quad x_i^+ = 0 \quad \text{if} \quad x_i \geq E(x)$$

In the example above, semi-variance $= \Sigma p_i (r_i^- - E(r))^2 = 0.023$.

Semi-variance is important to risk-averse investors who are more concerned with downside risk (losses) than gains.

4. First, recall the definition of covariance.

$$\text{cov}(x, y) = E[(x - E(x))(y - E(y))]$$

Multiplying the factors in brackets on the right-hand side, we have

$$\text{cov}(x, y) = E[(xy - xE(y) - yE(x) + E(x)E(y)]$$

and taking the expectation of the right-hand side we have

$$\text{cov}(x, y) = E(xy) - E(x)E(y) - E(y)E(x) + E(x)E(y)$$

$$\text{cov}(x, y) = E(xy) - E(x)E(y)$$

Therefore,

$$E(xy) = \text{cov}(x, y) + E(x)E(y)$$

5. Let σ_x^2 be the variance of the stock. The variance of a perfectly hedged portfolio is

$$var = a^2\sigma_x^2 + 2ab \ cov(x,\ x) + b^2\sigma_x^2$$

The long position means 100% in X and the short position means –100% in X. Therefore,

$$a = 1$$

$$b = -1$$

Therefore, the variance is

$$var = \sigma_x^2 - 2 \ cov(x,\ x) + \sigma_x^2$$

$$\sigma_x^2 - 2\sigma_x^2 + \sigma_x^2 = 0$$

and the position is perfectly risk free.

6. Using matrix notation, the variance is

$$V = X' \Sigma X$$

where

V = variance

X = vector of weights

X' = transpose of the vector of weights

Σ = the variance-covariance matrix

(a) Therefore, the variance of an equally weighted portfolio is

$$V = [1/3 \quad 1/3 \quad 1/3]\begin{bmatrix} 24 & -10 & 25 \\ -10 & 75 & 32 \\ 25 & 32 & 12 \end{bmatrix}\begin{bmatrix} 1/3 \\ 1/3 \\ 1/3 \end{bmatrix}$$

$$V = [1/3 \quad 1/3 \quad 1/3]\begin{bmatrix} 8 & - & 10/3 & + & 25/3 \\ -10/3 & + & 25 & + & 32/3 \\ 25/3 & + & 32/3 & + & 4 \end{bmatrix}$$

$$V = [1/3 \quad 1/3 \quad 1/3]\begin{bmatrix} 13 \\ 32\,1/3 \\ 23 \end{bmatrix}$$

$$V = \frac{13}{3} + \frac{32\,1/3}{3} + \frac{23}{3} = 22.78$$

(b) The covariance is

$$cov = [.1 \quad .8 \quad .1] \begin{bmatrix} 24 & -10 & 25 \\ -10 & 75 & 32 \\ 25 & 32 & 12 \end{bmatrix} \begin{bmatrix} 1.25 \\ -.10 \\ -.15 \end{bmatrix}$$

$$cov = [.1 \quad .8 \quad .1] \begin{bmatrix} 27.25 \\ -24.80 \\ 26.25 \end{bmatrix}$$

$$cov = [.1(27.25) - .8(24.80) + .1(26.25)] = -14.49$$

7. (a)

p_i	X_i	p_iX_i	$X_i - E(X)$	$[X_i - E(X)]^2$	$p_i[X_i - E(X)]^2$	Y_i	p_iY_i
.2	18	3.6	9.0	81.00	16.2	0	0
.2	5	1.0	−4.0	16.00	3.2	−3	−.6
.2	12	2.4	3.0	9.00	1.8	15	3.0
.2	4	.8	−5.0	25.00	5.0	12	2.4
.2	6	1.2	−3.0	9.00	1.8	1	.2
		E(X) = 9.0			var(X) = 28.0		E(Y) = 5.0

$Y_i - E(Y)$	$[Y_i - E(Y)]^2$	$p_i[Y_i - E(Y)]^2$	$p_i[X_i - E(X)][Y_i - E(Y)]$
−5	25	5.0	−9.0
−8	64	12.8	6.4
10	100	20.0	6.0
7	49	9.8	−7.0
−4	16	3.2	2.4
		var(Y) = 50.8	cov(X, Y) = −1.2

(b) Mean = aE(X) + (1 − a)E(Y)

$$\text{Variance} = a^2\sigma_x^2 + 2ab \; cov(X, Y) + (1-a)^2\sigma_y^2$$

% in X	% in Y	$E(R_p)$	$var(R_p)$	σ_p
125	−25	10.0	47.675	6.905
100	0	9.0	28.000	5.292
75	25	8.0	18.475	4.298
50	50	7.0	19.100	4.370
25	75	6.0	29.875	5.466
0	100	5.0	50.800	7.127
−25	125	4.0	81.875	9.048

The opportunity set is shown in Figure S5.2 on the following page.

(c) The minimum variance portfolio is given by equation 5.21.

$$a^* = \frac{\sigma_y^2 - r_{xy}\sigma_x\sigma_y}{\sigma_x^2 + \sigma_y^2 - 2r_{xy}\sigma_x\sigma_y}$$

Recognizing the relationship between r_{xy} and cov(x, y),

$$cov(x, y) = r_{xy}\sigma_x\sigma_y$$

and substituting cov(x, y) into equation 5.21,

$$a^* = \frac{\sigma_y^2 - cov(x, y)}{\sigma_x^2 + \sigma_y^2 - 2\,cov(x, y)}$$

$$= \frac{50.8 - (-1.2)}{28.0 + 50.8 - 2(-1.2)}$$

$$= .64$$

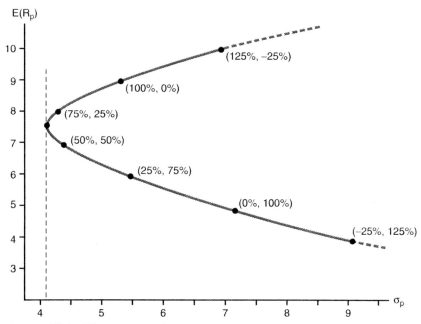

Figure S5.2   The opportunity set

Thus, the minimum variance portfolio has 64 percent invested in asset x and 36 percent in asset y. The portfolio mean and variance at this point are:

$$E(R_p) = .64(9.0) + .36(5.0) = 7.56$$

$$var(R_p) = (.64)^2(28.0) + 2(.64)(.36)(-1.2) + (.36)^2(50.8)$$

$$= 11.469 - .553 + 6.584$$

$$= 17.5$$

$$\sigma_p = 4.183$$

(d) Portfolio A is 75 percent in X and 25 percent in Y; portfolio B is 25 percent in X and 75 percent in Y. The covariance between the two is

$$cov(A, B) = [.75 \quad .25]\begin{bmatrix} 28.0 & -1.2 \\ -1.2 & 50.8 \end{bmatrix}\begin{bmatrix} .25 \\ .75 \end{bmatrix}$$

$$= [.75 \quad .25]\begin{bmatrix} 6.1 \\ 37.8 \end{bmatrix}$$

$$= .75(6.1) + .25(37.8) = 14.025$$

(e) The covariance between the minimum variance portfolio, V_{min}, and portfolio A is

$$cov(V_{min}, A) = [.64 \quad .36]\begin{bmatrix} 28.0 & -1.2 \\ -1.2 & 50.8 \end{bmatrix}\begin{bmatrix} .75 \\ .25 \end{bmatrix}$$

$$= [.64 \quad .36]\begin{bmatrix} 20.7 \\ 11.8 \end{bmatrix} = 17.5$$

The covariance between the minimum variance portfolio, V_{min}, and portfolio B is

$$cov(V_{min}, B) = [.64 \quad .36]\begin{bmatrix} 28.0 & -1.2 \\ -1.2 & 50.8 \end{bmatrix}\begin{bmatrix} .25 \\ .75 \end{bmatrix}$$

$$= [.64 \quad .36]\begin{bmatrix} 6.1 \\ 37.8 \end{bmatrix} = 17.5$$

(f) It is no coincidence that the covariance between the minimum variance portfolio and portfolios A and B is the same (except for rounding error). It can be proven that the covariance between the global minimum variance portfolio and *any* portfolio along the efficient set is a constant. (See Merton (1972).)

(g) The variance of the global minimum variance portfolio is

$$var(V_{min}) = [.64 \; .36]\begin{bmatrix} 28.0 & -1.2 \\ -1.2 & 50.8 \end{bmatrix}\begin{bmatrix} .64 \\ .36 \end{bmatrix}$$

$$= [.64 \; .36]\begin{bmatrix} 17.488 \\ 17.520 \end{bmatrix} = 17.5$$

Again, this is not a coincidence. The variance of the minimum variance portfolio equals the covariance between the minimum variance portfolio and any other portfolio along the efficient set.

8. (a) Using the definition of expected value,

$$E(ax + by) = \sum p_i (ax_i + by_i)$$

$$= \sum p_i(ax_i) + \sum p_i(by_i)$$

$$= a \sum p_i x_i + b \sum p_i y_i$$

$$= aE(x) + bE(y)$$

(b) Using the definition of variance,

$$
\begin{aligned}
\text{var}(ax + by) &= \sum p_i \, [(ax_i + by_i) - E(ax_i + by_i)]^2 \\
&= \sum p_i \, [(ax_i + by_i) - (aE(x) + bE(y))]^2 \\
&= \sum p_i \, [a(x_i + E(x)) + b(y_i - E(y))]^2 \\
&= \sum p_i [(a^2(x_i - E(x))^2 + 2ab(x_i - E(x)) \, (y_i - E(y)) \\
&\quad + b^2(y_i - E(y))^2] \\
&= a^2 \sum p_i (x_i - E(x))^2 + 2ab \sum p_i (x_i - E(x)) \, (y_i - E(y)) \\
&\quad + b^2 \sum p_i (y_i - E(y))^2 \\
&= a^2 \, \text{var}(x) + 2ab \, \text{cov}(x, y) + b^2 \, \text{var}(y)
\end{aligned}
$$

(c) Using the definition of covariance,

$$
\begin{aligned}
\text{cov}[(ax + bz), y] &= \sum p_i \, (ax_i + bz_i - E(ax_i + bz_i))(y_i - E(y)) \\
&= \sum p_i \, [a(x_i - E(x)) + b(z_i - E(z))](y_i - E(y)) \\
&= a \sum p_i (x_i - E(x))(y_i - E(y)) \\
&\quad + b \sum p_i \, (z_i - E(z))(y_i - E(y)) \\
&= a \, \text{cov}(x, y) + b \, \text{cov}(z, y)
\end{aligned}
$$

(d) Using the definition of the covariance of x with itself,

$$
\begin{aligned}
\text{cov}(x, x) &= E[(x - E(x))(x - E(x))] \\
&= E[x^2 - E(x)x - xE(x) + E(x)E(x)] \\
&= E(x^2) - E(x)E(x) - E(x)E(x) + E(x)E(x) \\
\text{cov}(x, x) &= E(x^2) - [E(x)]^2 \\
\text{var}(x) &= E(x^2) - [E(x)]^2 \\
E(x^2) &= [E(x)]^2 + \text{var}(x)
\end{aligned}
$$

(e) Prove that if $r_{xy} = 1$, then $\sigma(x + y) = \sigma_x + \sigma_y$:

$$
\begin{aligned}
\text{var}(x + y) &= \text{var}(x) + \text{var}(y) + 2 \, \text{cov}(x, y) \\
\text{cov}(x, y) &= r_{xy}\sigma_x\sigma_y
\end{aligned}
$$

Therefore, if $r_{xy} = 1$,

$$
\begin{aligned}
\text{var}(x + y) = \sigma^2(x + y) &= \sigma_x^2 + \sigma_y^2 + 2\sigma_x\sigma_y \\
\sigma^2(x + y) &= (\sigma_x + \sigma_y)^2 \\
\sigma(x + y) &= \sigma_x + \sigma_y
\end{aligned}
$$

Prove that, if $r_{xy} = -1$, then $\sigma(x + y) = \sigma_x - \sigma_y$:

$$
\begin{aligned}
\text{var}(x + y) &= \sigma_x^2 + \sigma_y^2 - 2\sigma_x\sigma_y \\
\sigma^2(x + y) &= (\sigma_x - \sigma_y)^2 \\
\sigma(x + y) &= \sigma_x - \sigma_y
\end{aligned}
$$

9. (a)

Table S5.3   Opportunity Set Computations

% in Asset 1	% in Asset 2	$E(R_p)$	$Var(R_p)$	$\sigma(R_p)$
150	−50	0.50%	7.250%	26.93%
100	0	3.00	2.000	14.14
75	25	4.25	1.063	10.31
50	50	5.50	1.250	11.18
25	75	6.75	2.563	16.01
0	100	8.00	5.000	22.36
−50	150	10.50	13.250	36.40

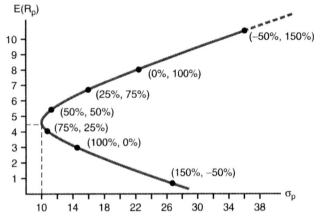

Figure S5.3   The opportunity set in mean-standard deviation space

(b) Using equation 5.21,

$$a^* = \frac{\sigma_y^2 - r_{xy}\sigma_x\sigma_y}{\sigma_x^2 + \sigma_y^2 - 2r_{xy}\sigma_x\sigma_y} \quad \text{where } r_{xy}\sigma_x\sigma_y = \text{cov}(x, y)$$

$$\text{then } a^* = \frac{.05 - (-.01)}{.02 + .05 - 2(-.01)} = \frac{.06}{.09} = .67$$

If we put two-thirds into asset 1, the portfolio's standard deviation is

$$\sigma_{p_{min}} = [(.67)^2(.02) + (.33)^2(.05) + 2(.67)(.33)(-.01)]^{1/2}$$

$$= (.01)^{1/2} = 10\%$$

$$E(R_{p_{min}}) = .67(.03) + .33(.08) = 4.65\%$$

The minimum variance portfolio is plotted in Figure S5.3.

(c) From Table S5.3, line 4:

$$E(R_p) = 5.50\%$$

$$\sigma(R_p) = 11.18\%$$

10. (a)

$$E(R_1) = .1(-1.0) + .8(.5) + .1(.5) = .35$$

$$Var(R_1) = .1(-1.0-.35)^2 + .8(.5-.35)^2 + .1(.5 - .35)^2$$

$$= .1(1.8225) + .8(.0225) + .1(.0225)$$

$$= .2025$$

$$E(R_2) = .1(.15) + .8(.15) + .1(1.65) = .30$$

$$Var(R_2) = .1(.15 - .30)^2 + .8(.15 - .30)^2 + .1(1.65 - .30)^2$$

$$= .1(.0225) + .8(.0225) + .1(.8225)$$

$$= .2025$$

$$Cov(R_1, R_2) = .1(-1.0-.35)(.15-.30) + .8(.5 - .35)(.15 - .30)$$

$$+ .1(.5 - .35)(1.65 - .30)$$

$$= .1(.2025) + .8(-.0225) + .1(.2025)$$

$$= .0225$$

(b) The table on the following page gives the mean and standard deviation of returns for various portfolios.

Table S5.4 Computing The Opportunity Set

% in 1	% in 2	$E(R_p)$	$\sigma^2(R_p)$	$\sigma(R_p)$
100	0	.3500	.2025	.450
75	25	.3375	.1350	.367
50	50	.3250	.1125	.335
25	75	.3125	.1350	.367
0	100	.3000	.2025	.450

Because the mean-variance efficient set is the upper half of the opportunity set, we also need to know the mean and variance of the minimum variance portfolio. Using equation 5.21, we have

$$a^* = \frac{\sigma_y^2 - r_{xy}\sigma_x\sigma_y}{\sigma_x^2 + \sigma_y^2 - 2r_{xy}\sigma_x\sigma_y}$$

$$= \frac{.2025 - .0225}{.2025 + .2025 - 2(.0225)}$$

$$= \frac{.18}{.36} = .5$$

The opportunity set is graphed below.

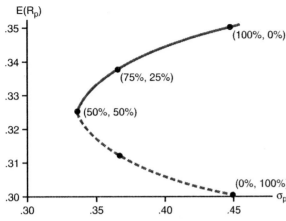

Figure S5.4   The opportunity set

(c) The efficient set is the solid line in the above figure. It starts with the minimum variance portfolio (50 percent in 1, 50 percent in 2) and ends with 100 percent in asset 1 (assuming no short sales).

(d) If mean and variance are the only relevant decision criteria (even though the returns are not jointly normally distributed), then asset 1 dominates asset 2 because it has a higher mean and the same variance. Asset 2 enters into efficient portfolios because of the diversification benefits it provides since it is not perfectly correlated with asset 1.

(e) Figure S5.5 below shows the new efficient set as the solid line.

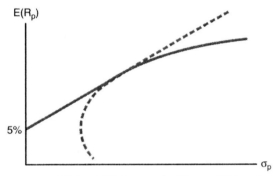

Figure S5.5   Efficient set with no riskless borrowing

11. Portfolio variance, in general, can be written as

$$Var(R_p) = \sum_i \sum_j w_i w_j \sigma_{ij}$$

Because the returns are independently distributed, all of the covariance terms are equal to zero, i.e., $\sigma_{ij} = 0$ for $i \neq j$. This means that the variance becomes

$$Var(R_p) = \sum_i w_i^2 \sigma_{ii}$$

Because the assets also have identical means (as shown in Figure S5.6), a risk-averse investor will simply choose the set of weights, w_i, which minimizes variance. Intuitively,

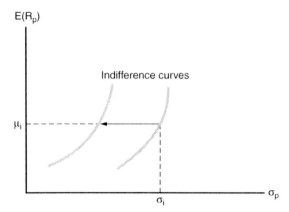

$E(R_p)$

μ_i

Indifference curves

σ_i

σ_p

Figure S5.6   Optimal portfolio composition

this implies putting an equal amount of wealth in each security. Proof is given by minimizing the variance subject to the constraint that the weights add to 100 percent, i.e., $\sum w_i = 1$. Forming a Lagrangian, we have

$$\Psi = \sum w_i^2 \sigma_{ii} - \lambda \left(\sum w_i - 1 \right)$$

The first-order conditions are

$$\frac{\partial \Psi}{\partial w_i} = 2w_i \sigma_{ii} - \lambda = 0; \quad N \text{ equations, } i = 1, \ldots, N$$

$$\frac{\partial \Psi}{\partial \lambda} = \sum w_i - 1 = 0$$

The ratio of the partials with respect to w_i is

$$\frac{2w_i \sigma_{ii}}{2w_j \sigma_{jj}} = \frac{\lambda}{\lambda}$$

Therefore

$$\frac{w_i}{w_j} = 1$$

Thus, we see that the minimum variance is achieved if all of the weights are equal. If there are N securities, the optimal weight is 1/N.

12. Going back to Chapter 3 (Utility Theory), we have the result that when returns are normally distributed, the marginal rate of substitution between risk and return is

$$\frac{dE}{d\sigma} = \frac{-\int U'(E + \sigma Z) Z f(Z; 0, 1) dZ}{\int U'(E + \sigma Z) f(Z; 0, 1) dZ}$$

When an asset is risk-free, the standard deviation of return is zero, the rate of return always equals its expected value, and since

$$R = E + \sigma Z$$

we have the result that Z = 0. Therefore, the marginal rate of substitution between expected return and risk, dE/dσ, is zero. As shown in the figure below, this implies that the slope of the risk-averter's indifference curve is always zero at the y-axis. As long as the ex-ante market rate of return is greater than the risk-free rate, the slope of the capital market line must be positive at the y-axis. Therefore, a tangency between a risk-averter's indifference curve and the CML at the y-axis is impossible. No risk averter will hold all of his wealth in the risk-free asset.

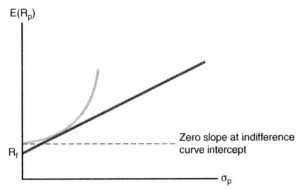

Figure S5.7   No risk-averse investor will hold 100% of his wealth in the risk-free asset

13. First compute the expected returns and standard deviations for asset X.

p_i	X_i	$p_i X_i$	$X_i - E(X)$	$[X_i - E(X)]^2$	$p_i[X_i - E(X)]^2$
.1	30	3.0	20	400	40
.2	20	4.0	10	100	20
.4	15	6.0	5	25	10
.2	10	2.0	0	0	0
.1	−50	−5.0	−60	3600	360
1.0		E(X) = 10.0			VAR(X) = 430

Using the probability properties, we can immediately write the expected value and variance of asset Y.

$$E(Y) = 6 + .2E(X)$$
$$= 6 + .2(10) = 8$$
$$VAR(Y) = (.2)^2 VAR(X)$$
$$= .04(430) = 17.2$$

Also, the standard deviations of X and Y are

$$\sigma_X = \sqrt{430} = 20.74 \qquad \sigma_Y = \sqrt{17.2} = 4.15$$

The simplest way to solve the problem is to make use of the fact that the opportunity set for a portfolio of two perfectly correlated assets is a straight line. The opportunity set is graphed in Figure S5.8. If we find the expected return represented by its intercept then we can determine the correct weights for the zero variance portfolio. The linear equation for the opportunity set is

$$E(R_p) = a + b\sigma(R_p)$$

We know the coordinates of the points X and Y, therefore the slope is

$$b = \frac{E(X) - E(Y)}{\sigma_X - \sigma_Y} = \frac{10 - 8}{20.74 - 4.15} = .1206$$

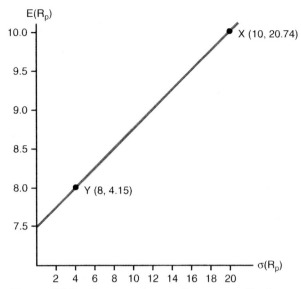

Figure S5.8   Opportunity set for two perfectly correlated assets

Using the coordinates for X and the slope we have

$$E(X) = a + .1206\sigma_X$$
$$10.0 = a + .1206(20.74)$$
$$a = 7.5$$

The zero variance portfolio has an expected return of 7.5%. If we let α be the percent invested in X then the proportions of X and Y in this portfolio are

$$E(R_p) = \alpha E(X) + (1-\alpha)E(Y)$$
$$7.5 = \alpha(10) + (1-\alpha)8$$
$$\alpha = -.25$$

Therefore, we should sell short 25% of our wealth in asset X and go long 125% in asset Y. To confirm this result we can plug the appropriate weights into the definition of the variance of a portfolio of two assets as follows:

$$VAR(R_p) = \alpha^2 VAR(X) + 2\alpha(1-\alpha)r_{XY}\sigma_X\sigma_Y + (1-\alpha)^2 VAR(Y)$$
$$= (-.25)^2 430 + 2(-.25)(1.25)(1.0)(20.74)(4.15) + (1.25)^2(17.2)$$
$$= 26.88 - 53.79 + 26.88 \approx 0$$

14. (a) The variance of the shareholders' equity position recognizes that the shareholders' portfolio has positive weights (long positions) in assets and negative weights (short positions) in liabilities. The return on equity can be written as

$$R_S = w_{STA}R_{STA} + w_{US}R_{US} + w_L R_L - w_{STL}R_{STL} - w_D R_D$$

We require that the sum of the weights add to 1.0, therefore each weight is defined as the value of the ith asset or liability, V_i, divided by the market value of equity, S.

$$w_i = \frac{V_i}{S}, V_i < 0 \text{ for liabilities}$$

The variance of the shareholders' position is

$$Var(R_S) = w' \Sigma w$$

where: $w' = [\, w_{STA} \quad w_{US} \quad w_L \quad -w_{STL} \quad -w_D \,]$

$$= [1.0 \quad 2.0 \quad 7.0 \quad -5.0 \quad -8.5]$$

$$\Sigma = \begin{bmatrix} (.02)^2 & 0 & 0 & 0 & 0 \\ 0 & (.04)^2 & .8(.04)(.07) & 0 & .3(.04)(.03) \\ 0 & .8(.04)(.07) & (.07)^2 & 0 & .2(.07)(.03) \\ 0 & 0 & 0 & (.02)^2 & 0 \\ 0 & .3(.04)(.03) & .2(.03)(.07) & 0 & (.03)^2 \end{bmatrix}$$

$$w' \Sigma w = [1.0 \quad 2.0 \quad 7.0 \quad -.5 \quad -8.5]$$

$$\begin{bmatrix} .00040 & 0 & 0 & 0 & 0 \\ 0 & .00160 & .00224 & 0 & .000360 \\ 0 & .00224 & .00490 & 0 & .000420 \\ 0 & 0 & 0 & .00040 & 0 \\ 0 & .00036 & .00042 & 0 & .000900 \end{bmatrix} \begin{bmatrix} 1.0 \\ 2.0 \\ 7.0 \\ -.5 \\ -8.5 \end{bmatrix}$$

$$w' \Sigma w = [1.0 \quad 2.0 \quad 7.0 \quad -.5 \quad -8.5] \begin{bmatrix} .00040 \\ .01582 \\ .03521 \\ -.00020 \\ -.00399 \end{bmatrix}$$

$$w' \Sigma w = .33003$$

The standard deviation is the square root of the variance

$$\sigma = \sqrt{.33003} = .574482$$

(b) The position in T-bond futures contracts is taken in order to minimize the standard deviation of the shareholders' claim. Equation (5.33) is the result of taking the derivative of the shareholders' portfolio variance (given that it has been augmented with futures contracts) with respect to the number of futures contracts.

$$N = -\sum_i \frac{V_i r_{i,TB} \sigma_i}{P_{TB} \sigma_{TB}}$$

Expanding this expression to fit the current problem, we have

$$N = -\frac{V_{US} r_{US,TB} \sigma_{US}}{P_{TB} \sigma_{TB}} - \frac{V_L r_{L,TB} \sigma_L}{P_{TB} \sigma_{TB}} - \frac{-V_D r_{D,TB} \sigma_D}{P_{TB} \sigma_{TB}}$$

$$N = -\frac{200(.9)(.04)}{.09(.08)} - \frac{700(.5)(.07)}{.09(.08)} - \frac{-850(.3)(.03)}{.09(.08)}$$

$$N = -1,000 - 3,403 + 1,063$$

$$N = -3,340$$

The conclusion is that the variance of shareholders' return can be minimized by short selling 3,340 futures contracts. The T-bond futures position will rise in value when interest rates fall, and this will offset the declines in the value of the bank's loan portfolio and government bond holdings.

The new shareholders' position is augmented with futures as follows.

$$R_S = w_{STA}R_{STA} + w_{US}R_{US} + w_L R_L - w_{STL}R_{STL} - w_D R_D + w_{TB}R_{TB}$$

The market value weight of the futures position is

$$w_F = \frac{NP_{TB}}{S} = \frac{-3340(.09 \text{ million})}{100 \text{ million}} = -3.0$$

and the variance of the revised shareholder position is

$$w'\Sigma w = [1.0 \quad 2.0 \quad 7.0 \quad -.5 \quad -8.5 \quad -3.0]$$

$$\begin{bmatrix} .00040 & 0 & 0 & 0 & 0 & 0 \\ 0 & .00160 & .00224 & 0 & .000360 & .00288 \\ 0 & .00224 & .00490 & 0 & .000420 & .00280 \\ 0 & 0 & 0 & .00040 & 0 & 0 \\ 0 & .00036 & .00042 & 0 & .000900 & .00072 \\ 0 & .00288 & .00280 & 0 & .000720 & .00640 \end{bmatrix}$$

$$\begin{bmatrix} 1.0 \\ 2.0 \\ 7.0 \\ -.5 \\ -8.5 \\ -3.0 \end{bmatrix}$$

$$w'\Sigma w = [1.0 \quad 2.0 \quad 7.0 \quad -.5 \quad -8.5 \quad -3.0] \begin{bmatrix} .00040 \\ .00718 \\ .02681 \\ -.00020 \\ -.00615 \\ .00004 \end{bmatrix}$$

$$w'\Sigma w = .253605$$

The new standard deviation is .503592.

Chapter 6
Market Equilibrium: CAPM and APT

1. The conditions are those necessary for two-fund separation, namely (in addition to those already assumed)

   - homogeneous expectations
   - asset markets frictionless with costless information simultaneously available to all individuals
   - all assets marketable and perfectly divisible
   - no market imperfections such as taxes or restrictions on selling short

2.

p_i	R_j	$p_i R_j$	$R_j - \bar{R}_j$	$p_i (R_j - \bar{R}_j)^2$
.1	−.30	−.03	−.45	.02025
.3	.00	.00	−.15	.00675
.4	.20	.08	.05	.00100
.2	.50	.10	.35	.02450
	$E(R_j^*) = .15$			$\sigma_j^2 = .0525$

R_m	$p_i R_m$	$R_m - \bar{R}_m$	$p_i (R_m - \bar{R}_m)^2$	$p_i (R_j - \bar{R}_j)(R_m - \bar{R}_m)$
−.15	−.015	−.25	.00625	.1(−.45)(−.25) = .01125
.05	.015	−.05	.00075	.3(−.15)(−.05) = .00225
.15	.060	.05	.00100	.4(.05)(.05) = .00100
.20	.040	.10	.00200	.2(.35)(.10) = .00700
				cov (R_j, R_m) = .02150
$E(R_m) = .10$		$\sigma_m^2 = .0100$		$\beta_j = \dfrac{\text{cov}(R_j, R_m)}{\sigma_m^2} = \dfrac{.0215}{.01} = 2.15$

(a) $E(R_m) = 10\%$

(b) $\sigma_m^2 = 1\%$, $\sigma_m = 10\%$

(c) $E(R_j^*) = 15\%$

(d) $cov(R_j, R_m) = 2.15\%$

(e) $E(R_j) = R_f + [E(R_m) - R_f]\beta_j$

   $E(R_j) = .06 + [.10 - .06]\beta_j$

(f) The required rate of return on Donovan Company is

$$E(R_j) = .06 + [.10 - .06]\frac{cov(R_j, R_m)}{\sigma_m^2}$$

$$= .06 + [.04]\frac{.0215}{.01}$$

$$= .06 + .04(2.15) = 14.6\%$$

The expected return, $E(R_j^*) = 15\%$ (see c above). Because Donovan earns more than is required, we might expect its price to increase so that in equilibrium its expected rate of return equals 14.6%.

3. Now we are dealing with sample data; therefore, we can use statistics formulae for sample mean and variance.

$$E(X) = \frac{\sum X_i}{N} \qquad var(X) = \frac{\sum(X_i - E(X))^2}{N-1}$$

Note that the sample variance is calculated by dividing the sum of mean deviations squared by N – 1, the number of observations minus one. We subtract one because we lose one degree of freedom in estimating the mean. Covariance calculations also are divided by N – 1.

$$cov(X, Y) = \frac{\sum(X_i - E(X))(Y_i - E(Y))}{N-1}$$

Year	R_m	$R_m - \bar{R}_m$	$(R_m - \bar{R}_m)^2$	R_j	$R_j - \bar{R}_j$	$(R_j - \bar{R}_j)(R_m - \bar{R}_m)$
1978	.27	.15	.0225	.25	.15	.0225
1977	.12	0	0	.05	−.05	0
1976	−.03	−.15	.0225	−.05	−.15	.0225
1975	.12	0	0	.15	.05	0
1974	−.03	−.15	.0225	−.10	−.20	.0300
1973	.27	.15	.0225	.30	.20	.0300
	$\sum R_m = .72$		$\sum(R_m - \bar{R})^2 = .09$	$\sum R_j = .6$		$\sum = .105$

$$E(R_m) = \frac{\sum R_m}{N} = \frac{.72}{6} = .12 \qquad var(R_m) = \frac{\sum(R_m - \bar{R}_m)^2}{N-1} = \frac{.09}{5} = .018$$

$$E(R_j) = \frac{\sum R_j}{N} = \frac{.6}{6} = .10 \qquad cov(R_j, R_m) = \frac{\sum(R_j - \bar{R}_j)(R_m - \bar{R}_m)}{N-1}$$

$$= \frac{.105}{5} = .021$$

(a) $E(R_m) = 12\%$

(b) $var(R_m) = 1.8\%$, $\sigma_m = 13.42\%$

(c) $E(R_j) = 10\%$

(d) $cov(R_j, R_m) = 2.1\%$

(e) $E(R_j) = R_f + \left[E(R_m) - R_f\right] \dfrac{cov(R_j, R_m)}{var(R_m)}$

(f) Required return $(R_j) = .066 + [.054](1.1667) = 12.9\%$

The market requires 12.9% and the expected (i.e., anticipated) rate of return is only 10%. Therefore, we would expect the Milliken company to decline in value.

4. See table S6.1, Panel A.

(a) $\overline{R}_m = \dfrac{\sum (col.\,5)}{10} = \dfrac{.7796}{10} \cong .078$

(b) $var(R_m) = \dfrac{\sum (col.\,7)}{10-1} = \dfrac{.0964}{9} = .0107$

(c) $\sigma(R_m) = \sqrt{.0107} = .1034$

5. See table S6.1, Panel B.

(a) $\overline{R}_j = \dfrac{\sum (col.\,5)}{10} = \dfrac{1.0221}{10} = .1022$

(b) $var(R_j) = \dfrac{\sum (col.\,7)}{10-1} = \dfrac{.2644}{9} = .0294$

(c) $cov(R_j, R_m) = \dfrac{\sum (col.\,8)}{10-1} = \dfrac{.0801}{9} = .0089$

(d) $\beta_j = \dfrac{cov(R_j, R_m)}{var(R_m)} = \dfrac{.0089}{.0107} = .8318$

6. Other than the usual perfect market assumptions, and given that we have rational, risk-averse, expected-end-of-period-utility-of-wealth maximizers, the key assumptions are that 1) investors have homogeneous expectations and 2) all assets are perfectly divisible and marketable. It is not necessary that there be risk-free assets. Given the two above assumptions, all individuals will perceive the same efficient set and all assets will be held in equilibrium. If every individual holds an efficient portfolio, and all assets are held, then the market

Table S 6.1

	Panel A:	Estimates of Market Parameters					
Year	S&P 500 Price Index	% Change in Price	Dividend Yield	Percent Return	Return Deviation	Market Variance	Bish-free rate
(t)	P_t	$\dfrac{P_t}{P_{t-1}} - 1$	$\dfrac{D_t}{P_t}$	R_{mt}	$(R_{mt} - \bar{R}_m)$	$(R_{mt} - \bar{R}_m)^2$	R_f
				$(3+4)$	$(5 - \bar{R}_m)$	(6^2)	
(1)	(2)	(3)	(4)	(5)	(6)	(7)	(8)
1960	55.85						
1961	66.27	.1866	.0298	.2164	.1384	.0192	.03
1962	62.38	−.0587	.0337	−.0250	−.1030	.0106	.03
1963	69.87	.1201	.0317	.1518	.0738	.0054	.03
1964	81.37	.1646	.0301	.1947	.1167	.0136	.04
1965	88.17	.0836	.0300	.1136	.0356	.0013	.04
1966	85.26	−.0330	.0340	.0010	−.0770	.0059	.04
1967	91.93	.0782	.0320	.1102	.0322	.0010	.05
1968	98.70	.0736	.0307	.1043	.0263	.0007	.05
1969	97.84	−.0087	.0324	.0237	−.0543	.0029	.07
1970	83.22	−.1494	.0383	−.1111	−.1891	.0358	.06
				.7796		.0964	
						$\bar{R}_f = .44/10 = .044$	

	Panel B:	Calculation of Beta for General Motors				
Year	GM Price	% Change in Price	Dividend Yield	Percent Return	Deviation of Returns	Variance of Returns	Covariance with Market
(t)	P_t	$\dfrac{P_t}{P_{t-1}} - 1$	$\dfrac{D_t}{P_t}$	R_{jt}	$(R_{jt} - \bar{R}_j)$	$(R_{jt} - \bar{R}_j)^2$	$(R_{jt} - \bar{R}_j)(R_{mt} - \bar{R}_m)$
				$(3+4)$	$(5 - \bar{R}_j)$	(6^2)	$(6 \times 6 \text{ [Panel A]})$
(1)	(2)	(3)	(4)	(5)	(6)	(7)	(8)
1960	48						
1961	49	.0208	.05	.0708	−.0314	.0010	−.0043
1962	52	.0612	.06	.1212	.0190	.0004	−.0020
1963	74	.4231	.05	.4731	.3709	.1376	.0274
1964	90	.2162	.05	.2662	.1640	.0269	.0191
1965	102	.1333	.05	.1833	.0811	.0066	.0029
1966	87	−.1471	.05	−.0971	−.1993	.0397	.0153
1967	78	−.1034	.05	−.0534	−.1556	.0242	−.0050
1968	81	.0385	.05	.0885	−.0137	.0002	−.0004
1969	74	−.0864	.06	−.0264	−.1286	.0165	.0070
1970	70	−.0541	.05	−.0041	−.1063	.0113	.0201
				1.0221		.2644	.0801

portfolio must also be efficient because it is merely the sum of all efficient portfolios held by all individuals.

7. Yes. Given a riskless asset, two-fund separation obtains, and if you can observe any one of the following: 1) the percent of the investor's portfolio held in the market portfolio, 2) the β of the investor's portfolio, or 3) the expected return on the investor's portfolio, you can tell how risk averse he is. These three measures are equivalent. To see this, note that

$$E(R_p) = R_f + [E(R_m) - R_f] \, \beta_p$$

$$E(R_p) = R_f(1 - \beta_p) + R_m \beta_p$$

Also

$$E(R_p) = R_f(1 - a) + R_m a$$

where a is the percent invested in the market portfolio. Therefore, $a = \beta_p$. Finally,

$$\beta_p = \beta_f(1 - a) + \beta_m a$$

where $\beta_f = 0$ is the beta of the risk-free asset. Therefore,

$$\beta_p = a \beta_m$$

and since $\beta_m = 1.0$

$$\beta_p = a$$

The greater the percentage, a, of the market portfolio held in the investor's total portfolio, the less risk averse the investor is. This result does not change in a world without a risk-free asset because the zero-β portfolio may be substituted for the risk-free asset without changing any results.

8. Systematic risk is defined as market risk, i.e., a portfolio's variance that can be explained in terms of market variance. With risk-free borrowing and lending, all efficient portfolios are linear combinations of the risk-free asset and the market portfolio. The capital market line is made up of a linear efficient set as in Figure 6.2. Because the risk-free asset has no variance, total variance in every efficient portfolio is contributed solely by the market portfolio. Thus, all risk is systematic.

    Algebraically, the variance in any efficient portfolio would be

$$var[a(R_m) + (1 - a)R_f] = a^2 \sigma_m^2 + (1 - a)^2 \sigma_{R_f}^2 + 2(a)(1 - a)\sigma_{m, R_f}$$

$$= a^2 \sigma_m^2 + 0 + 0$$

where a represents the percentage of the efficient portfolio invested in the market portfolio. The percentage, a, is equal to the portfolio's β_p, as proven in problem 6.7. β is the measure of systematic risk.

    Thus, $\sigma_p = \beta_p \sigma_m$.

9.
$$E(R_j) - R_f + [E(R_m) - R_f]\beta_j$$

$$\frac{.2 - .05}{.15 - .05} = \beta_j = 1.5$$

We know that efficient portfolios have no unsystematic risk. The total risk (equation 6.12) is

$$\sigma_j^2 = \beta_j^2 \sigma_m^2 + \sigma_\varepsilon^2$$

and since the unsystematic risk of an efficient portfolio, σ_ε^2, is zero,

$$\sigma_j = \beta_j s_m = 1.5(.2) = .3 \text{ or } 30\%, \quad \sigma_j^2 = .09 \text{ or } 9\%$$

The definition of correlation (from Chapter 5, equation 17) is

$$r_{jm} = \frac{\text{cov}(R_j, R_m)}{\sigma_j \sigma_m}$$

To find cov (R_j, R_m), use the defination of β_j

$$b_j = \frac{\text{cov}(R_j, R_m)}{\sigma_m^2}$$

$$1.5 (.2)^2 = \text{cov}(R_j, R_m) = .06$$

Since $r_{jm} = 1.0$, we again have the result that efficient portfolios are perfectly correlated with the market (and with each other).

10. Assuming equilibrium, all assets must be priced so that they fall along the security market line. Therefore, we can find the β_k for Rapid Rolling. β_k is its systematic risk.

$$E(R_k) = R_f + [E(R_m) - R_f]\beta_k$$

$$\beta_k = \frac{.25 - .05}{.15 - .05} = 2.0$$

Total risk is defined by equation 6.12. We can use it to find Rapid Rolling's unsystematic risk, σ_ε^2

$$\sigma_k^2 = \beta_k^2 \sigma_m^2 + \sigma_\varepsilon^2$$
$$.52 = (2.0)^2 (.2)^2 + \sigma_\varepsilon^2$$
$$\sigma_\varepsilon^2 = .52 - 4(.2)^2 = .36 \text{ or } \sigma_\varepsilon = .6$$

11. (a) We know by the CAPM:

$$R_j = R_f + [E(R_m) - R_f]\beta_j$$
$$.10 = .06 + (.14 - .06)\beta_j$$
$$.04 = .8\beta_j$$
$$\beta_j = .5$$

The CAPM assumes that the market is in equilibrium and that investors hold efficient portfolios, i.e., that all portfolios lie on the security market line.

(b) Let "a" be the percent invested in the risk-free asset. Portfolio return is the point on the security market line where

$$E(R_p) = aR_f - (1-a)E(R_m)$$

$$10\% = a(6\%) + (1-a)(14\%)$$

$$a = \frac{.10 - .14}{-.08} = .5$$

Therefore, $(1 - a) = 50\%$, i.e., the individual should put 50% of his portfolio into the market portfolio.

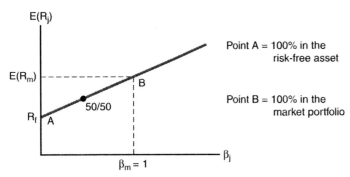

Figure S6.1 (Problem 6.11)   The security market line

12. Assuming that the company pays no dividends, the one period rate of return, R_j, is

$$E(R_j) = \frac{E(P_1) - P_0}{P_0}$$

where $E(P_1) = \$100$. Using the CAPM, we have

$$E(R_j) = \frac{E(P_1) - P_0}{P_0} = R_f + [E(R_m) - R_f]\beta_j$$

Substituting in the appropriate numbers and solving for P_0, we have

$$\frac{\$100 - P_0}{P_0} = .08 + [.18 - .08]2.0$$

$$\$100 - P_0 = .08P_0 + .2P_0$$

$$1.28P_0 = \$100$$

$$P_0 = \$78.125$$

13. (a) A zero-beta portfolio has zero covariance with the market portfolio, by definition. Also, using matrix notation, the covariance between two portfolios is

$$cov = W_1' \Sigma W_2$$

where

$W_1^{'}$ = the row vector of weights in the zero-β portfolio

$\sum$ = the variance-covariance matrix of two risky assets

W_2 = the column vector of weights in the index portfolio

By setting cov = 0, we can solve for $W_1^{'}$.

$$\text{cov} = [X_1 \quad X_2] \begin{bmatrix} .01 & 0 \\ 0 & .0064 \end{bmatrix} \begin{bmatrix} .5 \\ .5 \end{bmatrix} = 0$$

$$[X_1 \quad X_2] \begin{bmatrix} .005 & + & 0 \\ 0 & + & .0032 \end{bmatrix} = 0$$

$$.005X_1 + .0032X_2 = 0$$

In order to have two equations and two unknowns, we also use the fact that the weights must always sum to one, i.e.,

$$X_1 + X_2 = 1$$

Solving this system of equations we have

$$.005X_1 + .0032X_2 = 0$$
$$\underline{.005X_1 + .0050X_2 = .005}$$

$$-.0018X_2 = -.005$$
$$X_2 = \frac{.0050}{.0018} = 2.78$$

This implies putting 278 percent of the portfolio wealth into asset 2 and −178 percent into asset 1. Therefore, the expected return on the zero-β portfolio is

$$E(R_p) = -1.78E(R_1) + 2.78E(R_2)$$
$$= -1.78(.2) + 2.78(.1) = -.078$$

(b) The vector of weights in the minimum variance portfolio can be found by using equation 5.21.

$$a^* = \frac{\sigma_y^2 - r_{xy}\sigma_x\sigma_y}{\sigma_x^2 + \sigma_y^2 - 2r_{xy}\sigma_x\sigma_y}$$

From the variance-covariance matrix, $\sum$, we know that

$$\sigma_x^2 = .01 \qquad \text{cov}(X, Y) = 0$$
$$\sigma_y^2 = .0064$$

Therefore, $r_{xy} = 0$, and

$$a^* = \frac{.0064 - 0}{.01 + .0064 - 0} = .390$$

Thus, the minimum variance portfolio consists of 39 percent in asset 1 and 61 percent in asset 2.

(c) Using the covariance definition again, we have

$$cov = W_1' \Sigma W_2$$

$$= [.39 \quad .61] \begin{bmatrix} .01 & 0 \\ 0 & .0064 \end{bmatrix} \begin{bmatrix} -1.78 \\ 2.78 \end{bmatrix}$$

$$= [.39 \quad .61] \begin{bmatrix} -.0178 \\ .0178 \end{bmatrix}$$

$$= -.006942 + .010858 = .003916$$

(d) The equation of the market line is

$$E(R_j) = E(R_z) + [E(R_1) - E(R_z)]\beta_{jI}$$

where

$E(R_j)$ = the expected return on the jth asset

$E(R_z)$ = the expected return on the zero–β portfolio

$E(R_1)$ = the expected return on the efficient index portfolio

$\quad \beta_{jI}$ = the covariance between the returns on the jth asset and the index portfolio, standardized by
       the variance of the index portfolio

Substituting in the estimated parameters, we have

$$E(R_j) = -.078 + [.15 - (-.078)]\beta_{jI}$$

$$E(R_j) = -.078 + .228\beta_{jI}$$

14. Using matrix notation, the definition of covariance is

$$cov(X,Y) = W_x' \Sigma W_y$$

where

W_x' = a row vector of weights in portfolio A

W_y = a column vector of weights in portfolio B

Σ = the variance-covariance matrix of A and B

Substituting in the appropriate numbers, we have

$$cov(X, Y) = [.1 \quad .9] \begin{bmatrix} .01 & -.02 \\ -.02 & .04 \end{bmatrix} \begin{bmatrix} .6 \\ .4 \end{bmatrix}$$

$$= [.1 \quad .9] \begin{bmatrix} .006 & - & .008 \\ -.012 & + & .016 \end{bmatrix}$$

$$= [.1 \quad .9] \begin{bmatrix} -.002 \\ .004 \end{bmatrix}$$

$$= -.0002 + .0036 = .0034$$

15. Using the definition of the correlation coefficient, we have

$$r_{k,m} = \frac{cov(k, m)}{\sigma_k \sigma_m}$$

Substituting the correct numbers and solving for cov(k, m),

$$.8 = \frac{\text{cov(k, m)}}{(.25)(.2)}$$

$$\text{cov(k, m)} = .8(.25)(.2) = .04$$

Using the definition of β we can calculate the systematic risk of Knowlode

$$\beta_k = \frac{\text{cov(k, m)}}{\sigma_m^2} = \frac{.04}{(.2)^2} = 1.0$$

The systematic risk of a portfolio is a weighted average of the asset's β's. If "a" is the percent of Knowlode,

$$\beta_p = (1 - a)\beta_i + a\beta_k$$

$$1.6 = (1 - a)(0) + a(1.0)$$

$$a = 1.6 \text{ or } 160\%$$

In this case the investor would borrow an amount equal to 60 percent of his wealth and invest 160 percent of his wealth in Knowlode in order to obtain a portfolio with a β of 1.6. (This analysis assumes investors may borrow at the risk-free rate.)

16. First, we need to know $E(R_m)$ and R_f. Since each of the assets must fall on the security market line in equilibrium, we can use the CAPM and $E(R_j)$.

$$\text{Asset 1: } E(R_1) = R_f + [E(R_m) - R_f]\beta_1$$

$$7.6 = R_f + [E(R_m) - R_f].2$$

$$\text{Asset 2: } 12.4 = R_f + [E(R_m) - R_f].8$$

This gives two equations with two unknowns. Multiplying the first equation by 4 and subtracting the second equation, we have

$$4(7.6) = 4R_f + [E(R_m) - R_f].8$$

$$-[12.4 = R_f + [E(R_m) - R_f].8]$$

$$18.0 = 3R_f$$

$$R_f = 6 \text{ (i.e., 6\%)}$$

Substituting the value of R_f into equation 1, we have

$$7.6 = 6 + [E(R_m) - 6].2$$

$$\frac{7.6 - 6}{.2} + 6 = E(R_m)$$

$$E(R_m) = 14 \text{ (i.e., 14\%)}$$

To double check, if the values of R_f and $E(R_m)$ are used in order to obtain $E(R_j)$ for assets 3 and 4, they should also fall on the security market line.

For asset 3, we have

$$E(R_3) = 6 + [14 - 6]1.2 = 15.6$$

and for asset 4 we have

$$E(R_4) = 6 + [14 - 6]\,1.6 = 18.8$$

The expected rate of return and β for the current portfolio are

$$E(R_p) = \sum_{i-1}^{5} W_i E(R_i)$$

$$= .1(7.6) + .1(12.4) + .1(15.6) + .2(18.8) + .5(6)$$

$$= 10.32$$

$$\beta_p = \sum_{i=1}^{5} W_i \beta_i$$

$$= .1(.2) + .1(.8) + .1(1.2) + .2(1.6) + .5(0)$$

$$= .54$$

In order to achieve a new portfolio with a 12 percent expected rate of return, we subtract X percent from our holdings in the risk-free asset and add X percent to new holdings in the market portfolio.

$$12 = E(R_p) = .1(7.6) + .1(12.4) + .1(15.6) + .2(18.8)$$

$$+ (.5 - X)(6) + X(14)$$

$$12 - 7.32 = 3 + 8X$$

$$\frac{1.68}{8} = X = .21$$

Therefore, the new portfolio holdings will be

	Return on Asset i	β_i	Percent in Asset i
1	7.6%	.2	10%
2	12.4%	.8	10%
3	15.6%	1.2	10%
4	18.8%	1.6	20%
R_f	6.0%	0	29%
R_m	14.0%	1.0	21%

The expected return of the new portfolio is 12 percent and its β is .75.

If you hold only the risk-free asset and the market portfolio, the set of weights that would yield a 12 percent expected return can be determined as follows:

$$W_1 = \text{amount in risk-free asset}$$

$$W_2 = \text{amount in market portfolio}$$

$$.06W_1 + .14W_2 = .12$$

$$W_1 + W_2 = 1$$

We have two equations with two unknowns. Multiplying the second equation by .06 and subtracting from the first gives

$$.06W_1 + .14W_2 = .12$$

$$-(.06W_1 + .06W_2 = .06)$$

$$.08W_2 = .06$$

$$W_2 = .75$$

$$W_1 + .75 = 1$$

$$W_1 = .25$$

A portfolio with 25 percent in the risk-free asset and 75 percent in the market portfolio has an expected return of 12 percent.

17. We know from the CAPM

$$E(R_j) = R_f + [E(R_m) - R_f]\beta_j$$

Substituting the correct numbers for β_j

$$.13 = .07 + (.08)\beta_j$$

$$\frac{.13 - .07}{.08} = \beta_j$$

$$\beta_j = .75$$

If the rate of return covariance with the market portfolio doubles, β_j will also double since

$$\beta_{j0} = \frac{(\sigma_{jm})_0}{\sigma_m^2} \text{ where } (\sigma_{jm})_0 = \text{original cov}(E(R_j), E(R_m))$$

$$\beta_{j1} = \frac{2(\sigma_{jm})_0}{\sigma_m^2} \text{ where } 2(\sigma_{jm})_0 = \text{subsequent cov}(E(R_j), E(R_m))$$

Therefore

$$\beta_{j1} = 2\beta_{j0}$$

so the new required return for the security will be

$$\text{Required } R_j = .07 + (.08)1.5 = .19 = 19\%$$

At the original rate of return, 13 percent, and given a present price of $P_0 = \$40$, the expected future price, P_1, was

$$P_0(1 + r) = P_1$$

$$40(1.13) = \$45.20$$

If the expected future price is still $45.20 but the covariance with the market has doubled, so that the required return is 19 percent, then the present price will be

$$P_0 = P_1(1 + r)^{-1} = 45.20/1.19$$

$$= \$37.98$$

18. (a) The required rate of return on a security with $\text{cov}(E(R_j), E(R_m)) = .01$ is

$$E(R_j) = R_f + [E(R_m) - R_f]\beta_j$$
$$= .08 + (.16 - .08).25$$
$$E(R_j) = .10$$

where

$$\beta_j = \frac{\sigma_{jm}}{\sigma_m^2} = \frac{.01}{(.2)^2} = .25$$

Since the expected rate of return is greater than the required rate of return, investment in the security would be advisable.

To find the percentage change in the security's price that would result in a return of 10 percent instead of 12 percent, solve for P^* in terms of P_0:

$$P_0(1.12) = P^*(1.10)$$
$$\frac{P^*}{P_0} = \frac{1.12}{1.1} = 1.01818$$

Thus, P^* is a 1.82 percent increase in price over P_0.

If the security's price increases more than 1.82 percent, reverse the investment decision.

(b) There are two possibilities for the low *ex post* return. First, the expected rate of return and the estimated risk could have been overestimated. The second possibility is that after the fact, the market unexpectedly fell. The *ex post* market rate of return which would have resulted in a 5 percent rate of return for the security in question is

$$R_j = R_f + [R_m - R_f]\beta_j$$
$$.05 = .08 + [R_m - .08].25$$
$$R_m = [.05 - .08]4 + .08 = -.04$$

The ex post security market line is depicted in Figure S6.2.

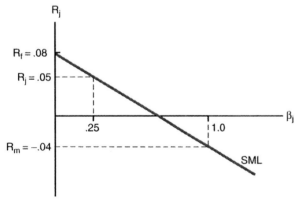

Figure S6.2   The *ex post* security market line

19. (a) Given that some assets are nonmarketable, the equilibrium pricing equation is given by Mayers (1972) in equation 6.26.

$$E(R_j) = R_f + \lambda[V_m \, cov(R_j, R_m) + cov(R_j, R_H)]$$

This implies that the individual will take into consideration not only the covariance of an asset with the market portfolio, but also its covariance with the portfolio of nonmarketable assets. This may be interpreted as a form of three-fund separation, where the three funds are 1) the risk-free asset, 2) the portfolio of risky marketable assets, and 3) the portfolio of risky nonmarketable assets. Separation is still valid in the sense that the marginal rate of substitution between risk and return is independent of individuals' utility preferences.

(b) If the risk-free rate is nonstochastic, then we can use Merton's (1973) continuous time model as shown in equation 6.28

$$E(R_j) = r_f + \gamma_1[E(R_m) - r_f] + \gamma_2[E(R_N) - r_f]$$

Once again, three-fund separation obtains. Every investor will hold one of three funds: 1) the risk-free asset, 2) the market portfolio, and 3) a hedge portfolio chosen to hedge against unforeseen changes in the future risk-free rate. We have separation because the market price of risk (the marginal rate of substitution between risk and return) is independent of individuals' utility functions.

20. (a) The covariance between investor I's index and asset A is

$$COV(R_A, R_I) = [1 \quad 0]\begin{bmatrix} .0081 & 0 \\ 0 & .0025 \end{bmatrix}\begin{bmatrix} .75 \\ .25 \end{bmatrix}$$
$$= .75(.0081) = .006075$$

The variance of investor I's index is

$$COV(R_I, R_I) = [.75 \quad .25]\begin{bmatrix} .0081 & 0 \\ 0 & .0025 \end{bmatrix}\begin{bmatrix} .75 \\ .25 \end{bmatrix}$$
$$= [.75 \quad .25]\begin{bmatrix} .006075 \\ .000625 \end{bmatrix}$$
$$= .0045563 + .0001563 = .0047126$$

Therefore, investor I computes a β of

$$\beta_I = \frac{COV(R_A, R_I)}{COV(R_I, R_I)} = \frac{.006075}{.0047126} = 1.289$$

Repeating the exercise for investor J we have

$$COV(R_A, R_J) = [1 \quad 0]\begin{bmatrix} .0081 & 0 \\ 0 & .0025 \end{bmatrix}\begin{bmatrix} .5 \\ .5 \end{bmatrix}$$
$$= .5(.0081) = .00405$$
$$COV(R_J, R_J) = [.5 \quad .5]\begin{bmatrix} .0081 & 0 \\ 0 & .0025 \end{bmatrix}\begin{bmatrix} .5 \\ .5 \end{bmatrix}$$
$$= [.5 \quad .5]\begin{bmatrix} .00405 \\ .00125 \end{bmatrix}$$
$$= .002025 + .000625 = .002650$$

And investor J estimates a β of

$$b_J = \frac{COV(R_A,R_J)}{COV(R_J,R_J)} = \frac{.00405}{.002650} = 1.528$$

(b) Both investors will require the same rate of return on asset A. They must. They have homogenous expectations therefore they perceive the same risk-return combination. The expected return on asset A is 30%.

(c) The key to understanding this problem is Roll's critique. The two investors choose different index portfolios, but both portfolios are efficient. They must be because this (over-simplified) world has only two risky assets. Any combination of them will lie on the mean variance opportunity set.

Consequently, even though the investors perceive different security market lines and different betas, they will perceive the same expected rate of return on any portfolio. In order to numerically demonstrate this result the zero-beta portfolios and security market lines for each investor are computed below.

The zero-beta portfolio is the minimum variance portfolio which has zero covariance with the index portfolio. Since all portfolios lie on the minimum variance opportunity set in this two-asset world, we need be concerned only with the zero covariance condition. If we define R_z as the return on the zero-beta portfolio and W_z as its vector of weights, then we require that

$$COV(R_z,R_I) = W_z' \Sigma W_I = 0$$

The appropriate numbers for investor I are:

$$COV(R_z,R_I) = [W_{z1} \quad W_{z2}]\begin{bmatrix} .0081 & 0 \\ 0 & .0025 \end{bmatrix}\begin{bmatrix} .75 \\ .25 \end{bmatrix} = 0$$

Solving, we have one equation and two unknowns

$$.75(.0081)W_{z1} + .25(.0025)W_{z2} = 0$$

However, we also know that the weights must add to one

$$W_{z1} + W_{z2} = 1$$

This gives two equations and two unknowns, as shown below

$$.006075W_{z1} + .000625W_{z2} = 0$$
$$W_{z1} + W_{z2} = 1$$

Solving, we have

$$W_{z1} = -.1147, \quad W_{z2} = 1.1147$$

Thus, for investor I the expected return on his zero-beta portfolio is

$$E(R_z) = W_{z1}E(R_A) + W_{z2}(R_B)$$
$$= -.1147(30\%) + 1.1147(20\%)$$
$$= 18.85\%$$

Therefore, the security market line perceived by investor I can be written as follows:

$$E(R_J) = E(R_z) + [E(R_I) - E(R_z)]\beta_I$$
$$= .1885 + [.2750 - .1885]\beta_I, \quad \text{SML for I}$$

Recalling that investor I estimated a β of 1.289 for asset A, we can now verify that investor I expects a 30% rate of return on asset A.

$$E(R_A) = .1885 + [.2750 - .1885]1.289$$
$$= 30\%$$

Next, we repeat the same procedure for investor J. The only difference is that investor J uses a different index portfolio. Investor J's zero-beta portfolio will be

$$COV(R_z, R_j) = W_z' \not{\Sigma} W_j = 0$$

$$COV(R_z, R_j) = [W_{z1} \quad W_{z2}] \begin{bmatrix} .0081 & 0 \\ 0 & .0025 \end{bmatrix} \begin{bmatrix} .50 \\ .50 \end{bmatrix}$$

The two simultaneous equations are

$$.50(.0081)W_{z1} + .50(.0025)W_{z2} = 0$$
$$W_{z1} + W_{z2} = 1$$

and their solution is

$$W_{z1} = -.4464, \quad W_{z2} = 1.4464$$

The expected rate of return on investor J's zero-beta portfolio is

$$E(R_z) = -.4464(30\%) + 1.4464(20\%) = 15.54\%$$

Investor J's security market line equation is

$$E(R_j) = .1554 + [.2500 - .1554]\beta_j, \text{ SML for J.}$$

Finally, recalling that investor J estimated a β of 1.528 for asset A, we see that his expected return on asset A is

$$E(R_A) = .1554 + [.2500 - .1554]1.528$$
$$= 30\%$$

This numerical example demonstrates that although investors I and J estimate different betas, they will have the same expected return for asset A.

21. (a) Using the CAPM, the expected return on her portfolio is

$$E(R_i) = R_f + [E(R_M) - R_f]\beta_i$$
$$= .08 + [.062]1.0$$
$$= .142$$

Using the fact that $E(R_i) = 14.2\%$ for her portfolio and using the APT equation, we have

$$E(R_i) = .142 = .08 + [.05]\beta_{i1} + [.11]\beta_{i2}$$
$$.142 = .08 + [.05](-.5) + [.11]\beta_{i2}$$

$$\frac{.142 - .08 - (.05)(-.5)}{.11} = \beta_{i2}$$
$$.7909 = \beta_{i2}$$

(b) Writing the APT equations once more, we have

$$E(R_i) = .142 = .08 + (.05)\beta_{i1} + (.11)\beta_{i2}$$

Substituting in the value of b_{i2} as zero, we have

$$.142 = .08 + .05\beta_{i1}$$

$$\frac{.142 - .08}{.05} = \beta_{i1}$$

$$1.24 = \beta_{i1}$$

Chapter 7
Pricing Contingent Claims: Option Pricing Theory and Evidence

1. We can use the Black-Scholes formula (equation 7.36 pricing European calls.

$$C = SN(d_1) - Xe^{-r_f T}N(d_2)$$

where

$$d_1 = \frac{\ln(S/X) + r_f T}{\sigma\sqrt{T}} + (1/2)\sigma\sqrt{T}$$

$$d_2 = d_1 - \sigma\sqrt{T}$$

Substituting the correct values into d_1, we have

$$d_1 = \frac{\ln(28/40) + .06(.5)}{\sqrt{.5}\sqrt{.5}} + .5(\sqrt{.5})(\sqrt{.5})$$

$$d_1 = \frac{-.356675 + .03}{.5} + .25 = -.40335$$

$$d_2 = -.40335 - (\sqrt{.5})(\sqrt{.5}) = -.90335$$

Using the Table for Normal Areas, we have

$$N(d_1) = .5 - .1566 = .3434$$

$$N(d_2) = .5 - .3171 = .1829$$

Substituting these values back into the Black-Scholes formula, we have

$$C = 28(.3434) - 40e^{-.06(.5)}(.1829)$$

$$C = 9.6152 - 40(.970446)(.1829)$$

$$= \$2.52$$

2. We know from put-call parity that the value of a European put can be determined using the value of a European call with the same parameters, according to equation 7.8

$$C_0 - P_0 = \frac{(1 + r_f)S_0 - X}{(1 + r_f)}$$

   Solving for P_0, the present value of a put, and converting the formula to continuous rather than discrete compounding, we have

$$P_0 = C_0 - S_0 + X^{-r_f T}e$$

First, calculate the value of the corresponding call option, according to the Black-Scholes formula (equation 7.36)

$$C = SN(d_1) - e^{-r_f T} XN(d_2)$$

where:

$$d_1 = \frac{\ln(S/X) + r_f T}{\sigma\sqrt{T}} + (1/2)\sigma\sqrt{T}$$

Solving for d_1, we have

$$d_1 = \frac{\ln(20/20) + (.08)(.5)}{(.6)(\sqrt{.5})} + (1/2)(.6)(\sqrt{.5})$$

$$= .3064$$

and d_2 is equal to

$$d_2 = d_1 - .6\sqrt{.5}$$

$$= .3064 - .4243$$

$$= -.1179$$

From the Table of Normal Areas, we have

$$N(d_1) = .5 + .12172$$

$$= .62172$$

$$N(d_2) = .5 - .04776$$

$$= .45224$$

Substituting these values into the Black-Scholes formula yields

$$C = 20(.62172) - e^{-(.08)(.5)}(20)(.45224)$$

$$= 12.434 - 8.690$$

$$= 3.744$$

Solving for the value of a put,

$$P = 3.744 - 20 + (20)e^{-(.08)(.5)}$$

$$= -16.256 + 19.216$$

$$= \$2.96$$

3. (a) Figure S7.1a shows the payoffs from selling one call (–C), selling one put (–P), and from the combination (–C–P).

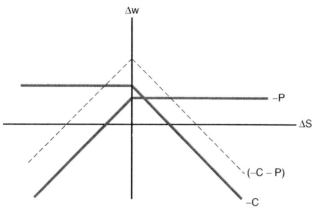

Figure S7.1a   Payoffs from selling one call and one put

The portfolio (–C–P) is the opposite of a straddle. It earns a positive rate of return if the stock price does not change much from its original value. If the instantaneous variance of the stock increases, the value of the call increases, since $\frac{\partial C}{\partial \sigma} > 0$. Suppose the value of the call increases by some amount a > 0,

$$C_1 = C_0 + a$$

Then by put-call parity, the value of the put also increases by a.

$$P_1 = C_1 - S + Xe^{-rt}$$
$$= C_0 + a - S + Xe^{-rt}$$
$$= P_0 + a$$

If you sold one call and one put for prices of C_0 and P_0, and the options' true values were $C_0 + a$ and $P_0 + a$, this represents an opportunity loss to you of –2a. Given the inside information, the portfolio strategy would be to buy both the put and the call (at P_0 and C_0) for a gain of 2a.

(b) Figure S7.1b shows the payoffs from buying one call (+C), selling one put (–P) and from the combination (C – P).

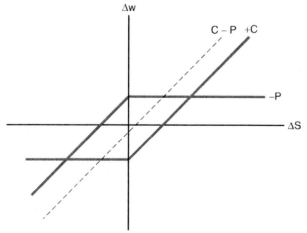

Figure S7.1b   Payoffs from buying one call and selling one put

The return from this portfolio (C − P) remains unchanged by an increase in the instantaneous variance, since, by put-call parity, the increase in the value of the long position in the call option is exactly offset by an increase in the value of the shorted put option. In the algebra of part (a) above,

$$C_0 + a - (P_0 + a) = C_0 + P_0.$$

Therefore, the strategy of this portfolio is neither advantageous nor disadvantageous, given inside information of an increase in the instantaneous variance.

4. The value of the call option can be calculated directly by the Black-Scholes formula for a European call, equation 7.32. Using the correct values from the problem,

$$C = 44.375N(d_1) - 45e^{-(.07)(156/365)} N(d_2).$$

First calculate d_1 and d_2:

$$d_1 = \frac{\ln(44.375/45) + (.07)(156/365)}{(\sqrt{.0961})(\sqrt{156/365})} + (1/2)(\sqrt{.0961})(\sqrt{156/365})$$

$$= \frac{-.01398 + (.07)(.4274)}{(.31)(.6538)} + (1/2)(.31)(.6538)$$

$$= .18$$

$$d_2 = .18 - (\sqrt{.0961})(.6538)$$

$$= -.02$$

Substituting these values into the Black-Scholes Formula,

$$C = 44.375N(.18) - 45e^{-.03}N(-.02)$$

Using the Table of Normal Areas, we can determine N(.18) and N(−.02). Substituting these values into the formula yields

$$C = 44.375(.5714) - 45(.9704)(.4920)$$

$$= 25.3559 - 21.4847$$

$$= \$3.87$$

5. Compare the payoffs at maturity of two portfolios. The first is a European put option with exercise price X_1, and the second is a European put option written on the same stock, with the same time to maturity, but with exercise price $X_2 < X_1$. The payoffs are given in Table S7.1.

Because portfolio A has a value either greater than or equal to the value of portfolio B in every possible state of nature, the put with a higher exercise price is more valuable.

$$P(S, T, X_1) > P(S, T, X_2) \quad \text{if } X_2 < X_1.$$

Table S7.1   State Contingent Payoffs of Put Portfolios

Portfolio	$S < X_2$	$X_2 \leq S < X_1$	$X_1 \leq S$
a) $P(S, T, X_1)$	$X_1 - S$	$X_1 - S$	0
b) $P(S, T, X_2)$	$X_2 - S$	0	0
Comparative Value of A and B	$V_A > V_B$	$V_A > V_B$	$V_A = V_B$

6. The total value of the firm, \$5MM, is

$$V = S + B$$

We can use the OPM to determine the market value of the stock (expressed as a call option on the firm), and subtract this from \$5MM to find B, the market value of the debt.

For $R_1 = .05$, we have

$$S = VN(d_1) - D\ e^{-r_f T} N(d_2)$$

where
S = market value of the stock
V = market value of the firm
D = face value of the debt

$$d_1 = \frac{\ln(5MM/4MM) + (.05)(10)}{(\sqrt{.5})(\sqrt{10})} + (1/2)\left(\sqrt{.5}\right)\left(\sqrt{10}\right)$$

Note that T, the time to maturity, is the time until the firm's debt matures, ten years.

$$d_1 = \frac{(.2231) + (.5)}{2.236} + 1.118$$

$$= 1.44$$

$$d_2 = d_1 - \sigma\sqrt{T}$$

$$= 1.44 - 2.236$$

$$= -.795$$

$$S = 5,000,000N(1.44) - 4,000,000e^{-(.05)(10)}N(-.795)$$

$$= 5,000,000\ (.5 + .42507) - 4,000,000(.6065)(.5 - .2865)$$

$$= 4,625,350 - 517,951$$

$$= \$4,107,399$$

The value of the debt is

$$\$5,000,000 - 4,107,399 = \$892,601.$$

For $r_1 = .10$, we have

$$d_1' = \frac{\ln(5MM/4MM) + (.1)(10)}{(\sqrt{.5})(\sqrt{10})} + (1/2)\left(\sqrt{.5}\right)\left(\sqrt{10}\right)$$

$$= \frac{(.2231 + 1)}{2.236} + 1.118$$

$$= 1.665$$

$$d_2 = d_1 - (\sqrt{.5})(\sqrt{10})$$

$$= 1.665 - 2.236$$

$$= -.571$$

$$S = 5{,}000{,}000N(1.665) - 4{,}000{,}000e^{-(.1)(10)}N(-.571)$$

$$= 5{,}000{,}000(.5 + .452) - 4{,}000{,}000\,(.3679)(.5 - .21603)$$

$$= 4{,}760{,}000 - 417{,}890$$

$$= \$4{,}342{,}110$$

The value of the debt decreases to

$$\$5{,}000{,}000 - 4{,}342{,}110 = \$657{,}890$$

Therefore, the rise in r_f benefits the stockholders. This is what we would expect, since $\dfrac{\partial C}{\partial r_f} > 0$, and the

stockholders in this example hold a call option on the value of the firm.

7. In order to standardize the results we assume that the stock price is equal to 1, (S = 1). The three tables below show the call price as a percentage of the stock price, plotted against the time to maturity (in Table S7.2), the risk-free rate (in Table S7.3), and the standard deviation (in Table S7.4). The relationships given by the tables are graphed in Figures S7.2, S7.3, and S7.4.

Table S7.2 C/S as a Function of T
         Assume: S = 1, r_f = 6%, σ = .2

T in Months	S/X = .9	S/X = 1.0	S/X = 1.1
2	.005	.038	.104
4	.016	.056	.118
6	.028	.072	.131
8	.039	.085	.142
10	.050	.098	.156
12	.060	.110	.167
14	.071	.121	.178
16	.081	.132	.188
18	.091	.142	.198

Table S7.3 C/S as a Function of r_f
         Assume: S = 1, T = 6 months, σ = .2

r_f	S/X = .9	S/X = 1.0	S/X = 1.1
.02	.024	.061	.118
.04	.025	.066	.123
.06	.028	.072	.131
.08	.031	.077	.138
.10	.034	.083	.146
.12	.037	.089	.153
.14	.041	.095	.160
.16	.045	.101	.167
.18	.049	.107	.175

Table S7.4   C/S as a Function of σ
Assume: S = 1, T = 6 months, r_f = 6%

σ	S/X = .9	S/X = 1.0	S/X = 1.1
.01	.000	.030	.118
.05	.000	.033	.118
.10	.005	.045	.119
.15	.015	.058	.124
.20	.028	.072	.131
.25	.041	.085	.141
.30	.054	.099	.152
.35	.068	.112	.163
.40	.082	.126	.175

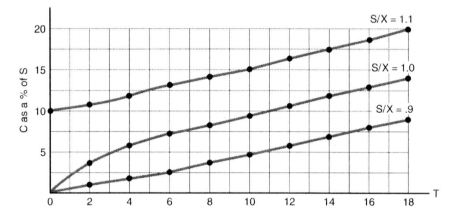

Figure S7.2   C/S as a function of T

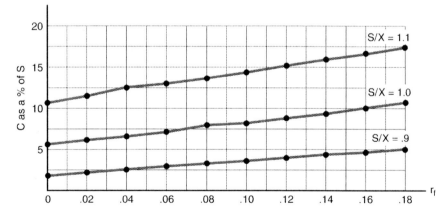

Figure S7.3   C/S as a function of r_f

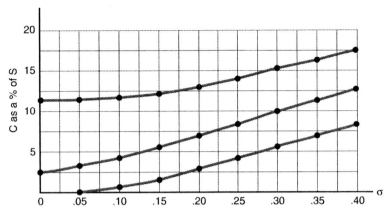

Figure S7.4   C/S as a function of σ

8. The owner of a put option profits when the stock price falls. However, the price cannot fall below zero. This fact limits the maximum profit from holding a put. At any point in time the put can be exercised for X – S dollars. If the date of exercise is t and the time of maturity is T, then the

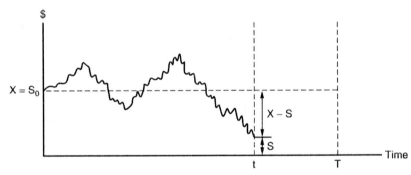

Figure S7.5   The early exercise of an american put option

future value if you exercise now is $(X-S)e^{r_f^{T-t}}$. Alternatively, if you hold the option to maturity it is worth X dollars at most. Therefore, the condition for early exercise is

$$(X-S)\,e^{r_f\,(T-t)} > X.$$

In words, this condition says that you can gain more from exercising immediately and putting the proceeds in a risk-free asset than you could from holding the put to maturity. The above condition can also be rewritten as follows:

$$S < X(1-e^{-r_f\,(T-t)})$$

If the stock price falls below a predetermined level on any given calendar date, it pays to exercise the put option early.

9. As far as the senior debt is concerned, there is no difference between having only common stock or having subordinated debt and common stock outstanding. In either case the senior debt-holders own the firm but have written a call option held by the junior securityholders to sell the firm for D_s at the calendar date, t^*. Therefore, the value of senior debt, B_s, equals the value of the firm minus the call option:

$$B_s = V - [VN(d_s) - D_s\,e^{-r_f T}\,N(d_s - \sigma\sqrt{T})]$$

$$d_s = \frac{\ln(V/D_s) + r_f T}{\sigma\sqrt{T}} + (1/2)\sigma\sqrt{T}$$

where T is the remaining time to maturity.

From the point of view of the common stockholders, there is no difference between senior or junior debt; all that matters is the exercise price they must pay to repurchase the firm at t^*. This is always equal to the face value of *all the debt* $D_S + D_J$. So the value of the stock is

$$S = VN(d_J) - (D_S + D_J)\, e^{-r_j T}\, N(d_{J+S} - \sigma\sqrt{T})$$

where

$$d_{J+S} = \frac{\ln(V/(D_S + D_J)) + r_f T}{\sigma\sqrt{T}} + (1/2)\sigma\sqrt{T}$$

Since the value of the firm equals the value of its securities, the value of the subordinated debt must be

$$B_J = V - B_S - S$$

The subordinate debtholders own a call option to purchase the firm from the senior debtholders for an exercise price of D_S but have written a call option owned by the stockholders allowing the stockholders to buy the firm at an exercise price of $D_S + D_J$.

10. An American put is always worth at least as much as the equivalent European put because the American put can be exercised before its maturity date. As shown in problem 7.8, there are conditions where it pays to exercise an American put early. Therefore, the option which can be exercised at any time is more valuable than the corresponding option which may be exercised only at maturity.

11. The Black-Scholes model estimated the price of the August 45's options to be \$0.09 while the actual market price was \$0.15. This implies either that (1) the August 45's are overpriced by the market or (2) the August 35s, which provided the estimate of implicit variance of 51.5 percent, are undervalued by the market. It really doesn't matter which price is out of line. All that matters is that two options, both written on the same asset, are out of line relative to each other. If the August 45's are overpriced relative to the August 35's, we can form a risk-free hedge by (1) writing $1/(\partial C_1/\partial S)$ August 45 calls and buying one share of stock and (2) buying $1/(\partial C_2/\partial S)$ August 35's calls and selling short one share of stock. If these two positions are combined, the stock holdings net out. Therefore, all we need to do is write $1/(\partial C_1/\partial S)$ August 45s and buy $1/(\partial C_2/\partial S)$ August 35's.

The Black-Scholes formula is

$$C = SN(d_1) - Xe^{-r_f T} N(d_2)$$

The partial derivative with respect to S is

$$\frac{\partial C}{\partial S} = N(d_1)$$

Therefore, the correct ratio of all contracts per share of stock is $[1/N(d_1)]$. According to the Black-Scholes model

$$d_1 = \frac{\ln(S/X) + r_f T}{\sigma\sqrt{T}} + (1/2)\sigma\sqrt{T}$$

Using the facts applicable to Krespy Kreme August 45s we have

$$d_1 = \frac{\ln(34.65/45) + (.0171)(30/365)}{(.515)(\sqrt{30/365})} + (1/2)(.515)(\sqrt{30/365})$$

$$= \frac{-.2614 + .0014}{.1477} + .0738$$

$$= -1.7603 + .0738 = -1.6865$$

and from the Table of Normal Areas

$$N(d_1) = .5 - .454 = .046$$

Repeating this exercise for the KK August 35s, we have

$$d_1' = \frac{\ln(46.75/35) + (.0171)(30/365)}{(.515)(\sqrt{30/365})} + (1/2)(.515)(\sqrt{30/365})$$

$$= \frac{.2815 + .0014}{.1476} + .0738 = 2.04$$

and from the Table of Normal Areas

$$N(d_1') = .5 + .4793 = .9793$$

Therefore, the hedged portfolio will be to write

$$1/(\partial C_1/\partial S) = 1/N(d_1) = 1/.046 = 21.74$$

of the August 35 calls and buy

$$1/(\partial C_2/\partial S) = 1/N(d_1') = 1/.9793 = 1.02$$

of the August 45 calls.

12. (a) Black and Scholes show that a riskless hedge can be created if we continuously adjust our portfolio so that for every share of stock we write (i.e., sell) $[1/(\partial C/\partial S)]$ call options. The Black-Scholes formula for the value of a European call is

$$C = SN(d_1) - X e^{-r_f T} N(d_2)$$

By taking the partial derivative with respect to S, we have

$$\frac{\partial C}{\partial S} = N(d_1)$$

Therefore, if we write $[1/N(d_1)]$ call contracts, we will have created the correct hedge. Given the facts of the problem, we can solve for $N(d_1)$.

$$d_1 = \frac{\ln(S/X) + r_f T}{\sigma\sqrt{T}} + (1/2)\sigma\sqrt{T}$$

$$= \frac{\ln(44.75/40) + (.065)(71/365)}{(.31)(\sqrt{71/365})} + (1/2(.31)(\sqrt{71/365})$$

$$= \frac{.112212 + .0126438}{.1367239} + .0683619$$

$$= .9131966 + .0683619 = .981559$$

From the Table of Normal Areas, we have

$$N(d_1) = .5 + .337 = .837$$

The inverse of $N(d_1)$ is the number of call options to write against each share.

$$1/(\partial C/\partial S) = 1/N(d_1) = 1.1947$$

Therefore, if you hold 100 shares of stock you should write 119.47 call options.

(b) If we assume that Honeybear options are European options, we can obtain an exact solution to the problem by using put-call parity. If the option is an American option, the solution is only approximate. If we write equation 7.10, the put-call parity formula in continuous time, we have

$$C - P = S_0 - X e^{-r_f T}$$

Solving for P:

$$P = X e^{-r_f T} - S + C$$

Substituting the Black-Scholes formula for the value of a European call, we have

$$P = X e^{-r_f T} - S + S N(d_1) - X e^{-r_f T} N(d_2)$$

$$= X e^{-r_f T} (1 - N(d_2)) - S(1 - N(d_1))$$

If you own one share of stock, a risk-free hedge can be formed if you purchase enough put contracts so that $\partial P/\partial S = -dS$; that is, a change in the stock price is offset by an equal and opposite change in the value of the put options held. From the equation for a put, we can find $\dfrac{\partial P}{\partial S}$:

$$\frac{\partial P}{\partial S} = -(1 - N(d_1))$$

Therefore, for each share of stock you hold, you would buy $1/(1 - N(d_1))$ put options. Since $N(d_1) = .837$, if you owned one share you would buy 6.135 puts.

$$\frac{1}{1 - N(d_1)} = \frac{1}{.163} = 6.135 \text{ put options}$$

If you own five put options, you would buy .815 shares.

$$1 \text{ share} = 6.135 \text{ puts}$$

$$\frac{1}{6.135} \text{ shares} = 1 \text{ put}$$

$$.163 \text{ shares} = 1 \text{ put}$$

$$.815 \text{ shares} = 5 \text{ puts}$$

(c) Again, if we assume that the puts and calls are European options, we can find an exact solution. The difference between the riskless position for stock and calls, and the position for stock and puts, will also be riskless. Mathematically, this is

$$1 \cdot S - \frac{1}{N(d_1)} C - (1 \cdot S + \frac{1}{N(d_1)} P) = V_H$$

The position in common stock nets out, leaving us with the necessary position in call and put contracts. In other words, if we buy $1/N(d_1)$ calls, we should also buy $1/(1 - N(d_1))$ puts. Therefore, if we hold one call contract, we should buy 5.135 puts, as shown below.

$$C = \frac{1/(1 - N(d_1))}{1/N(d_1)} P$$

$$= \frac{N(d_1)}{1 - N(d_1)} P$$

$$= \frac{.837}{.163} P$$

$$= 5.135P$$

13. To answer this question, all we need to do is appeal to the logic of the CAPM. The call buyer will have a positive β. The call writer will have a negative β of equal magnitude and opposite sign. Figure S7.6 shows one possible instantaneous frequency function for the price of the underlying asset, S. Given an exercise price of X, the call writer "wins" if the share price is below X, while the call buyer "wins" if the share price is above X. A priori, neither knows what the final outcome will be. In an efficient market, the option would be priced to reflect the perceived probability of winning or losing. It is only after the fact (i.e., after the option expires) that one investor wins and the other loses. Initially they both anticipate returns commensurate with the systematic risk of their position. Otherwise they would not enter into the contract.

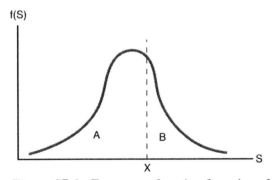

Figure S7.6   Frequency function for price of S

14. The contract is really an application of put-call parity. At maturity the only possible events are:

(1) The store is worth more than \$X at the end of 5 years. In this case she buys the store for \$X and you receive \$X in cash.

(2) The store is worth less than \$X at the end of 5 years. If this happens she must buy it for \$X, and you receive \$X.

Either way you receive \$X at the end of 5 years (assuming that the contract will be honored no matter what happens). The only question is how to establish the exercise price, \$X, so that you earn 20% per year.

If we assume discrete compounding, the put-call parity relationship is

$$S_0 + P_0 - C_0 = \frac{X}{(1+r)^5}.$$

The amount lent is \$80,000, therefore

$$S_0 + P_0 - C_0 = \$80,000.$$

Thus,

$$80,000 = \frac{X}{(1.2)^5}$$

and the exercise price is $X = \$199,065.60$

Chapter 8
The Term Structure of Interest Rates, Forward Contracts, and Futures

1. (a) Assuming that the unbiased expectations hypothesis (as given by Eq. 8.2) is valid, we can solve the problem by computing the following ratio:

$$\frac{(1+_0R_3)^3}{(1+_0R_2)^2} = \frac{(1+_0R_1)(1+_1f_2)(1+_2f_3)}{(1+_0R_1)(1+_2f_2)} = 1+_2f_3$$

$$\frac{(1.15)^3}{(1.14)^2} = \frac{1.5209}{1.2996} = 1.1703 = 1+_2f_3$$

Therefore, the implied forward rate for the third year is

$$_2f_3 = 17.03\%$$

(b) The rate of interest on a bond held from the beginning of the third year and held to the beginning of the fifth year is a two-year rate of interest equal to the product of the expected forward rates during the third and fourth years. The formula is given below:

$$\left(1+_2f_3\right)(1+_3f_4) = \frac{(1+_0R_4)^4}{(1+_0R_2)^2}$$

$$= \frac{(1+_0R_1)(1+_1f_2)(1+_2f_3)(1+_3f_4)}{(1+_0R_1)(1+_1f_2)}$$

$$= \frac{(1.155)^4}{(1.140)^2} = \frac{1.7796}{1.2996} = 1.3693$$

The two-year rate of interest is 36.93%. The average one-year rate is $(1.3693)^{.5} - 1 = 17.02\%$.

2. Vasicek (1977) assumes the following mean-reverting process for the short-term rate (Eq. 8.4):

$$dr = v(\mu - r)dt + \sigma dz$$

where μ is the long-term mean of the short-term rate, v is the speed of adjustment of the short-term rate to the long-term mean and σ is the instantaneous standard deviation. There is mean reversion in the process specified in equation (8.4) since a higher (lower) current short-term rate, r, as compared to the long-run mean, μ, impliea a negative (positive) drift, which, in turn, implies that, an average, the short-term rate will decrease (increase) towards the long-run mean.

The price at time t of a zero-coupon bond that pays $1 at time T is then given by (Eq. 8.5):

$$B(t, T) = A(t, T)e^{-b(t, T)r(t)}$$

where

$$r(t) = \text{the short rate at } t$$

$$b(t, T) = \frac{1 - e^{-v(T-t)}}{v}$$

$$A(t, T) = e^{\left[\dfrac{(b(t,T)-T+t)\left(v^2\mu - \dfrac{\sigma^2}{2}\right)}{v^2} - \dfrac{\sigma^2 b^2(t,T)}{4v} \right]}$$

Since $B(t, T) = e^{-(_t R_T)(T-t)}$, where $_t R_T$ is the interest rate at time t for a term of $(T - t)$, we get:

$$_t R_T = \frac{1}{T-t}\left[b(t,T)r(t) - A(t,T)\right]$$

Equation (8.6) suggests that the entire yield curve can be obtained as a function of r(t) once the three process parameters: the long-term mean of the short-term rate, μ, the speed of adjustment, v, and the instantaneous standard deviation, σ are specified. The term structure can be upward-sloping, downward-sloping or humped depending on the values of the various parameters.

In this question, the current short-term rate, r(t) is 2%, the long-run mean, μ, is 6%, the instantaneous standard deviation, σ, is 10% and the rate of adjustment, v, is 0.4. These set of parameters result in the following term structure of interest rates:

Time to Maturity in Years (T – t)	b(t, T)	A(t, T)	Value of a Zero-Coupon Bond [B(t, T)]	Interest Rate [$_t R_T$]
1	0.8242	0.9907	0.9745	2.58%
2	1.3767	0.9707	0.9443	2.87%
3	1.7470	0.9464	0.9139	3.00%
4	1.9953	0.9208	0.8848	3.06%
5	2.1617	0.8951	0.8572	3.08%

3. Cox, Ingersoll and Ross (1985) (CIR) propose a mean reverting process for the short rate where the standard deviation of the changes in interest rates are proportional to the square root of the level of the rate. In the model, the short-term interest rate process is Eq. (8.7):

$$dr = v(\mu - r)dt + \sigma(\sqrt{r})dz$$

The price of a zero-coupon bond in this framework is given by the equation (8.8):

$$B(t, T) = A(t, T)e^{-b(t,T)r(t)}$$

where

$$b(t,T) = \frac{2\left(e^{r(T-t)} - 1\right)}{2\gamma + (\nu + \gamma)(e^{\gamma(T-t)} - 1)}$$

$$A(t,T) = \left(\frac{2\gamma e^{(\nu+\gamma)(T-t)/2}}{2\gamma + (\nu + \gamma)\left(e^{\gamma(T-t)} - 1\right)}\right)^{2\nu\mu/\sigma^2}$$

$$\gamma = \sqrt{\nu^2 + 2\sigma^2}$$

The interest rate from t to T, $_tR_T$, would be given by Equation (8.9):

$$_tR_T = \frac{1}{T-t}[b(t,T)r(t) - A(t,T)]$$

where b(t, T) and A(t, T) are as defined above.

   In this question, the current short-term rate is 2%, the long-run mean is 6%, the instantaneous standard deviation is 10% and the rate of adjustment is 0.4. These set of parameters result in the following term structure of interest rates:

Time to Maturity in Years (T – t)	b(t, T)	A(t, T)	Value of a Zero-Coupon Bond [B(t, T)]	Interest Rate [$_tR_T$]
1	0.8231	0.9895	0.9734	2.70%
2	1.3705	0.9634	0.9373	3.24%
3	1.7326	0.9279	0.8963	3.65%
4	1.9712	0.8874	0.8531	3.97%
5	2.1284	0.8447	0.8095	4.23%

4.   Ho and Lee propose a binomial model for bond prices of all following form:

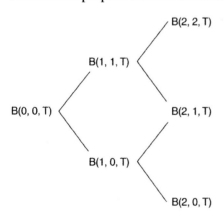

where B(t, i, T) is the price of a bond at time t and state i that pays \$1 at time T. Note that B(0, 0, T) is the initially observed term structure of bond prices. The evolution of bond prices is based on perturbation functions h(τ) and h*(τ) such that (Eqs. 8.10a, 8.10b, 8.10c)

$$B(t,i+1,T) = \frac{B(t-1,i,T)}{B(t-1,i,t)} h(T-t)$$

$$B(t,i,T) = \frac{B(t-1,i,T)}{B(t-1,i,t)} h*(T-t)$$

$$h(0) = h*(0) = 1$$

The above equations when divided imply that (Eq. 8.11):

$$\frac{B(t,i+1,T)}{B(t,i,T)} = \frac{h(T-t)}{h*(T-t)}$$

The no-arbitrage condition implies that (Eq. 8.12)

$$B(t,i,T) = [\pi B(t+1,i+1,T) + (1-\pi)B(t+1,i,T)]B(t,i,t+1)$$

where π is the probability associated with the perturbation h(τ). Combining the no arbitrage condition with the perturbation equations yields the following constraint on the perturbation function (Eq. 8.13):

$$\pi h(\tau) + (1-\pi)h*(\tau) = 1$$

Ho and Lee also show that for path independence to hold such that the order of the perturbations is not important, h(τ) and h*(τ) have to satisfy the following conditions(Eq. 8.14):

$$h(\tau) = \frac{1}{\pi + (1-\pi)\delta^\tau} \text{ and } h*(\tau) = \frac{\delta^\tau}{\pi + (1-\pi)\delta^\tau}$$

for some constant $0 \le \delta \le 1$.

In this question, π and δ to be 0.5 and 0.9, respectively. In addition, 1, 2 and 3-year rates are at 4, 5 and 6%, respectively. These inputs would result in the following values for h(T), h*(T) and B (0, 0, T):

Maturity (T)	h(T)	h*(T)	B(0, 0, T)
1	1.053	0.947	0.9615
2	1.105	0.895	0.9070
3	1.157	0.843	0.8396

Applying the no-arbitrage condition to B(0, 0, 2), we get:

$$B(0, 0, 2) = [0.5B(1,1,2) + 0.5B(1,0,2)]B(0,0,1)$$

The perturbation conditions imply that:

$$\frac{B(1,1,2)}{B(1,0,2)} = \frac{h(1)}{h*(1)}$$

Substituting values from the table into the above two equations yields B(1,1,2) = 0.9496 and B(1, 0, 2) = 0.9021. This implies that with a perturbation of h or h*, the value of a bond that pays \$1 in 2 periods is going to be 0.9496 or 0.9021 in one period.

Applying the same logic and process at different nodes yields the following tree of bond prices:

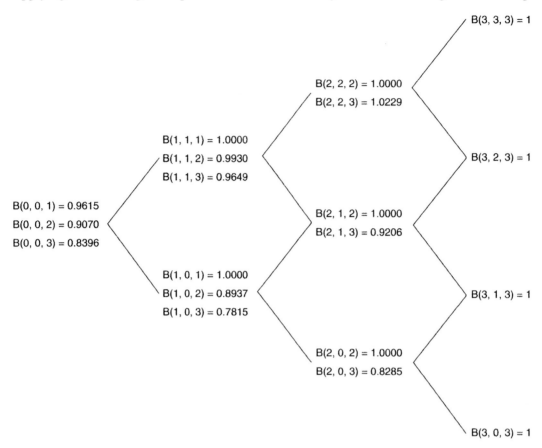

B(3, 3, 3) = 1

B(2, 2, 2) = 1.0000
B(2, 2, 3) = 1.0229

B(1, 1, 1) = 1.0000
B(1, 1, 2) = 0.9930
B(1, 1, 3) = 0.9649

B(3, 2, 3) = 1

B(0, 0, 1) = 0.9615
B(0, 0, 2) = 0.9070
B(0, 0, 3) = 0.8396

B(2, 1, 2) = 1.0000
B(2, 1, 3) = 0.9206

B(1, 0, 1) = 1.0000
B(1, 0, 2) = 0.8937
B(1, 0, 3) = 0.7815

B(3, 1, 3) = 1

B(2, 0, 2) = 1.0000
B(2, 0, 3) = 0.8285

B(3, 0, 3) = 1

5. There are several possible answers to this question. First, using the insight provided by Samuelson in Eq. (8.30), we note that the variance of futures contracts declines for longer-lived contracts. Far distant contracts have relatively lower variance because autoregressive prices have a long interval to correct themselves. As a result, there may be no market for long-lived contracts because their prices would not fluctuate enough to create any trading volume. A second, and related, answer is that hedgers may have no need to protect themselves against price fluctuations more than 18 months in the future.

6. (a) The first step is to compare the product of short-term rates against the longer-term rate.

$$(1.10)^{167/360} > (1.125)^{90/360}(1.06)^{77/360}$$

$$1.045205 > (1.029884)\,(1.012541)$$

$$1.045205 > 1.042799$$

The results tell us that a higher yield can be obtained if we are long in the 167 day T-bill and short in the futures contract and the short-term (77-day) T-bill.

(b) To make a riskless arbitrage profit we need to borrow enough to purchase one futures contract that will deliver a $1,000,000 face value 90-day T-bill on March 22. If the 167-day T-bill yields 10 percent, it costs

$$PV = \$1,000,000(1.10)^{-167/360}$$

$$= \$1,000,000(.95674983)$$

$$= \$956,749.83$$

We will borrow this amount at 6 percent for 77 days. Therefore, on March 22 we will repay

$$FV = \$956,749.83(1.06)^{77/360}$$

$$= \$956,749.83(1.012541)$$

$$= \$968,748.49$$

Simultaneously, we will sell short a T-bill futures contract with a $1,000,000 face value. On March 22, to cover our short position, we deliver our $1,000,000 face value T-bill that now has 90-days to maturity. In return, we receive the following amount of cash

$$PV = \$1,000,000(1.125)^{-90/360}$$

$$= \$1,000,000(.97098354)$$

$$\doteq \$970,983.54$$

After repaying the loan, our profit (on March 22) is

Cash received	$970,983.54
Loan payment	968,748.49
Pre-tax profit	$ 2,235.05

7. (a) Trends or seasonality in spot prices have no effect on futures prices. See Section D.2
    (b) Trends in spot prices can affect the variance of futures prices. Since spot prices are expected to rise from February through May, the autoregressive coefficient, a, in Eq. 8.21 is greater than one; and the variance of the futures price will decrease as we get closer to maturity.

8. (a) We can create a synthetic forward contract by buying a European call, C, on the underlying asset with maturity T and exercise price X equal to the forward price $_0F_T$; and simultaneously writing a European put, P, with the same time to maturity and exercise price. The put-call parity equation is

$$C_0 - P_0 = S_0 - X e^{-r_f T}$$

and the exercise price must equal the forward price, therefore,

$$C_0 - P_0 = S_0 - {_0F_T} e^{-r_f T}$$

$$C_0 - P_0 = 30 - 35 e^{-.07(.5)}$$

$$= 30 - 35(.965605)$$

$$= 30 - 33.79619$$

$$= -3.80$$

Consequently, it would be necessary to borrow $3.80 in order to have zero cash outlay.

    (b) If you believe the stock price will be $42 six months from now, you profit at delivery will be

$$Profit = S_T - {_0F_T}$$

$$= \$42.00 - S_0 e^{r_f T}$$

$$= \$42.00 - \$30.00 e^{.07(.5)}$$

$$= \$42.00 - \$30.00(1.03562)$$

$$= \$42.00 - \$31.07$$

$$= \$10.93$$

9. (a) Presumably, you are planning to close out your positions in March of 1987 when the shorter-lived contract expires. If the two contracts are highly correlated, you bear little risk until March 1987.
    (b) The profitability of your position depends on the spot price of silver. According to Eq. (8.34) the price of a T-period futures contract is

$$_tF_T = S_t e^{t_t T} + {}_tW_T - {}_tC_T$$

Your position is the difference between two futures contracts which will be held for the same period of time. Hence the carrying costs and convenience yields should be the same for your expected 3-month holding period. The risk of changes in expected convenience yields and carrying costs beyond the March 1987 contract expiration date are assumed to be small. If so, the difference in the values of the two contracts is

$$_tF_{3/88} - {}_tF_{3/87} = S_t e^{(15/12)(.08)} - S_t e^{(3/12)(.08)}$$

$$\$6.008 - \$5.610 = S_t (1.105171 - 1.020201)$$

$$\frac{\$.398}{.084970} = S_t = \$4.684$$

Consequently, if the spot price of silver is greater than \$4.684 per ounce, you will make a profit.

10. To alleviate timing or market risk, you can sell short stock index futures contracts. If the market index falls, losses in your portfolio will be offset by gains in your stock index position (and vice versa).

11. An effective strategy, called a time spread, would be to sell long-term T-bill futures and buy short-term T-bill futures, then close out your position after the yield spread widens. Note that this is not a hedged position. If the yield spread narrows you will lose money.

12. This is a cross-hedging problem, similar to what was covered in Chapter 5 (Portfolio Theory). The general idea is to minimize shareholders' risk by augmenting their current position with T-bond contracts. Since T-bonds are positively correlated with the market value of loans, a short position is required. As interest rates rise, the market value of fixed rate loans falls, but would be offset by gains from a short position in T-bonds. This effect is counterbalanced by the positive correlation between T-bonds and demand deposits (a liability). To find the optimal number of contracts, write out the variance of the shareholders' position, take the derivative with respect to the number of futures contracts, and set the result equal to zero. From Chapter 5, the result is

$$N = -\sum_{i=1}^{N} - \frac{\rho_{i,F}\sigma_i V_i}{\sigma_F P_F}$$

where:

N = the optimal number of futures contracts
$\rho_{i,F}$ = the correlation between the ith asset (liability) and futures contracts
σ_i = the standard deviation of the ith asset (liability)
P_F = the price of a futures contract
V_i = the market value of the ith asset (liability)

Substituting in the facts of the problem, we have

$$N = -\frac{(.30)(.06)(820 \text{ mm})}{.08(.08 \text{ mm})} - \frac{(.15)(.02)(-900 \text{ mm})}{.08(.08 \text{ mm})}$$

$$= -2,306.3 + 421.9$$

$$= -1,884.4 \text{ contracts}$$

Therefore, the optimal hedge is to go short 1,884.4 T-bond futures contracts.

Chapter 9
Multiperiod Capital Budgeting under Uncertainty: Real Options Analysis

1. (a) First, what is the project's NPV without the option to expand?

NPV cannot capture the flexibility of the project. Without the option to expand the NPV of the project is 10. The up and down movement for the binomial tree are estimated as follows:

Annual Volatility (σ) = 15%

$$u = e^{\sigma\sqrt{t}} = e^{0.15\sqrt{t}} = 1.16$$

$$d = \frac{1}{u} = \frac{1}{1.16} = 0.86$$

uV = 1.16*30 = 34.86

PV = 30

–Initial investment = –20

Net Present Value = 10

34.86

25.82

40.50

30.00

22.22

Time

0   1   2

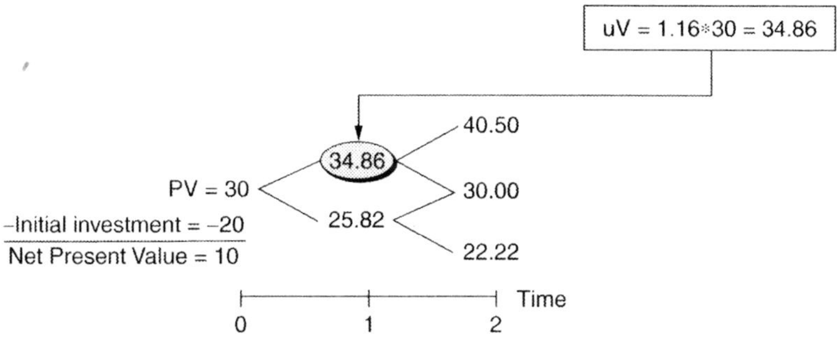

Figure S9.1A   Present value event tree

(b) What is the project's ROA value with the option to expand? (Prove your answer).

The real option to expand turns out to be valuable because the project can be optimally expanded under certain scenarios. The ROA value of the project is $11.53, which is higher than its NPV of $10

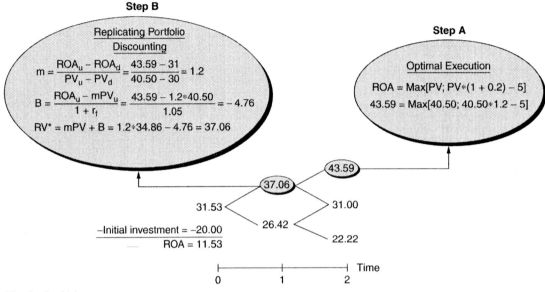

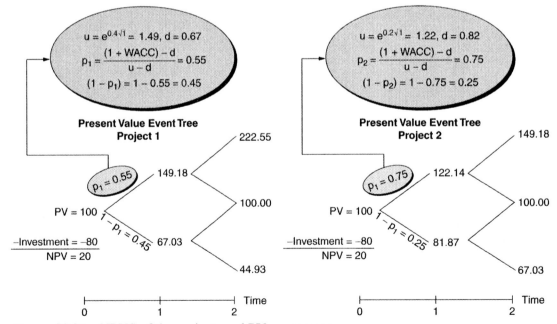

*Replication Value
RV = mPV + B

Figure S9.1B   ROA decision tree

2.   (a) First, we must estimate the NPV of the two mutually exclusive projects.

Present Value Event trees and objective probabilities for each project are given below. The NPV of both projects is $20

Figure S9.2A   NPVS of the projects and PV event trees

Using a Decision Tree Analysis (DTA), answer the following questions: Which project should the company select? Since the DTA value of Project 1 is higher and positive it should be selected for execution. Note that DTA discounts using the WACC even though risk has changed.

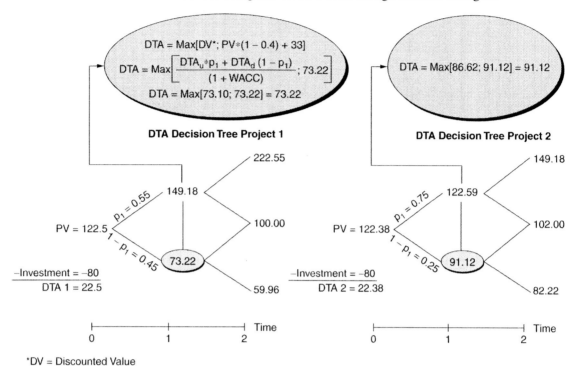

*DV = Discounted Value

Figure S9.2B   Decision tree for the projects

Using Decision Tree Analysis (DTA), answer the following question: when and under what conditions would the options to contract be executed with each project? With Project 1 and Project 2, the option to contract should be executed next year if their present values continuously decline. With Project 2, the option should also be executed at the end of the second year if the present value is at its current level

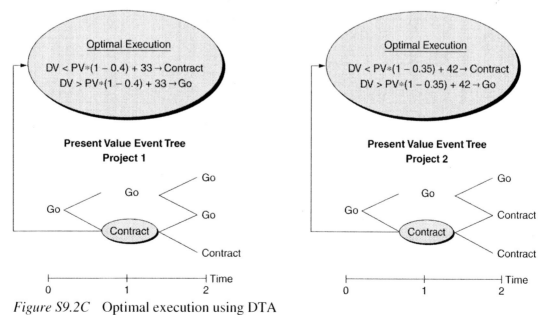

Figure S9.2C   Optimal execution using DTA

Using a Decision Tree Analysis (DTA), answer the following question: What is the value of the option to contract with Project 1 and Project 2? As the option to contract is the only flexibility accounted for in the DTA valuation, its value is equal to the difference between the DTA value and the NPV

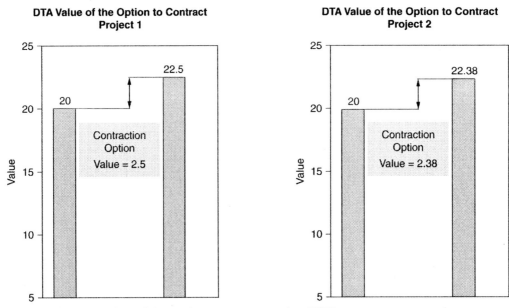

Figure S9.2D   Value of the option to contract using DTA

(b) Using Real Option Analysis (ROA), which project should the company select? As the ROA value of Project 2 is higher and positive, it should be selected for execution

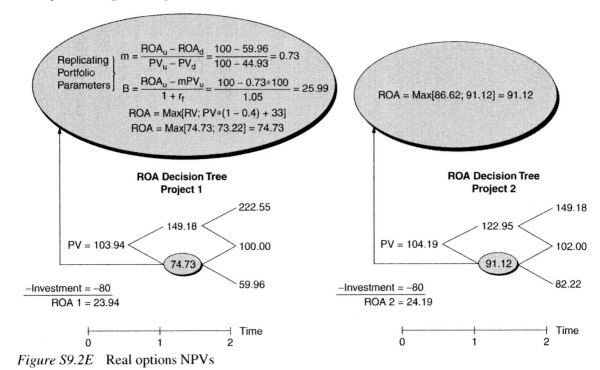

Figure S9.2E   Real options NPVs

Using a Real Option Analysis (ROA), answer the following question: When and under what conditions would the options to contract be executed with each project? With Project 1, contract at the end of year two if the present value has been falling successively. With Project 2, contract if the PV of the project drops during the first period, or if the present value is at its current level at the end of the second period. This optimal execution is different when using ROA versus DTA.

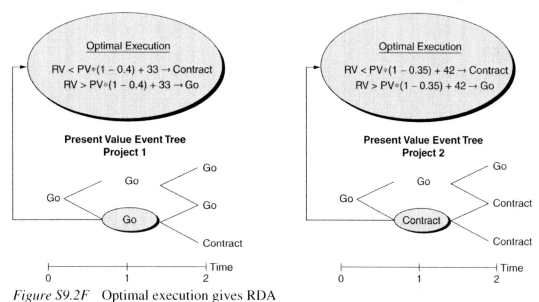

Figure S9.2F   Optimal execution gives RDA

What is the value of the option to contract with Project 1 and Project 2 using ROA? As the option to contract is the only flexibility accounted for in the ROA valuation, its value is equal to the difference between the ROA value and the NPV

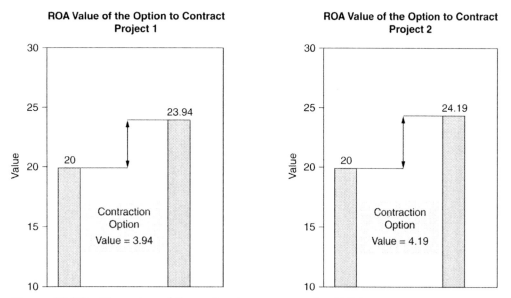

Figure S9.2G   The value of the option to contract using ROA

(c) Do the DTA and ROA valuation suggest the same optimal execution for the options, the same value for each of the two projects? The DTA and ROA valuations suggest different optimal execution of the option to contract for Project 1. With DTA we wrongly select Project 1, and with ROA we correctly select Project 2.

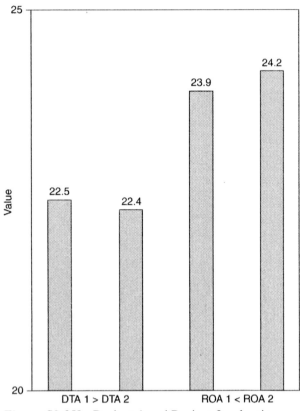

Figure S9.2H   Project 1 and Project 2 valuations

3. Two companies are developing a 50/50 joint venture with an NPV of $25 million. The annual volatility of the venture is 20%. The risk-free rate is 5%. One of the companies wants to buy the right from the other to acquire its 50% share in a year for $15 million.

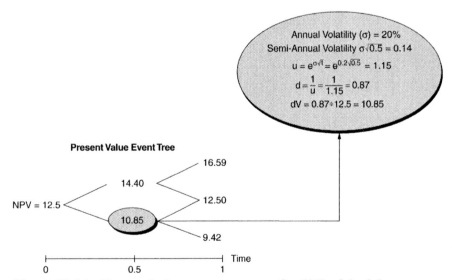

Figure S9.3A   Two period per year event tree for 50% of the joint venture

(a) Using a two period model (six months per period,), what is the maximum price the company should be ready to pay for the option?

Valued with two period per year, the real option to acquire half of the joint venture in a year is worth 0.46 million

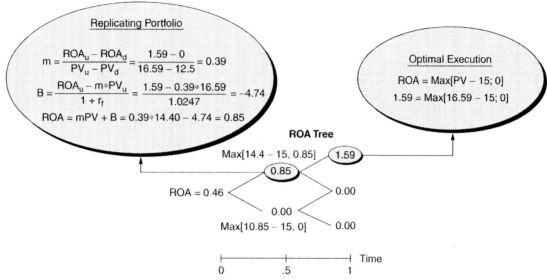

Note: Given an annual rate of 5%,
The six-month rate is $(1.05)^{-5} - 1 = 0.0247$

Figure S9.3B   PV of the right to acquire 50% of the JV

(b) Given 3 periods per year, the estimate of u and d changes, but the NPV remains the same.

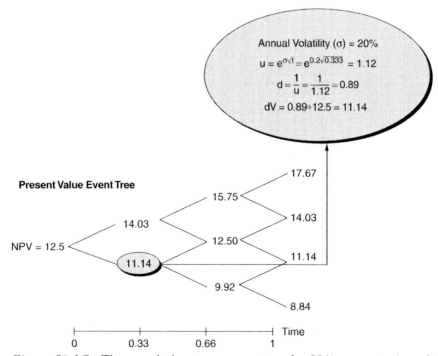

Figure S9.3C   Three period per year event tree for 50% present value of the joint venture

Using a three period model (four months per period) how does the option price change? Valued with three periods per year using the replication method, the real option to acquire half of the joint venture in a year is worth 0.41 million

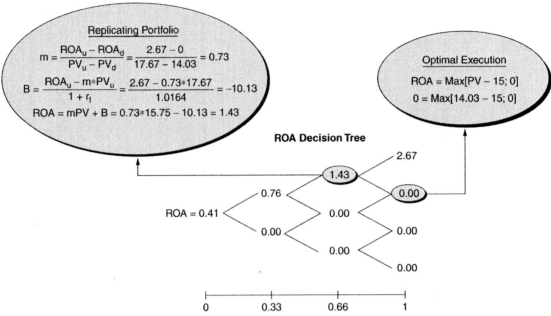

Figure S9.3D   Different Estimate of value, assuming 3 Binomial Trials per year

(c)   How can we use the Black-Scholes formula to solve this problem? What is the option price if we use the Black-Scholes formula? As the option to acquire half of the joint venture in a year is a European Call Option we can use the Black-Scholes formula to value it. The value is 0.41 million

Inputs for Comparison Calculations

- Present value of underlying (V_0): 12.5
- Risk-free rate (r_f): 5%
- Exercise price (X): 15
- Annual Volatility (σ):20%
- Time Span (T): 1

Step 1:   Calculate d_1 and d_2 for Black-Scholes formula

$$d_1 = \frac{ln(V_0/X) + r_f T}{\sigma\sqrt{T}} + \frac{1}{2}\sigma\sqrt{T}$$

$$d_1 = \frac{ln(12.5/15) + 0.05*1}{.20\sqrt{1}} + \frac{1}{2}0.20\sqrt{1}$$

$$d_1 = \frac{-0.1823 + 0.05}{.20} + 0.1 = -0.562$$

Step 2:   Calculate cumulative normal probabilities

$$N(d_1) = N(-0.562) = 0.287$$

$$d_2 = d_1 - \sigma\sqrt{T} = -0.562 - .2$$

$$= -0.762$$

$$N(d_2) = N(-0.762) = 0.223$$

Step 3:   Calculate option value

$$C_0 = V_0 N(d_1) - Xe^{-r_f T} N(d_2)$$

$$= 12.5 * 0.287* - 15e^{-0.05}(0.223)$$

$$= 3.588 - 3.182 = 0.41$$

(d) Which of the three prices would you use to make a decision and why? What price would you use if the buyer wants the right to buy the share at any time during the year? The Black-Scholes formula provides the most correct valuation and so 0.41 million is the correct price

(e) We can use the same price if the option is American and could be exercised at any time. As the joint venture does not pay dividends the option should always be exercised at the end of the year.

4. (a) First create on event tree for the underlying risky asset

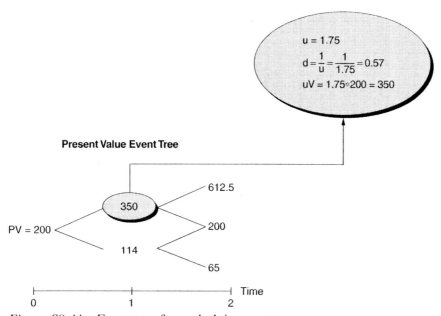

Figure S9.4A   Event tree for underlying asset

(b) Execution of the option must occur at the end of the decision tree (it is a European put) Use of replicating portfolios to value the project with the abandonment put option

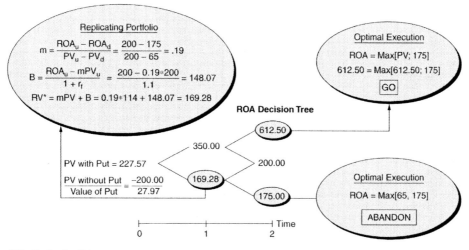

*RV = Replication Value

Figure S9.4B   ROA of the European put

5. (a) **Event tree for the underlying risky asset.** Note that the value of the underlying ex dividend is ten percent less when the dividend is paid at the end of each period

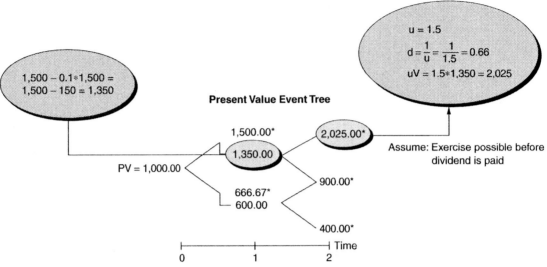

Figure S9.5A   Event tree with divided payment

(b) Note, in this case, we have optimal execution of the option at the end of the decision tree and we used replicating portfolios to value the call option

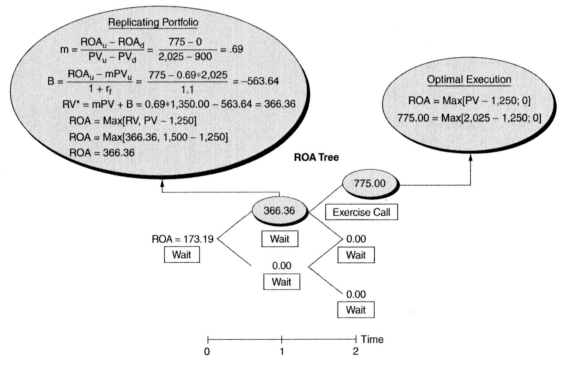

*RV = Replication Value

Figure S9.5B   Valuation of the American call

6. (a) The first step is to create the event tree for the underlying risky asset

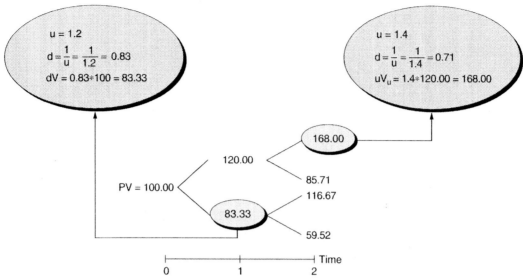

Figure S9.6A   Event tree for the underlying risky asset (Non-recombining)

(b) The second step is to use replicating portfolios to value the call option, assuming optimal execution of the option at the end of the decision tree

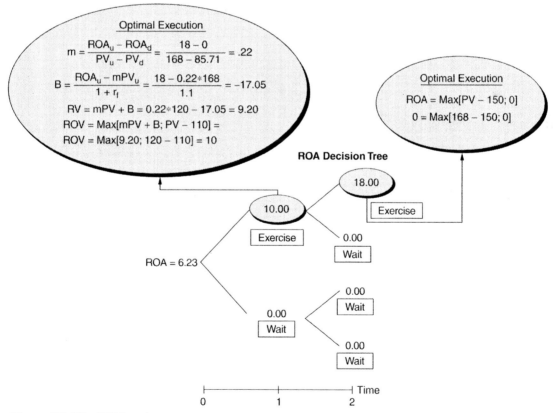

Figure S9.6B   ROA value

7.   Figure S9.7A shows the calculations. For example, at node D you can expand, contract or keep your options open, the values of these alternatives are respectively $2545, $1600 and $2554. Therefore, the best action at node D is simply to keep your option open.

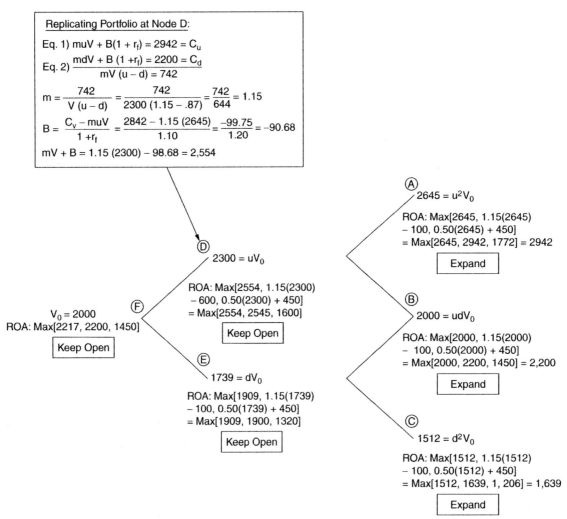

> **Replicating Portfolio at Node D:**
>
> Eq. 1) $muV + B(1 + r_f) = 2942 = C_u$
>
> Eq. 2) $\dfrac{mdV + B(1 + r_f) = 2200 = C_d}{mV(u - d) = 742}$
>
> $m = \dfrac{742}{V(u - d)} = \dfrac{742}{2300(1.15 - .87)} = \dfrac{742}{644} = 1.15$
>
> $B = \dfrac{C_v - muV}{1 + r_f} = \dfrac{2842 - 1.15(2645)}{1.10} = \dfrac{-99.75}{1.20} = -90.68$
>
> $mV + B = 1.15(2300) - 98.68 = 2,554$

Ⓐ
$2645 = u^2V_0$

ROA: Max[2645, 1.15(2645)
– 100, 0.50(2645) + 450]
= Max[2645, 2942, 1772] = 2942

Expand

Ⓓ
$2300 = uV_0$

ROA: Max[2554, 1.15(2300)
– 600, 0.50(2300) + 450]
= Max[2554, 2545, 1600]

Keep Open

Ⓑ
$2000 = udV_0$

ROA: Max[2000, 1.15(2000)
– 100, 0.50(2000) + 450]
= Max[2000, 2200, 1450] = 2,200

Expand

Ⓕ
$V_0 = 2000$
ROA: Max[2217, 2200, 1450]

Keep Open

Ⓔ
$1739 = dV_0$

ROA: Max[1909, 1.15(1739)
– 100, 0.50(1739) + 450]
= Max[1909, 1900, 1320]

Keep Open

Ⓒ
$1512 = d^2V_0$

ROA: Max[1512, 1.15(1512)
– 100, 0.50(1512) + 450]
= Max[1512, 1639, 1, 206] = 1,639

Expand

Figure S9.7A

8.   To solve the problem, we have made the following assumptions:

- If the mine is open to begin with, it produces 4,000 tons immediately, so that if the mine stays open it will require 2 time periods to be exhausted.

- If the mine should be closed at time zero, there is no production a time zero (inventory is not reduced) and the closing cost is paid immediately.

This is a switching option. If open (at a cost of $20,000) the mine depletes the inventory (12,000 tons) at the rate of 4,000 tons per year. If closed (at a cost of $30,000) there is no production.

Price and free cash flow event trees with objective probabilities for the extraction project are given in Figure S9.8A, assuming the mine is open.

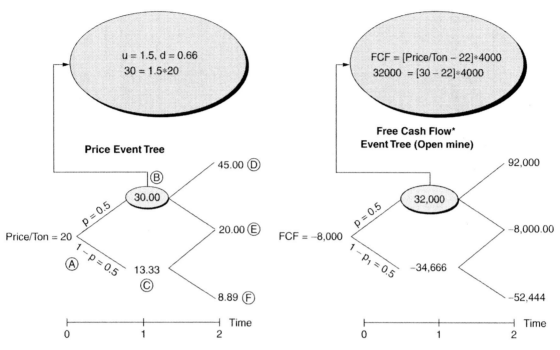

*FCF = (Price/Ton – Extraction Cost/Ton) Production Rate

Figure S9.8A   Price and cash flow event tree

Since all decisions are based on value, we need to construct the **present value event tree for the project in operation**, as shown in Figure S9.8B. Of course, *if the project is not in operation, all cash flows (FCF$_C$) and the present value (PV$_C$) are zero.*

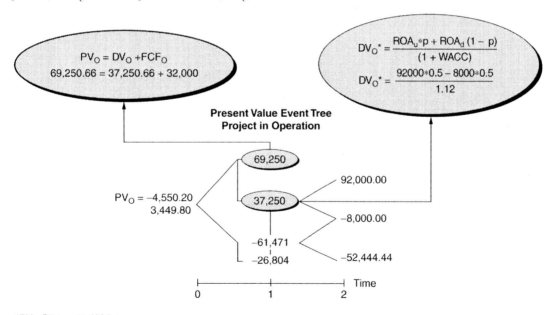

*DV - Discounted Value

Figure S9.8B   Value event tree (open mine)

The Solution Logic is the following

1. Identify optimal action for each node on the event tree entering in "Open" and "Closed" mode, starting from the back of the tree

2. Each decision compares the marginal cost of closing/opening (lost cash flow from current operations and closing cost) with the present value of keeping the mine open/closed

3. If we close the mine at a node with remaining deposits in the ground, the cash flow in the valuation of the mine is zero even though it may be reopened in the future if the price is sufficiently high

4. The optimal reopening of the mine in the future should be decided by solving the same type of problem at each future node while deposits remain.

ROA value of the extraction project entering in each state (price level) in mode "Closed"

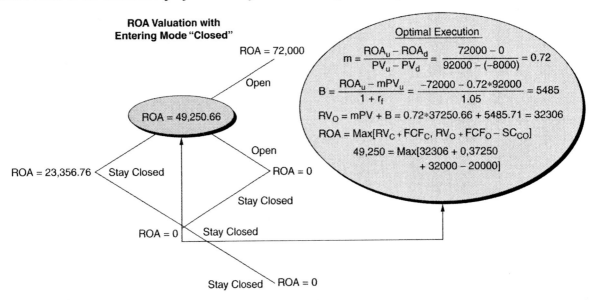

Note: The solution in this figure underestimates the value of the project because it only covers three years of operation and because there is a full inventory of 12,000 tons if either of the two lower paths were experienced on the way to year 3.

Figure S9.8C   Present value assuming the mine starts in a "Closed" mode

ROA value of the extraction project entering in each state (price level) in mode "Open"

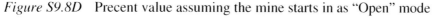

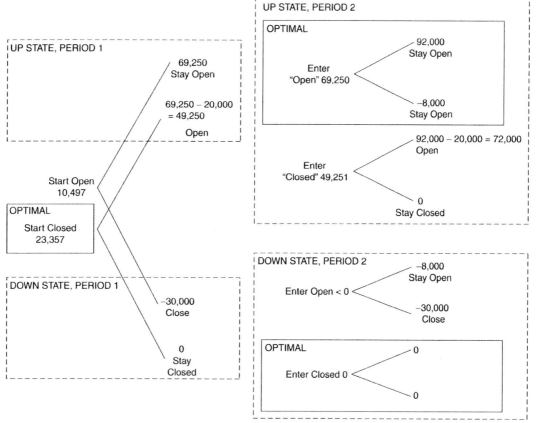

Figure S9.8D Precent value assuming the mine starts in as "Open" mode

The final solution starts by comparing the period 2 values of starting the period open or closed, changes the optimum (enter open) then works back to period 1—using a "backward forward" algorithm

Figure S9.8E Solution to switching option

How does the answer change if the price of the mineral is currently $26?

Price and free cash flow event trees with objective probabilities for the extraction project given the current price of $26 per ton and shown in Figure S9.8F.

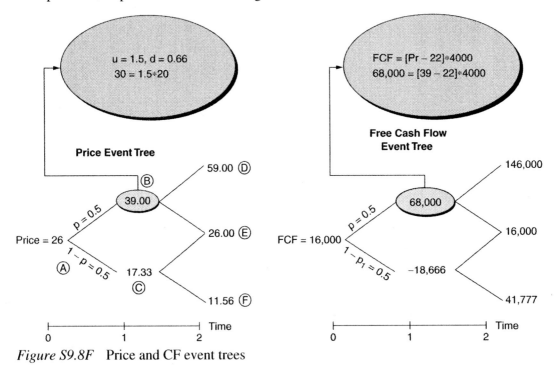

Figure S9.8F   Price and CF event trees

Present value event tree for the project in operation, assuming a current price of $26 per ton. If the project is not in operation, all cash flows (FCF_c) and the present value (PV_c) are zero.

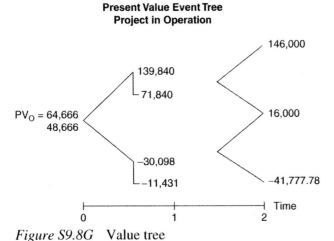

Figure S9.8G   Value tree

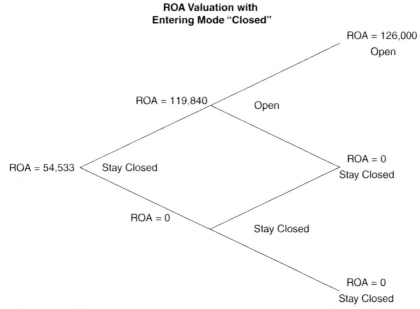

Figure S9.8H   Values of the project entering in mode "Closed"

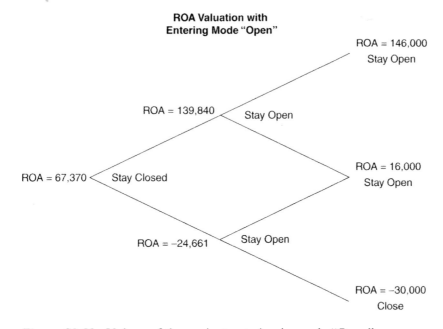

Figure S9.8I   Values of the project entering in mode "Open"

The higher price per ton changes the optimal starting mode of operation to "open" and raises the value of the project to $67,370

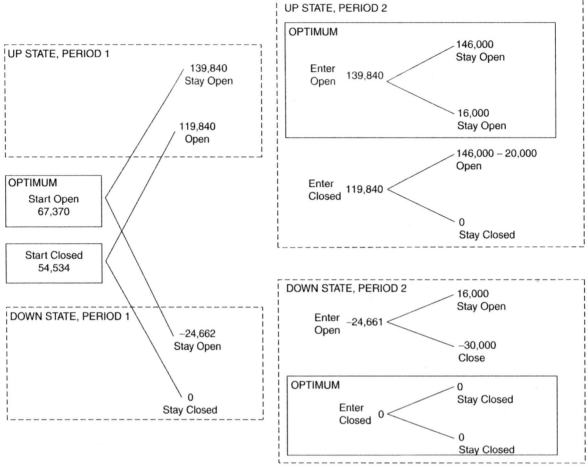

Figure S9.8J   New solution, give price of $26

9. This is an example of a simultaneous compound option. The binomial event tree for the underlying unlevered form is given in Figure S9.9A.

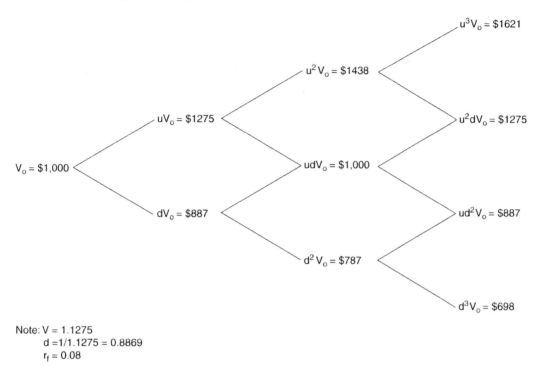

Note: V = 1.1275
    d = 1/1.1275 = 0.8869
    r_f = 0.08

Figure S9.9A   Binomial event tree for the unlevered firm

The equity of the levered firm is a call option on the firm. Its exercise price is the $800 face value of the zero-coupon debt and its maturity date is 3 years. Figure S9.9B values the equity. The value of the equity is $484, therefore the present value of the debt is $516 and its yield to maturity is 15.7%

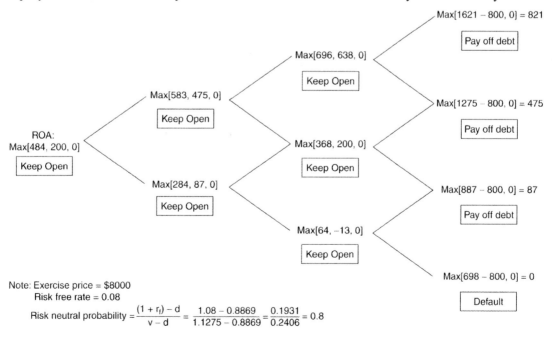

Note: Exercise price = $8000
    Risk free rate = 0.08
    Risk neutral probability $= \frac{(1 + r_f) - d}{v - d} = \frac{1.08 - 0.8869}{1.1275 - 0.8869} = \frac{0.1931}{0.2406} = 0.8$

Figure S9.9B   Equity valued as on option on the levered firm

Finally, the equity is the underlying asset for the American call that has an exercise rice of $400. Its value is calculated in Figure S9.9C as $260

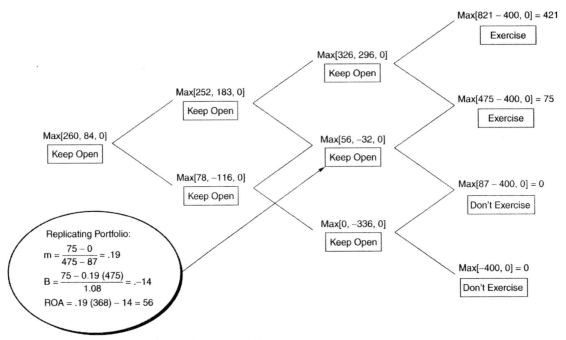

Figure S9.9C   Call on equity of a levered firm

10. Figure S9.10 shows the underlying. The first option, chronologically, is contingent on the value of the second, therefore the option values of the second option are the underlying for the first. The problem statement failed to provide a risk-free rate, therefore we assume it is 8%.

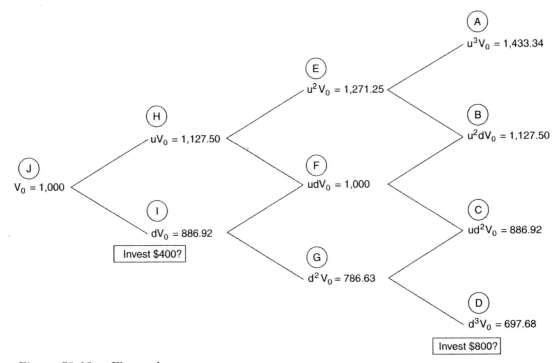

Figure S9.10a   Firm value event tree.

Figure S9.10b shows the valuation of the second option. At node E, for example, if we use the replicating portfolio method, we have

$$mu^3 V + (1 + r_t)B = 1,433 - 800 = 633$$

$$mu^2 dV + (1 + r_t)B = 1,128 - 800 = 328$$

$$m(1,433 - 1,128) = 305$$

$$m = \frac{305}{305} = 1$$

$$mu^3 V + (1 + r_t)B = 633$$

$$1,433 + (1.08)B = 633$$

$$B = \frac{633 - 1,433}{1.08} = \frac{-833}{1.08} = -771$$

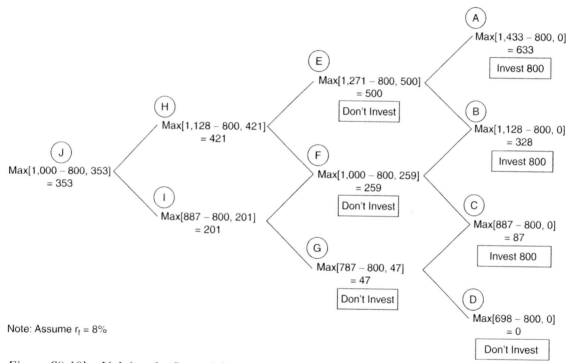

Note: Assume r_f = 8%

Figure S9.10b   Valuing the Second Option

Therefore, the option is worth

$$m u^2 V_0 + B = 1(1,271) - 771 = 500$$

at node E. The value if the option is exercised, is $1,271 − $800 = $471. Because the option is worth $29 more if it is not exercised, no investment will be made at node E. The option value at nodes F and G can be calculated in the same way. At node H, m = 0.89% and B = −583.

Next, we calculate the value of the first option as shown in Figure S9.10c. If exercised at the end of the first year, the payout of the first option is the value of the second option chronologically. Again, using the replicating portfolio approach at node A, we have

$$m\,421 - 1.08B = 21$$

$$\underline{\quad m\,201 - 1.08B = 0 \quad}$$

$$m = \frac{21 - 0}{421 - 201} = \frac{21}{220} = .10$$

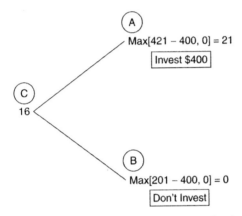

Figure S9.10c   Valuing the First Option

and solving for B, we have

$$m\,(421) - 1.08\,B = 21$$

$$B = \frac{21 - 42}{1.08} = -19$$

Finally, the value of the compound option at the zero is

$$mV + B = .10\,(393) - 19 = 16$$

Chapter 10
Efficient Capital Markets: Theory

1. (a) Clark Capital Corp. stock is a fair game because in the long run the expected payoff is equal to the actual payoff; in fact, in this example the expected and actual payoffs are precisely equal at every instant.

    If we want to graph the price of Clark Capital common stock over time, we know that just after the ex dividend date, it is worth

$$S_0 = \frac{D_1}{r_f} = \frac{\$10}{.05} = \$200$$

    The day before it goes ex dividend it is worth $200 plus the $10 dividend. The price is graphed in Figure S10.1.

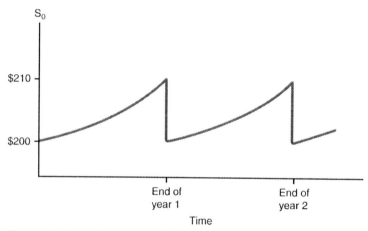

Figure S10.1 The price of Clark Capital Corporation common stock over time

   (b) At t the price at t + 1 is known with certainty. Even so, it is impossible to earn an arbitrage return because everyone knows what the price will be. The rate of return earned on the stock would be the same as the risk-free rate, which would make the investment a submartingale.

    The market is efficient in its strongest form, because all relevant information is known and impounded into the price of the stock instantaneously.

2. (a) The information which enables the brokerage firm to earn a consistent 3 percent abnormal profit is not costless. If the computer costs exceed the excess 3 percent profits from stocks, the firm is actually earning worse than normal returns. If the computer costs are less than the 3 percent profit, semi-strong capital market efficiency may be refuted. Also, brokerage fees may wipe out any trading profits.

   (b) The hypothesis of an efficient capital market is not contradicted. Except for very bad years, the average (and expected) return on the market is positive. This is considered a normal return. It is also a fair game. The fact that some investors enjoy higher returns than others is the result of the uncertainty in stock returns. Given any probability distribution, some observations will lie above the mean and some will lie below.

(c) Semi-strong (as well as weak) capital market efficiency is contradicted. You have discovered a trading rule based on past, nearly costless, price information that enables you to forecast future prices with better-than-random accuracy. Thus, all relevant publicly available information has not been instantaneously incorporated into stock prices.

(d) The semi-strong form of efficient capital markets assumes *publicly available* information is instantaneously impounded into prices; thus, benefits from insider information are accommodated under this hypothesis. In the example given, where apparent abnormal profits were available to insiders, strong form efficiency is refuted but semi-strong and weak efficiency are unchallenged.

3. The value of credit check information can be calculated according to equation 10.1:

$$V(\eta) = \sum q(m) \; \max_a \; \sum_e p(e|m)U(a, e) - V(\eta_0)$$

where

m_1 = favorable credit check

m_2 = unfavorable credit check

$q(m_1) = .8$

$q(m_2) = .2$

e_1 = customer pays loan

e_2 = customer defaults

a_1 = First National grants the loan

a_2 = First National refuses the loan

The information structure is

	m_1	m_2
e_1	.9	.5
e_2	.1	.5

The benefit function, U(a, e) is

	a_1	a_2
e_1	.18	−.18
e_2	−1.00	0.00

Notice the benefit function includes the opportunity cost, −18 percent, of not granting a loan when it would have been paid.

In order to find the correct values for the last sum in equation 10.1, we need to find optimal actions given a specific message, which are calculated according to the formula

$$\max_a \sum p(e|m) \, U(a, e)$$

If the message is m_1 :

$$\text{for } a_1\text{: } \sum p(e|m_1)U(a_1,e) = (.9)(.18) + (.1)(-1.00) = .062$$

$$\text{for } a_2\text{: } \sum p(e|m_1)U(a_2,e) = (.9)(-.18) + (.1)(0) = -.162$$

Therefore, given m_1, the optimal action is a_1 (grant the loan) for an expected return of 6.2 percent.
    If the message is m_2 :

$$\text{for } a_1: \sum p(e|m_2)U(a_1,e) = (.5)(.18) + (.5)(-1.00) = -.41$$

$$\text{for } a_2: \sum p(e|m_2)U(a_2,e) = (.5)(-.18) + (.5)(0) = -.09$$

Therefore, the optimal action given m_2 is a_2 (refuse the loan) with an expected opportunity loss, E(R) = –9 percent.
    Finally, calculate the difference between the value of the optimal action without information, and the value of the optimal actions with information.

Without information

$$\text{value of } a_1 = (.82)(.18) + (.18)(-1.00) = -3.24\%$$

$$\text{value of } a_2 = (.82)(-.18) + (.18)(0) = -14.76\%$$

Therefore, in the absence of information, the bank would choose always to grant the loan (a_1), for an expected loss of 3.24 percent. Recall that the loan program has been losing money.

With information

From previous calculations, we know $\sum p(e|m) U(a, e)$ is .062 given m_1, and –.09 given m_2. Substituting these values into equation 10.1 as follows:

$$V(\eta) = .8(.062) + .2(-.09) = 3.16\%$$

Since the cost of information = 5 percent, and the value of information, $V(\eta) - V(\eta_0)$, = 3.16 – (–3.24) = 6.4 percent, the credit check should be implemented.

4. (a) If the firm is risk neutral it will maximize expected pro-profits. First, we need to estimate the value of the optimal action without any test market. If we cancel the product our payoff is determined by multiplying the payoffs in various market conditions by their prior probabilities as follows:

$$V(\text{cancel}) = \sum p_i (\text{payoff})_i$$

$$= .6(0) + .3(0) + .1(0) = 0.$$

The expected payoff from going nationwide (without any test market) is

$$V(\text{nationwide}) = .6(-10) + .3(10) + .1(80) = 5.$$

Of these two actions it is best to go nationwide, with an expected payoff of $5 million. This represents the optimal action given that the firm does not use a test market.
    If we decide to test market the Kidwich product we can determine the optimal action given the outcome of the test marketing experience. If the experiment predicts no acceptance for Kidwich the optimal action is to cancel the product. The calculations are shown below:

$$V(\text{stop}|\text{no acceptance}) = .9(0) + .1(0) + 0(0) = 0$$

$$V(\text{nationwide}|\text{no acceptance}) = .9(-10) + .1(10) + 0(80)$$

$$= -8$$

If the test market indicates marginal acceptance, the optimal decision is to go nationwide.

$$V \text{ (stop|marginal)} = .1(0) + .7(0) + .2(0) = 0$$

$$V \text{ (nationwide|marginal)} = .1(-10) + .7(10) + .2(80) = 22.$$

Finally, if the experiment predicts success the optimal action is to go nationwide.

$$V \text{ (stop|success)} = .1(0) + .3(0) + .6(0) = 0$$

$$V \text{ (nationwide|success)} = .1(-10) + .3(10) + .6(80) = 50.$$

The value of information is defined as

$$V(\eta) = \sum_m q(m) \underset{a}{MAX} \sum_e p(e|m) \, V \, (a, e)$$

Having determined the optimal action given the test market results the value given the test market results is

$$V(\eta) = .6(0) + .3(22) + .1(50) = 11.6.$$

The value of the optimal action with no information at all was $5 million, therefore the value of the test market information is

$$V(\eta_1) - V(\eta_0) = 11.6 - 5 = \$6.6 \text{ million.}$$

The cost of the test market is $5 million therefore the net value of the information is $1.6 million.

(b) If you said to yourself "There's no such thing as a utility function for a firm," you are correct. Nevertheless, it is interesting to see how risk aversion might affect the value of information, at least for this simple example. The major difference is that the payoff matrix must first be converted into utiles so that expected utility can be computed. Given that

$$U(W) = \ln (W + 11)$$

the payoff matrix, expressed in utiles, is

Market Conditions	Action	
	Cancel	Go Nationwide
No acceptance	2.398	0
Marginal	2.398	3.045
Success	2.398	4.511

If there is no test market the optimal action is to cancel the product because it has higher expected utility.

$$U \text{ (stop)} = .6(2.398) + .3(2.398) + .1(2.398) = 2.398$$

$$U \text{ (nationwide)} = .6(0) + .3(3.045) + .1(4.511) = 1.365.$$

On the other hand, if there is a test market and if it predicts success, the optimal action is to go nationwide, as shown below.

$$U \text{ (stop|success)} = .1(2.398) + .3(2.398) + .6(2.398) = 2.398$$

$$U \text{ (nationwide|success)} = .1(0) + .3(3.045) + .6(4.511)$$

$$= 3.620.$$

If the experiment predicts marginal success the best action is to go nationwide.

$$U\text{ (stop|marginal)} = .1(2.398) + .7(2.398) + .2(2.398)$$

$$= 2.398$$

$$U\text{ (nationwide|marginal)} = .1(0) = .7(3.045) + .2(4.511)$$

$$= 3.034.$$

And if the experiment predicts no acceptance it is best to cancel the product.

$$U\text{ (stop|no acceptance)} = .9(2.398) + .1(2.398) + 0(2.398)$$

$$= 2.398$$

$$U\text{ (nationwide|no acceptance)} = .9(0) + .1(3.045) + 0(4.511)$$

$$= .305.$$

Given the information provided by a test market and the optimal action given each experimental outcome the expected utility given the information is

$$U(\eta_2) = .6(2.398) + .3(3.034) + .1(3.620) = 2.711.$$

The corresponding level of wealth is

$$V(\eta_2) = \$4.04 \text{ million.}$$

And since the optimal action given no information (i.e., cancelling the product) has a value of zero, $V(\eta_0)=0$, the value of information is

$$V(\eta_2) - V(\eta_0) = 4.04 - 0 = \$4.04 \text{ million.}$$

Because the test market costs $5 million. It would not be undertaken in the risk average case because its net value is $4.04 − $5 = $-.96 million.

5. There is nothing in the efficient markets hypothesis which says that arbitrageurs cannot make profits. However, it is important to look at their net profits after costs. One would expect that, at the margin, revenue from arbitrage just equals costs. If this were not true, more individuals would enter the arbitrage business until it became true. Costs include the cost of gathering information and a fair rate of return on physical and human capital.

6. (a) A fair game means that, on the average, outcomes conform to expectations. If our expect to lose 83 percent of the time and if, over a period of time, you do in fact lose 83 percent of the time, the game has been fair.

   (b) The options market is a fair game so long as investors' expected returns are equal to their long-run average returns. The options market would be a martingale if expected returns were equal to zero. If options are expected to expire unexercised 80 percent of the time, then the options market would follow a martingale if and only if the expected net present value of an exercised option was four times as great as the expected investment loss.

   Martingale: [Prob (loss)] · [Expected value (loss)]

   + [Prob (gain)] · [Expected value (gain)] = 0

In this example, a martingale holds if

$$-(.8)(L) + (.2)(G) = 0$$

$$G = (.8/.2) L$$

$$G = 4L \quad \text{for} \quad L > 0$$

If the expected NPV of a gain were more than four times the value of an investment loss, then the options market would follow a submartingale. If we assume a is some positive amount, then

$$E(R) = (.2)(4L + a) - (.8)(L)$$

$$= .2a > 0$$

This result is a submartingale with E(R) > 0.

7. In an efficient securities market, the NPV of any security is zero, since all securities are priced according to their perceived appropriate risk, and NPV's are discounted according to (the same) appropriate risk. The net result is NPV = 0. This is just another way of saying that you get what you pay for.

8. Assuming that the market portfolio is known to all investors so that systematic risk can be appropriately measured, then it is possible to measure ex post excess returns via the CAPM or the APM. If we make a second assumption, namely that the starting market value of the firm reflected no excess profits (or monopoly rents), then the residuals from the security market line will reflect the presence or absence of any abnormal returns above those which could be expected from a perfectly competitive firm of equivalent risk. However, the second assumption is unrealistic. It reflects one of the "weaknesses" of equilibrium models like the CAPM or the APM; namely, that although the model may be used to test for abnormal returns in an efficient capital market, it cannot tell us whether or not the initial market value of a firm reflects abnormal returns, i.e., whether or not product markets are efficient. Thus, if the assumptions of the CAPM or the APM are a reasonable approximation of reality, we can test for excess profits to investors in the capital market, but we cannot determine whether or not the value of the firm reflects excess profits above a competitive return in the product market.

9. The second-order stochastic dominance criterion assumes that all individuals have positive but decreasing marginal utility. In other words, they are greedy and risk averse. Given a world with investors of this type, if asset A dominates asset B and if they have the same present value, then every investor will sell B and buy A. This will continue, driving up the price of A relative to B, until the market price of A relative to B is high enough to make the marginal investor indifferent between A and B. But the higher price for A (and lower price for B) implies lower expected returns for A (and higher expected returns for B). This has the effect of altering the expected distributions of returns until there is no second-order stochastic dominance in equilibrium.

Chapter 11
Efficient Capital Markets: Evidence

1. Roll's critique (1977) is based on the assumption that capital markets are in equilibrium. What happens when the market is not in equilibrium? Suppose new information is revealed such that the market must adjust toward a new equilibrium which incorporates the news. Or suppose that a new security is introduced into the marketplace, as was the case of new issues studied in the Ibbotson (1975) paper. Given such a situation, the abnormal performance of an asset can be measured by the arbitrage profits available as its price is adjusted to a new market equilibrium. Before the disequilibrium situation as well as afterward, Roll's critique applies and we cannot expect to observe any abnormal performance relative to an efficient index. However, the adjustment process itself can be used to detect abnormal performance relative to the market index prior to equilibrium. In this way, Ibbotson's results can be interpreted either as 1) selection of an inefficient index, or 2) detection of abnormal performance during disequilibrium.

2. (a) The securities market can be efficient even though the market for information is not. All that is required for efficient securities markets is that prices fully reflect all available information. Should an individual—for example, a corporate insider—have monopoly access to valuable information, then the market cannot reflect the information because it is not publicly available. This is not a deficiency in the securities market, but rather a deficiency in the market for information.

   The quote taken from the special committee of the Securities and Exchange Commission is correct when it says that the efficient markets theory is silent as to the optimum amount of information required—that issue can be decided by better understanding of the supply of and demand for information.

   (b) Information is material if it has an impact on securities prices when it becomes publicly available for the first time. If it has no impact on prices, it is largely irrelevant, although it may cause portfolio adjustments that leave prices unchanged.

3. The empirical evidence on block trading is consistent with the semi-strong form of the efficient markets hypothesis, because once the block trade becomes public information, it is not possible to earn an abnormal return.

   The evidence may or may not be inconsistent with the strong form of the efficient markets hypothesis. If an individual can employ a strategy (using the –4.56 percent trading rule of Dann, Mayers and Raab) where he purchases shares at the block price, then sells at the closing price, he can earn a risk-adjusted abnormal return after transactions costs. However, the "abnormal return" is defined relative to the risk-adjusted return which would be predicted by the capital asset pricing model. It may be the case that the return is actually a fair return for the liquidity services rendered to the individual who sold the block.

4. (a) As shown by the Ball and Brown study (1968), almost all of the "information" in an annual report has already been discounted into the security price before the annual report is released. Therefore, it is unlikely that the latest copy of the annual report will allow an investor to earn an abnormal return.

   (b) The evidence on block trading indicates that it is highly unlikely that anyone can react fast enough to make a profit from the ticker tape announcement of a block trade.

(c) Empirical evidence of announcement abnormal returns for a pure split sample of stocks that had not dividends indicates a significant positive return (Grinblatt, Masulis and Titman [1984]). Thus, splits per se can be interpreted as good news about the future prospects of the firm. Brennan and Copeland [1987] model splits as costly signals to show that they can convey information in a rational expectations equilibrium.

(d) As indicated by the Ibbotson (1975) study, it is possible to earn large risk-adjusted abnormal returns if you buy a new issue at the offering price and sell at the end-of-month market price. However, as with block trades, this "abnormal" return may be simply a liquidity premium charged for services provided by buyers of the stock to the owners of the ABC Company. After all, a large new issue is also a large block.

5. Mr. A should not purchase the service. If he purchased it, he could be the victim of fraud. Consider the following scheme. A solicitation is mailed out to 270,000 investors. Ninety thousand are told the market will move up by more than 10 points, ninety thousnd are told it will stay within a 10 point range, and the remainder are told it will fall by more than 10 points. After the first month the group of ninety thousand which received the correct "forecast" is split into three groups. And finally, by the end of the third month there remains a group of 10,000 investors who have received three successive correct "predictions."

It goes without saying that the "success" of the solicitation in predicting the market for three months straight has absolutely nothing to do with their ability to forecast the next month's index.

The same thing can be said of individual investors who point to their past success in the market as evidence that they are clairvoyant. If there is a 50–50 chance of "winning" in the market during a year's time, then over a ten year interval, the probability of wining every year is

$$(1/2)^{10} \cong .000977$$

If there are 10 million investors in the market, then approximately 9,770 of them will have beat the market every year for ten years.

6. Ponzi frauds follow the adage "you can fool some of the people some of the time." The plan described has paid out 2 percent per month for 18 months. It would operate as follows:

If the first participant put in $1,000, his first dividend would be paid out of the money he put in. If no one else joined the "fund," the first individual would be paid $20 per month out of his original $1,000, until the money was gone and the fund was declared officially bankrupt. This would take 50 months if the perpetrators of the scheme kept their portion of the capital equal to zero. The investor's loss can be determined as follows:

If he had originally invested his $1,000 in the risk-free asset, he would have

$$\$1,000(1 + R_f)^T$$

where T = time until declaration of the Ponzi Fund's bankruptcy.

If X were the amount extorted by the founders of the Ponzi fund, and $20 per month was paid as "dividends," the time until bankruptcy would be

$$T = \frac{1,000 - X}{20} \le 50$$

If the investor participated in the Ponzi Fund, and immediately reinvested all dividend payments in the risk-free asset, his earnings would be

$$20(1 + R_f)^{T-1} + 20(1 + R_f)^{T-2} + \cdots + 20$$

where the first term represents the earnings from his first dividend paid, and the last term, $20 = 20(1 + R_i)^{T-1}$, represents his last dividend. Thus, his total loss would be

$$-\$1,000(1 + R_i)^T + \sum_{t=1}^{T} 20(1 + R_i)^{T-t} < 0$$

However, if enough new people joined the Ponzi Fund over time, it could go on indefinitely. When the scheme could not attract new participants, it would quickly go bankrupt. An individual investor who could accurately predict the time until bankruptcy, T, may be able to profit from the investment if the dividends paid to him (after his initial investment was recovered) exceeded the amount he would have received had be initially invested in a legitimate asset of equal risk. In this instance, the risk involved is his ability to predict the fraud's demise. In the aggregate, of course, the fund's investors lose money because no investments in real assets are being made.

7. Mutual funds do, in fact, attract more customers in a year which follows abnormal performance. The mystery is why. If investors are rational, then they should know that last year's performance is typically unrelated to this year's performance. Therefore, at any point in time their choice of a mutual fund should be a matter of indifference. But it isn't.

    Either way, their behavior is not inconsistent with efficient capital markets. It simply doesn't make any difference. The flows of dollars which they provide to mutual funds will not affect the way in which security prices adjust to new information.

8. The major problem is that the portfolios' performances in Figure Q11.8 have not been adjusted for risk. If portfolio 1 is riskier than the other portfolios, then one would expect it to have higher returns also. What should be reported is risk-adjusted abnormal rates of return. A second problem is that returns are reported without subtracting the transactions costs involved in readjusting the portfolios each week. Third, the chart does not say whether or not the returns recorded there include dividends as well as capital gains. Fourth, any differential effects of taxation are unaccounted for.

    It is not possible to discern whether or not the portfolios' actual performances are consistent with the efficient securities market until we test for abnormal performance based on net cash flows (i.e., capital gains plus dividends, net of taxes and transactions costs).

9. (a) A selection bias discredits any results implied by this study. Firms continuously listed on Compustat tapes from 1953 to 1973 are firms that, by definition, have not failed, since the records of bankrupt firms are completely deleted from the tape.

    (b) It is not surprising that stock brokers' preferences are correlated with rate of return differences across industries. It would be surprising if their preferences can be used to *predict* rate of return differences. If the information is predictive, then, on average, brokers can beat the market.

    (c) The results of this research provide evidence against capital market efficiency because past, publicly available data provides predictive power for future price changes. A study of this nature, by Niederhoffer, is reported in *The Journal of Business*, April, 1971.

    (d) The evidence is not creditable because the model has not been tested on independent date. Any model can be worked over to fit a set of data if enough variables are allowed. The relevant test would be in the model's predictive ability.

Chapter 12
Information Asymmetry and Agency Theory

1. In this question, at time 1, good firms have a value, $V_a = 250$, greater than bad firms with value $V_b = 150$. If there is no uncertainty in the market and pricing is risk neutral, the time 0 values of the two types of firms would be given by

$$V_{0a} = \frac{V_{1a}}{1+r} = \frac{250}{1.1} = 227.27$$

and

$$V_{0b} = \frac{V_{1b}}{1+r} = \frac{150}{1.1} = 136.36$$

where: r = the risk-free interest rate = 10%

The manager's compensation schedule is given by

$$M = (1+r)\gamma_0 V_0 + \gamma_1 \begin{Bmatrix} V_1 \text{ if } V_1 > D \\ V_1 - C \text{ if } V_1 \leq D \end{Bmatrix}$$

where $\gamma_0 = 0.2$, $\gamma_1 = 0.2$, V_1 is the value of the firm at time 1, D is the face value of debt issued by the firm at time 0 and C is a penalty imposed on the manager if $V_1 < D$.

Assume that D* is the maximum amount of debt a bad firm can carry without going into bankruptcy. Further assume that if $D > D^*$, investors perceive the firm to be good and if $D \leq D^*$, investors perceive the firm to be bad. Based on the signal (debt level) chosen by the manager of a good firm, her compensation would be

$$M^A(D) = \begin{Bmatrix} (0.2)(250) + (0.2)(250) = 100 \text{ if } D^* < D \leq 250 \\ (0.2)(150) + (0.2)(250) = 80 \quad \text{if } D \leq D^* \end{Bmatrix}$$

The manager of a good firm would have the incentive to issue the correct signal (choose a debt level higher than D*) as long as her compensation from signaling correctly is greater than her compensation based on an false signal. In this case, since the marginal payoff from telling the truth is greater than that from a lie, that is $100 > 80$, she will give the correct signal.

The compensation of the manager of a bad firm is given by

$$M^B(D) = \begin{Bmatrix} (0.2)(250) + (0.2)(150 - C) = 80 - 0.2C \text{ if } D^* < D \leq 250 \\ (0.2)(150) + (0.2)(150) = 60 \text{ if } D \leq D^* \end{Bmatrix}$$

The manager of a bad firm will have the incentive to signal correctly if $80 - 0.2C < 60$ or if $C > 100$. Therefore, the minimum cost of false signalling should be 100.

2. The equilibrium dividend, D*(t), and value response, V(D) schedules are

$$D^*(t) = At$$

and

$$V[D^*(t)] = (\tau_p + \beta A)D^*(t)$$

Where A is given by:

$$A = -\left[\frac{\tau_p}{\beta}\right]\left[\frac{1+r}{1+2r}\right] + \left[\frac{\tau_p}{\beta}\right]\left[\frac{1+r}{1+2r}\right]\sqrt{1+\frac{\beta(1+2r)}{\tau_p^2(1+r)^2}}$$

Where τ_p is the personal tax rate, r is the after tax rate of interest, β is the shortfall penalty and t is the upper bound on the cash flows. In this case, $\tau_p = 25\%$, r = 20%, $\beta = 50\%$ and t = 500. Therefore,

$$A = -\left[\frac{0.25}{0.5}\right]\left[\frac{1.2}{1.4}\right] + \left[\frac{0.25}{0.5}\right]\left[\frac{1.2}{1.4}\right]\sqrt{1+\frac{(0.5)(1.4)}{(0.25)^2(1.2)^2}} = 0.8412$$

The equilibrium dividend, D*(t), and value response, V(D) schedules are

$$D^*(t) = (0.8412)(500) = 420.59$$

and

$$V[D^*(t)] = (0.25 + (0.5)(0.8412))(420.59) = 282.05$$

If the tax rate is 30%

$$A = -\left[\frac{0.3}{0.5}\right]\left[\frac{1.2}{1.4}\right] + \left[\frac{0.3}{0.5}\right]\left[\frac{1.2}{1.4}\right]\sqrt{1+\frac{(0.5)(1.4)}{(0.3)^2(1.2)^2}} = 0.7869$$

The equilibrium dividend, D*(t), and value response, V(D) schedules are

$$D^*(t) = (0.7869)(500) = 393.45$$

and

$$V[D^*(t)] = (0.3 + (0.5)(0.7869))(393.45) = 272.84$$

If the shortfall cost is 70%,

$$A = -\left[\frac{0.25}{0.7}\right]\left[\frac{1.2}{1.4}\right] + \left[\frac{0.25}{0.7}\right]\left[\frac{1.2}{1.4}\right]\sqrt{1+\frac{(0.7)(1.4)}{(0.25)^2(1.2)^2}} = 0.7494$$

The equilibrium dividend, D*(t), and value response, V(D) schedules are

$$D^*(t) = (0.7494)(500) = 374.70$$

and

$$V[D^*(t)] = (0.25 + (0.7)(0.7494))(374.70) = 290.23$$

If the discount rate is 40%

$$A = -\left[\frac{0.25}{0.5}\right]\left[\frac{1.4}{1.8}\right] + \left[\frac{0.25}{0.5}\right]\left[\frac{1.4}{1.8}\right]\sqrt{1+\frac{(0.5)(1.8)}{(0.25)^2(1.4)^2}} = 0.7347$$

The equilibrium dividend, $D^*(t)$, and value response, $V(D)$ schedules are

$$D^*(t) = (0.7347)(500) = 367.33$$

and

$$V[D^*(t)] = (0.25 + (0.5)(0.7347))(367.33) = 226.79$$

3. Stein considers a three-date model (time 0, 1 and 2) with three types of firms (good, medium and bad). Each firm has access to a project with required investment at time 0 of I and expected net present value of B. The discount rate is assumed to be zero, all agents are risk-neutral, the amount required for investment has to be raised from external sources and the firm is completely owned by its manager prior to the infusion of capital. Each firm receives a cash flow from the investment of either b_L or b_H at time 2 ($b_L < I < b_H$). Firms differ in the ex ante probability of receiving b_H with good types receiving b_H with certainty, medium types receiving b_H with probability p and bad types receiving b_H with probability q ($q < p < 1$). Firm types are private information at time 0 and the true value of bad firms is volatile between time 0 and time 1. At time 1, the firm type is revealed and for bad firms, the value of the probability q is updated to either 0 or p. The probability of deterioration is assumed to be z and for consistency $q = (1-z)p$. The firm has three financing options at time 0—straight debt that matures at time 2, convertible debt that matures at time 2 but can be called to force conversion at time 1 at a predetermined conversion ratio and equity. Debt financing is associated with a potential for costly financial distress where a deadweight cost of c is imposed on the owner-manager. The costs of financial distress are such that $c > (I - b_L)$. Under these circumstances, there is a separating equilibrium in which good firms issued debt with face value I, bad firms issue a fraction $\frac{1}{qb_H+(1-q)b_L}$ of equity and medium firms issue convertible bonds with face value $F > b_L$, a call price K, $b_L < K < I$ and is convertible to $\frac{1}{pb_H+(1-p)b_L}$ of equity. For this to be a separating equilibrium, the firms should not want to mimic each other.

    For example, consider a situation in which the bad firm issues straight debt. If it does so, it issues debt with a true value of $qI + (1-q) b_L$. Since the bad firm raises an amount I from the debt issue, the debt is overpriced by $I - [qI + (1-q) b_L] = (1-q) (1-b_L)$. The expected costs of financial distress are $(1-q)c$. Since it has been assumed that $c > (1 - b_L)$, this implies that $(1-q)c > (1-q) (1-b_L)$, that is, the expected cost of financial distress is greater than the underpricing. Therefore, it does not pay for a bad firm to mimic a good firm.

    Now consider the situation in which a medium firm issues straight debt. If it does so, it issues debt with a true value of $pI + (1-p)b_L$. Since the medium firm raises an amount I from the debt issue, the debt is overpriced by $I - [pI + (1-p) b_L] = (1-p) (I-b_L)$. The expected costs of financial distress are $(1-p)c$. Since it has been assumed that $c > (I - b_L)$, this implies that $(1-p) c > (1-p) (I-b_L)$, that is, the expected cost of financial distress is greater than the underpricing. Therefore, it does not pay for a medium firm to mimic a good firm.

    Finally, consider the situation in which a medium firm chooses to issue equity. Equity issuance makes sense for a bad firm since the equity issue helps it avoid the costs of financial distress. On the other hand, the medium firm bears the cost of underpricing if it issues equity but gets no offsetting gain. This follows from the fact that the medium firm cannot reduce the costs of financial distress by issuing equity since it perceives these costs to be zero. To see this, note than the medium firm knows that the conversion value of the convertible bond will always be I at time 1. Since this conversion value always exceeds the call price K, the firm can force conversion with certainty and is never left with any debt.

4. The optimal sharing rule is:

$$\frac{U'[s-c(s,p)]}{V'[c(s,p)]} = \lambda$$

where U is the principal's utility function, V is the agent's utility function, s is the final outcome, p is a performance measure, c is the contract between the principal and agent, λ is a constant, $U' = \frac{\partial U}{\partial W}$ and $V' = \frac{\partial V}{\partial W}$. In this question both utility functions are of the form $-\alpha_i e^{-W/\alpha_i}$, i = $agent, principal$ and α_i is i's risk tolerance. Therefore, $U' = e^{-W_P/\alpha_P}$ and $V' = e^{-W_A/\alpha_A}$, where $W_P = s - c$ and $W_A = c$. Substituting these expressions in the optimal sharing rule yields:

$$\frac{e^{-(s-c)/\alpha_P}}{e^{-c/\alpha_A}} = \lambda \text{ or } e^{\left[\frac{\alpha_A}{\alpha}s + c\right]\left(\frac{\alpha}{\alpha_A\alpha_P}\right)} = \lambda$$

where $\alpha = \alpha_A + \alpha_P$.
Taking natural logs of both sides and some simple algebra yields:

$$c = \beta + \left(\frac{\alpha_A}{\alpha}\right)s$$

$$\text{where } \beta = \left(\frac{\alpha_A\alpha_P}{\alpha}\right)\ln \lambda.$$

5. The optimal sharing rule is this case is:

$$\frac{U'[s-c(s)]}{V'[c(s)]} = \lambda + \mu\frac{f_a(s|a)}{f(s|a)}$$

where U is the principal's utility function, V is the agent's utility function, s is the final outcome, p is a performance measure, c is the contract between the principal and agent, a is the agent's action, λ is a constant, f(s|a) is the density function for the outcome conditional on the effort, $f_a(s|a) = \frac{\partial f(s|a)}{\partial a}$ $U' = \frac{\partial U}{\partial W}$ $V' = \frac{\partial V}{\partial W}$.

In this question, the principal is risk neutral, $V(c) = [1/(1 - \gamma)](\delta_0 + \delta_1 c)^{(1-\gamma)}$ and $\frac{f_a(s|a)}{f(s|a)}$ is linear in s.

In this case, $V'(c) = \delta_1/(\delta_0 + \delta_1 c)^\gamma$ and the sharing rule can be written as:

$$\left(\frac{1}{\delta_1}\right)(\delta_0 + \delta_1 c)^\gamma = \lambda + \mu\frac{f_a(s|a)}{f(s|a)}$$

Solving the above equation for the compensation function yields:

$$c(s) = -\left(\frac{\delta_0}{\delta_1}\right) + (\delta_1)^{\left(\frac{1}{\gamma}-1\right)} = \left(\lambda + \mu - \frac{f_a(s|a)}{f(s|a)}\right)^{\frac{1}{\gamma}}$$

Therefore, if $0 < \gamma < 1$, the compensation function is a convex function of s. It is linear if γ is one and concave if γ is larger than 1.

6. Given a tenure of T and an opportunity cost of i, the manger will use a hurdle rate of r* for project accept/reject decisions, where r* is given by:

$$r^* = \frac{i}{1-(1+i)^{-T}}$$

The following table provides the relation between the tenure of the manager and the hurdle rate employed for an opportunity cost of 25 percent (=i).

Manager Tenure (T years)	Project Hurdle Rate (r* percent)
2	69.44
5	37.18
10	28.01
15	25.91
20	25.29
40	25

Chapter 13
The Role of the CFO, Performance Measurement, and Incentive Design

1. Assume that the cash flows of the firm are a constant perpetuity. In this case the DCF definition of the entity value of the firm is

$$V_0 = \frac{E(EBIT_t - dep_t - I_t)}{WACC_t}$$

and since a perpetuity has $I_t = dep_t$, (where I_t = new plus replacement investment) this reduces to

$$V_0 = \frac{E(EBIT_t)}{WACC_t}$$

The economic profit approach definition of value is (I_{t-1} is beginning-of-year invested capital).

$$V_0 = \frac{E(ROIC_t - WACC_t)IC_{t-1}}{WACC_t} + IC_{t-1}$$

$$V_0 = \frac{E(ROIC_t)IC_{t-1}}{WACC_t} - \frac{(WACC_t)IC_{t-1}}{WACC_t} + IC_{t-1} = \frac{E(EBIT_t)}{WACC_t}$$

Note the last two terms cancel, and that $E(ROIC_t) IC_{t-1} = E(EBIT_t)$, therefore the economic profit approach is isomorphic to the DCF approach (before or after taxes).

2. Let's take a look at the data provided in Table S13.2. (Note that I_0 = \$10,000, not \$1,000 as found in early printings and the corresponding sale price is \$11,000.)

Table S13.2 Data for Q13.2

	Base Case	(a) Bottleneck	(b) Cut Costs	(c) Sell for 10% Premium
WACC	10%	10%	10%	10%
I_0	\$10,000	\$10,000	\$10,000	\$10,000
ΔI_0	\$0	400	0	0
ΔCF_1	\$300	500	350	—
ΔCF_2	\$300	500	350	—
ΔCF_3	\$300	500	350	—
Sale Price	—	—	—	\$11,000

(a) The first alternative is debottlenecking. It will require an incremental investment of $400 and will bring in additional cash flows of $200 for three years. Its net present value is

$$\text{NPV}(\textit{debottlenecking}) = -400 + \frac{200}{1.1} + \frac{200}{1.1^2} + \frac{200}{1.1^3}$$

$$= -400 + 182 + 165 + 150 = 97 > 0$$

Traditional NPV analysis would favor accepting this project even though the business unit ROIC is only $300/$10,000 = 3% in the base case and $500/$10,400 = 4.8% after the debottlenecking.

(b) The second alternative is cost cutting. The incremental investment is zero and incremental cash flows increase by $50 per year, therefore the NPV is

$$\text{NPV}(\text{cost } \textit{cutting}) = \frac{\$50}{1.1} + \frac{\$50}{1.1^2} + \frac{\$50}{1.1^3} = 45 + 41 + 38 = 124 > 0$$

Again, traditional NPV would cause us to accept the project although the ROIC, originally at 3%, rises to only 3.5%. Note that this is a lower business unit ROIC but higher NPV than debottlenecking.

(c) If the sale takes place immediately and is not taxed (or if we interpret $11,000 as after tax proceeds), then this is by far the best alternative with NPV of $11,000 (remember that the basic value of $10,000 is a sunk cost).

By way of contrast, if the cash flows of the other two alternatives were perpetuities their NPVs would be

$$\text{NPV (debottlenecking perpetuity)} = -400 + \frac{500}{.1} = 4,600$$

$$\text{NPV (base case perpetuity)} = \frac{300}{.1} = 3,000$$

$$\text{NPV (cost cutting perpetuity)} = \frac{350}{.1} = 3,500$$

$$\text{NPV (sale)} = \$11,000$$

3.   Table S13.3 provides an example where revenue growth averages 8.3% per year, net income grows at an average of 3.4%, yet ROIC declines every year because incremental return on new capital is less than the cost of capital (assumed to be 10%). New investment that earns less than the cost of capital destroys value.

Table S13.3   ROIC falls while the Top and Bottom Lines both Grow

	1	2	3	4	5	6
Revenue	1,000	1,100	1,210	1,331	1,464	1,611
− Operating Costs	−600	−675	−755	−839	−951	−1,063
= Earnings before interest and taxes	400	425	455	492	513	548
− interest on debt (5%)	−10	−20	−31	−43	−56	−71
= Earnings before taxes	390	405	425	449	457	477
− taxes (50%)	−195	−202	−212	−224	−228	−238
= Net income	195	203	213	225	229	239
Invested Capital	2000	2200	2420	2662	2928	3221
Return on invested capital (after tax)	10.0%	9.7%	9.4%	9.2%	8.8%	8.5%
Return on new capital (after tax)	—	6.3%	6.8%	7.6%	3.9%	6.0%
Debt	200	400	620	862	1128	1421

4.   EPS (earnings per share) and the growth in EPS are uncorrelated with the total return to shareholders because they ignore balance sheet information and because they fail to capture the changes in expectations that drive TRS. EVA® and the change in EVA® contain information about earnings, invested capital and the cost of capital, but omit expectations. Consequently, they also have a very low correlation with TRS.

5.   The facts are summarized in Table S13.5. Let's assume that ROIC is after tax.

Table S13.5

	WACC	Announced Capital	Announced ROIC	Revised ROIC	Expected EBIT Announced	Expected EBIT Revised
Project A	10%	$5 million	30%	30%	$1.5 million	$1.5 million
Project B	10%	$30 million	40%	30%	$12.0 million	$9.0 million
Total					$13.5 million	$10.5 million
Project A	10%	$5 million	30%	30%	1.5 million	1.5 million
No Project B	10%	$30 million	40%	10%	12.0 million	3.0 million
Total					$13.5 million	$4.5 million

If the company makes public its revised estimate of the return on Project B, its stock price will fall because the expected total EBIT will fall from $13.5 to $10.5 million. The alternative is to announce that Project B will not be taken. In this alternative the shareholders would be presumed to earn the opportunity cost of capital, i.e., 10%. If so, the stock price would fall even more because expected earnings would fall from $13.5 to $4.5 million. Therefore, Project B should be taken. Any new investment should be accepted when its expected return in greater than the cost of capital.

6. The 3 alternative types of compensation are illustrated in Figure S13.6 below.

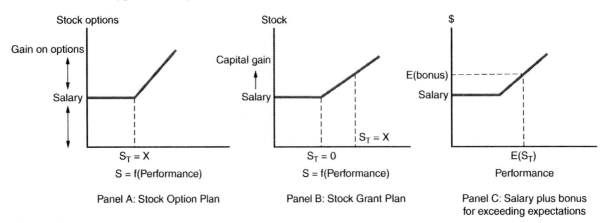

Figure S13.6

Tax considerations are not discussed in the answer to this problem. For tax policy see Chapter 14. The structure of all three incentives is roughly the same. Fixed salary provides a floor and non-salary incentives all provide gains that increase with performance. However, the graphed relationships break down if the measure of performance is not highly correlated with the stock price. Panel C is the only one that stipulated performance is based on expectations and that will be correlated with TRS.

Chapter 14
Valuation and Tax Policy

1. The standard industrial valuation model (see Chapter 14) discounts free cash flows at a weighted average cost of capital to value the enterprise. The value of equity is then derived by subtracting the market value of debt from the enterprise value. This entity approach assumes that the act of issuing debt (or not issuing it) is independent of the forecast of operating free cash flows, and that (other than providing an interest tax shield) no shareholder value results from issuing debt. Simply, it is assumed that (assuming trivial transactions costs) the firm receives $1 of cash for each $1 of debt that it issues.

   (a) Banks are different because of their franchise to provide demand deposits and certificates of deposit. These liabilities provide (insured) liquidity service to customers of the bank who demand less than their opportunity cost. Consequently these liabilities are an important part of the operations of the bank, and they earn a positive spread that creates value for shareholders. For this reason we recommend an equity cash flow approach for valuing banks. Free cash flow to equity include after-tax interest income and expense, and increases in deposit liabilities. This stream of free cash flow to equity is then discounted at the cost of equity.

   (b) Insurance companies also create shareholder value on the liabilities side of the balance sheet because their insurance reserves (the present value of their expected insurance benefits) yield investment rates of return below the opportunity cost to policyholders. Therefore, the equity approach is also appropriate for valuing insurance companies.

2. (a) In 2003 excess cash is $472/6,830 = 6.9\%$ of current assets and by 2010 it is $7,736/17.165 = 45.1\%$. This does not make sense until we realize that it does not affect the DCF value of the firm and it is merely a plugged number (whose counterpart, called unscheduled debt, is combined with long term debt in Table 14.7). Although the *current* amount of excess cash and marketable securities is added to the DCF of operating cash flows, future amounts are not because they are assumed to have zero NPV.

   (b) There are two ways to bring excess cash into line. One is to forecast growing dividend payments. However, that has already been done in Table 14.6 because the forecast has assumed that dividends are 65% of net income. The second approach is to go to financing flows in Table 14.8 and subtract an amount from excess cash each year and add the same amount to "decrease in common and treasury stock." In this case you are assuming that the excess cash is used in a share repurchase program.

   (c) Neither dividend payments nor share repurchases affect the value of the firm (unless there is a signaling effect) because both are ways of delivering value—not creating value.

3. Table S14.3a provides the calculations of the multiples and Table S14.3b compares the forecast

    Table S14.3a   Multiple Calculations

	2000	2010
Entity Value	$128.91	$194.80
EBIT	3.71	10.44
Multiple	34.8	18.7

    Table S14.3b   Assumptions

Averages for 2000–2010		Perpetuity Assumptions	
NOPLAT Growth	**ROIC**	**g**	**r**
12.1%/year	34.4%	5%/year	30%

    assumptions during 2000–2010 with those of the perpetuity (years 11 and on). Note that the NOPLAT growth rate is 12.1% during the explicit forecast, but more than halves from then to infinity. The ROIC also comes down—but it is assumed to remain well above the cost of capital. These assumptions are consistent with a multiple that declines from 34.8 in 2000 to 18.7 in 2010.

4. (a) Equation 14.21 is the finite supernormal growth model:

    $$V_0 = \frac{EBIT_1(1-T_c)}{k_u} + T_c B + K[EBIT_1(1-T_c)]N\left[\frac{r - WACC}{WACC(1 + WACC)}\right] \tag{14.21}$$

    Substituting in the suggested parameters, we get an estimate of continuing value as of year 10

    $$V_0 = \frac{4,000(1-.33)}{.0845} + .33(6,000) + .15[4,000(1-.33)] + 10\left[\frac{.52(1-.33)-.083}{.083(1.083)}\right]$$

    $$= 31,716 + 2,000 + 4.020\left[\frac{.265}{.090}\right]$$

    $$= 31,716 + 2,000 + 11,837 = 45,553.$$

    (b) The spreadsheet value estimate used EBIT $(1 - T) = \$2,487$ in 2000 whereas the formula above assumes EBIT $(1 - T) = \$2,680$—a small difference, not large enough to explain why the spreadsheet indicates that $V_0 = \$128.9$ billion and the finite supernormal growth formula has $V_0 = \$45.5$ billion. The WACC assumptions are the same. What creates the difference are the following:

       1) First, $K = g/r$ therefore $g = rK$ and $g = .52 (1 - .33)(.15) = 5.2\%$ whereas the spreadsheet assumes $g = 12.1\%$ for the next 10 years then $g = 5\%$ thereafter.

       2) Second the finite supernormal growth model assumes ROIC $= .52 (1 - .33) = .35$ for N = 10 years, then declines to equal WACC (on new capital invested). The spreadsheet assumed r = 30% forever.

(c) To simplify, let's assume that an extra revenue growth of 1% translates into 1% EBIT growth. Thus, EBIT, becomes \$4,040. Growth in NOPLAT rises from 5.2% to 6.2% and assuming that K remains at 15%, ROIC rises from 35% to $r = g/k = .062/15 = 41.3\%$ after tax. N stays at 10 years. Substituting these into Eq. 14.21, we have

$$V_0 = \frac{4,040(1-.33)}{.0845} + .33(6,000) + .15[4,040(1-.33)]10\left[\frac{.413-.083}{.083(1.083)}\right]$$

$$= 32,033 + 2,000 + 14,906 = 48,939.$$

This is an increase of \$3,386 million or 7.4%.

5. Because we have NOPLAT in the 10th year, let's perform the valuation as of year 10 and use the value-driver model

$$V_{10} = \frac{EBIT_{11}(1-T_c)(1-g/r)}{WACC-g}$$

Note: $NOPLAT = EBIT(1 - T_c)$, $10,000 = 1,667(1-T_c)$, $T_c = 0.4$

$$= \frac{1,667(1+.1)(1-.4)(1-.10/.12)}{.12-.10} = \frac{1,834(.6)(.167)}{.02} = \frac{182.8}{.02} = 9,138$$

If the growth in NOPLAT increases from 10% to 15%, and ROIC stays at 12%, the new retention rate will be

$$K = g/r$$

$$K = .15/.12 = 1.25 = 125\%$$

This implies that the company can grow with negative capital requirements. While possible for some companies to have negative working capital (e.g., magazine publishers who receive payment before delivering the goods) it is more likely, in this case, that ROIC goes up to achieve the higher growth that K does not change. If so

$$r = g/k$$

$$r = .15/.15 = 100\%$$

and the new valuation becomes infeasible because $WACC - g = .12 - .15 < 0$ in the denominator. Clearly, the firm cannot grow at 15% forever, so let's use the finite supernormal growth model assuming that N = 4 years.

$$V_{10} = \frac{EBIT_{11}(1-T_c)}{WACC} + K[EBIT_{11}(1-T_c)]N\left[\frac{r-WACC}{WACC(1+WACC)}\right]$$

$$V_{10} = \frac{1,667(1.1)(1-.4)}{.12} + .15[1,667(1.1)(1-.4)]4\left[\frac{1.00-.12}{.12(1.12)}\right]$$

$$= 9,169 + 4,322 = 13,138.$$

Note that it is not appropriate to compare the result of the value driver formula (that assumes g = .10 and r = .12 forever) and the result of the finite supernormal growth model (that assumes r = 1.00 for 4 years then r = WACC thereafter.

Chapter 15
Capital Structure and the Cost of Capital: Theory and Evidence

1. (a) Following an approach similar to the Modigliani-Miller derivation of equation 15.3, and with the same assumptions, the total cash flows paid by the firm to shareholders, debtholders and holders of preferred stock are:

$$NI + k_dD + r_pFP = (EBIT\,(1-T) - k_dD - Xr_pFP)\,(1-\tau_c) - (1-X)\,r_pFP$$

$$+ k_dD + r_pFP$$

where:

NI = cash flows after interest, preferred dividends and taxes

k_d = the coupon rate on debt

D = the face value of debt

r_p = the preferred dividend rate

FP = the face value of preferred stock

X = the percent of preferred dividends which may be expensed

$EBIT\,(1-T)$ = the cash flows from operations

The right-hand side of the above equation may be rearranged as follows:

$$= EBIT\,(1-T)\,(1-\tau_c) - k_dD + \tau_ck_dD + k_dD - Xr_pFP + X\tau_cr_pFP$$

$$- r_pFP + Xr_pFP + r_pFP$$

$$= EBIT\,(1-T)\,(1-\tau_c) + \tau_ck_dD + X\tau_cr_pFP$$

Each of these cash flow streams is discounted at the appropriate risk-adjusted rate in order to obtain the value of the levered firm.

$$V^L = \frac{EBIT\,(1-T)\,(1-\tau_c)}{\rho} + \frac{\tau_ck_dD}{k_b} + \frac{X\tau_cr_pFP}{k_p}$$

where:

ρ = the cost of equity for an all-equity firm

k_b = the cost of debt

k_p = the cost of preferred

This equation is equal to

$$V^L = V^U + \tau_cB + X\tau_cP$$

where:

$$V^U = \text{the value of an unlevered firm} = \frac{EBIT(1-T)(1-\tau_c)}{\rho}$$

$$B = \text{the market value of debt} = \frac{k_d D}{k_b}$$

$$P = \text{the market value of preferred} = \frac{r_p FP}{k_p}$$

(b) Given the above result for the value of the levered firm, the weighted average cost of capital, k_0, may be written directly as

$$k_0 = \rho\left(1 - \tau_c\,\frac{B}{B+P+S} - X\tau_c\,\frac{P}{B+P+S}\right)$$

Note that if 100 percent of the preferred dividends may be expensed, $X = 1$ and the third term becomes

$$\tau_c\,\frac{P}{P+B+S}$$

If $X = 0$, it is equal to zero.

2. The object is to find the appropriate weighted average cost of capital for the project assuming that it has 50 percent debt. Assume that Carternut has the same operating risk as the project. If so, its unlevered β and its 100 percent equity cost of capital will be the same as that of the project.

For Carternut (assuming it has risk-free debt), the cost of equity is given by the CAPM.

$$k_s = R_f + [E(R_m) - R_f]\beta$$

$$= .06 + [.18 - .06]2.0 = 30\%$$

Next, use the MM definition of the cost of equity (equation 15.18) in order to obtain the 100 percent equity cost of capital for Carternut.

$$k_s = \rho + (\rho - k_b)(1-\tau_c)\frac{B}{S}$$

$$.30 = \rho + (\rho - .06)(1-.5)\frac{1}{9}, \quad \text{since} \quad \frac{B}{B+S} = \frac{1}{10}$$

$$\frac{9(.30)}{.5} = \frac{9\rho}{.5} + \rho - .06$$

$$\frac{5.4 + .06}{19} = \rho = 28.74\%$$

Next, in order to solve for the weighted average cost of capital if the project has 50 percent debt, use the MM definition of the weighted average cost of capital (equation 15.13).

$$WACC^{\tau} = \rho \left(1 - \tau_c \frac{B}{B+S} \right)$$

$$= .2874 (1 - .5 (.5)) = 21.55\%$$

Therefore, accept the project since it earns 25 percent while the opportunity cost of capital, $WACC^{\tau}$, is only 21.55 percent. (Note: There are at least three other ways to obtain the same answer.)

3. We need to know the appropriate weighted average cost of capital for the project. One should be immediately suspect that 100 percent debt financing is unrealistic. Consequently, a better approach is to calculate the new weighted average cost of capital for the firm after the addition of $500,000 of debt to the firm's capital structure.

    Before the project, assuming the MM theorems apply, the WACC is 9 percent. Therefore, the cost of equity if the firm were all equity would be

$$WACC = \rho \left(1 - \tau_c \frac{B}{B+S} \right) \qquad (15.13)$$

$$\rho = \frac{.09}{1 - .4(.5)} = \frac{.09}{.8} = .1125$$

The new capital structure is

$$\frac{B}{B+S} = \frac{1,000,000}{1,500,000} = .667$$

Therefore, the new WACC is

$$WACC^{\tau} = .1125(1 - .4(.667))$$

$$= .0825$$

Because the project earns more than the new WACC, it should be accepted.

    The treasurer's reason for accepting the project is highly suspect. No project has 100 percent debt capacity. However, if a more reasonable debt capacity were assumed for the project, and if the project has the same operating risk as the firm but higher debt capacity, then it is reasonable to expect the project to have a lower WACC than the firm.

4. (a) Using the Miller (1977) argument, the gain from leverage is

$$G = B \left[1 - \frac{(1-\tau_c)(1-\tau_{PS})}{(1-\tau_{PB})} \right]$$
(15.24)

If the corporate tax rate decreases, *ceteris paribus*, the gain from leverage will decrease. Therefore, as shown in Figure S15.1, corporations will repurchase debt and the aggregate amount of debt will decrease.

(b) Given the assumptions of Miller (1977), then in equilibrium the gain from leverage will be zero, both before and after the change in the corporate tax rate. Therefore, there is no optimal capital structure is either case. Hence, there can be no systematic change in optimal capital structure from the point of view of a single firm.

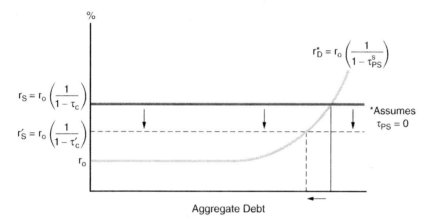

r_D = demand for debt
r_S = supply of debt before decrease in τ_c
r_S' = supply of debt after decrease in τ_c
r_0 = rate paid on debt of tax-free institutions

Figure S15.1   Changes in the Aggregate Amount of Debt Given a Decrease in the Corporate Tax Rate, τ_c

5. (a) According to Miller (1977), the gain from leverage is

$$G = B \left[1 - \frac{(1-\tau_c)(1-\tau_{PS})}{(1-\tau_{PB})} \right]$$

The gain is zero if the following condition is met:

$$(1 - \tau_c)(1 - \tau_{PS}) = (1 - \tau_{PB})$$

Both changes proposed by Congress affect the tax rate on income from common stock, τ_{PS}. If the reduction in the personal tax on dividend income exactly offsets the increase in capital gains tax for every individual, then there will be no effect on the equilibrium condition and no effect on optimal capital structure from the point of view of an individual firm. Even if the tax effects are not exactly offsetting, there will be no optimal capital structure from the firm's point of view. Equilibrium will be such that the gain from leverage will be zero both before and after the change.

(b) Figure S15.2 shows the supply and demand curves for aggregate debt.

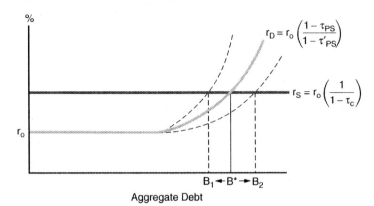

r_D = demand for debt
r_S = supply of debt
r_0 = rate paid on debt of tax-free institutions

Figure S15.2   Supply and Demand Curves for Aggregate Debt

If the effective tax on income from shares decreases, then we might expect the aggregate demand for debt to decline because equity capital is relatively more attractive. This, in fact, is the more likely effect of the proposed tax changes because the capital gains tax can be deferred, or offset. Hence, one might expect the reduction in the dividend tax to be overriding. The result would be to reduce the aggregate amount of debt in equilibrium from B^* to B_1. Of course, if the effective tax on income from shares increases, we would observe the opposite result, namely, an increase in aggregate debt from B^* to B_2.

6. (a) The cost of capital, WACC, is given by equation 15.19:

$$WACC = (1 - \tau_c)k_b \left(\frac{B}{B + S} \right) + k_s \left(\frac{S}{B + S} \right)$$

k_s can be found by the equation for the security market line, assuming a market in equilibrium, where

$$k_s = R_f + (E(R_m) - R_f)\beta$$

For firm B:

$$k_s = .06 + (.12 - .06)(1)$$

$$= .12$$

WACC (B) = .12 because B is an all-equity firm.
For firm C:

$$k_s = .06 + (.12 - .06)1.5$$

$$= .15$$

$$(1 - \tau_c)\,k_b = R_f\,(1 - \tau_c)$$

$$= .06\,(.5)$$

$$= .03$$

To find the WACC, transform the target debt-equity ratio, B/S, to B/(B + S):

$$\frac{B}{S} = 1$$

$$B = S$$

$$\frac{B}{B + S} = .5$$

Then, WACC (C) = .5 (.03) + .5 (.15) = .09.

The value of firm B can be computed using equation 15.1:

$$V^U = \frac{E\,(EBIT_1)(1 - \tau_c)}{\rho}$$

where

$$E\,(EBIT_1\,(1 - \tau_c)) = 180\,(1 - .5)$$

$$= 180\,(.5)$$

$$= 90$$

Therefore,

$$V^U = \frac{90}{.12}$$

$$= 750$$

For firm C, the equation for the value of a perpetuity can be used, since $E\,(EBIT_1\,(1 - \tau_c))$ is a perpetual stream. The income stream should be capitalized at the rate of the weighted average cost of capital for firm C.

$$V^L = \frac{E\,(EBIT_1)\,(1 - \tau_c)}{WACC}$$

$$= \frac{90}{.09}$$

$$= 1,000$$

(b) Since we know each project's correlation between its unlevered free cash flows and the market, r_{mj}, we can calculate the β^u appropriate to the project and use this to determine the project's cost of equity and WACC. Of course, the WACC is the required rate of return on the project.

For project 1,

$$\beta_j^u = \frac{cov\,(E\,(R_j),\ E\,(R_m))}{var\,(R_m)}$$

$$= \frac{r_{jm}\sigma_j\sigma_m}{\sigma_m^2}$$

$$= \frac{(.6)(.10)(.12)}{(.0144)} = .5$$

The required rate of return given 100% equity financing of project 1 is

$$\text{Required } E(R_j) = R_f + (E(R_m) - R_f)\beta_j$$

$$= .06 + (.12 - .06).5$$

$$= .09$$

This is also the WACC for firm B.

In order to compute the cost of equity given that firm C uses 50% debt financing, we need to estimate the levered β_e^L for the project then use the CAPM. We know that

$$\beta_e^L = \beta^u \left[1 + (1 - \tau_c) \frac{B}{S} \right]$$

$$= .5 [1 + (1 - .5)1] = .75$$

Using the CAPM to compute the cost of the levered equity in firm C, we have

$$k_s = R_f + [E(R_m) - R_f] \beta_e^L$$

$$= .06 + [.12 - .06] .75 = .105$$

The required rate of return for debt financing on project 1 is

$$R_f (1 - \tau_c) = .03$$

The expected return for project 1 is

$$E(R_j) = \frac{E(EBIT_j (1 - \tau_c))}{cost_j}$$

$$= \frac{9}{100} = .09$$

Therefore, for firm B (all-equity), the required return on project 1 is equal to the expected return (.09), and the project is marginally acceptable. For firm C, the total required return on project 1 is

$$k_s \left(\frac{S}{B + S} \right) + k_b \left(\frac{B}{B + S} \right) = .105(.5) + .03(.5)$$

$$= .0675$$

Therefore the expected return, .09, is higher than the required return, and the project is profitable.

Similar calculations for projects 2, 3, and 4 are summarized in Tables S15.1 and S15.2. In a world with corporate, but no personal, taxes a leveraged firm will always have a lower required rate of return on projects than an unleveraged firm. This is because the differential tax structure in effect subsidizes debt. There is a gain from leverage. Project 2 is rejected by firm B, the unlevered firm, but accepted by firm C with 50% leverage.

Table S15.1.   Project Evaluation for Firm B (All-Equity)

Project j	β_j^L	Required Rate on Equity Financing Equals the WACC	Expected Rate of Return on the Project $\left[= \dfrac{EBIT_j(1-\tau_c)}{cost_j} \right]$	Decision
1	.5	.09	.09	marginally acceptable
2	.6416	.0985	.0916	reject
3	.8	.108	.1125	accept
4	1.5	.15	.12	reject

Table S15.2.   Project Evaluation for Firm C $\left(LEVERED : \dfrac{B}{B+S} = .5 \right)$

Project j	β_j^L	Required Return on Equity Financing	Required Return on Debt Financing	Required Return Given $\dfrac{B}{B+S} = .5,$ WACC	Expected Return: $\dfrac{E(EBIT_j(1-\tau_c))}{cost_j}$	Decision
1	.75	.1050	.03	.0675	.09	accept
2	.9624	.1178	.03	.0739	.0916	accept
3	1.2	.1320	.03	.0810	.1125	accept
4	2.25	.1950	.03	.1125	.12	accept

7. There are two possible assumptions about the appropriate capital structure: a) that it cannot support any debt, or b) that since it does not change the operating risk of the firm, it can support a debt to total assets ratio of 50 percent. The second assumption is more reasonable. We also assume that the MM model in a world with only corporate taxes is appropriate.

If the firm's current WACC is 10.4 percent, we can compute the all-equity cost of capital, ρ, from equation 15.13.

$$WACC = \rho \left(1 - \tau_c \ \frac{B}{B+S} \right)$$

Substituting in the appropriate numbers and rearranging, we have

$$\rho = \frac{.104}{1 - .4(.5)} = .13$$

If we had adopted the first assumption, namely, that the project cannot support any debt, then this would be the required rate of return.

Proceeding on the basis of the second assumption, we see that after the firm takes on the project, it will have $1,250,000 in assets. It will still have $500,000 in debt. Therefore, the new debt to equity ratio, which is relevant for valuing the project, is

$$\frac{B}{B+S} = \frac{500,000}{1,250,000} = .4$$

The new WACC can be computed from equation 15.13. It is the rate of return which the project must earn in order to be acceptable.

$$WACC = .13 \, (1 - .4(.4)) = .1092$$

8. Using the standard equation for the weighted average cost of capital, we have (in a world without taxes)

$$WACC = k_b \, \frac{B}{B+S} + k_s \, \frac{S}{B+S}$$

$$= .09\left(\frac{4}{12}\right) + .18\left(\frac{8}{12}\right) = 15\%$$

Next, use the CAPM and solve for variables $E(R_m)$ and β_f. (β_f = the beta for the firm.)

$$E(R) = R_f + [E(R_m) - R_f] \, \beta_f$$

$$.15 = .05 + [E(R_m) - .05] \, \beta_f$$

$$[E(R_m) - .05] \, \beta_f = 10\%$$

Next, using the CAPM for the project, we have an estimate of the return that is required:

$$E(R_i) = R_f + [E(R_m) - R_f] \, \beta_i, \qquad \text{where } \beta_i = \text{beta for the project}$$

$$= .05 + [E(R_m) - R_f] \, (\beta_f \, 1.3), \qquad \text{since, } \beta_i = 1.3\beta_f$$

$$= .05 + (.10) \, (1.3), \qquad \text{since } [E(R_m) - .05] \, \beta_f = .10$$

$$= 18\%$$

Therefore, the expected rate of return on the project, 17 percent, is less than the required rate of 18 percent. Reject the project.

9. Varhard's recommendation is obviously wrong. The value of the firm will decline if there is any gain to leverage. In a MM world with only corporate taxes

$$V^L = V^U + \tau_c \, B$$

Reducing leverage reduces the value of the debt tax shield. The investment decisions of the firm remain unchanged while the financing decision increases the firm's weighted average cost of capital.

For a numerical answer, assume away the effect of growth. When growth is zero, the appropriate valuation model is

$$V^L = \frac{E \, (EBIT(1-T)) \, (1-\tau_c)}{\rho} + \tau_c \, \frac{k_d D}{k_b}$$

$$V^L = \frac{E \, (EBIT(1-T))}{\rho} + \tau_c B$$

where

$$E \, (EBIT \, (1-T)) = E(EBIT \, (1-T)) \, (1-\tau_c)$$

$$B = \frac{k_d D}{k_b}$$

Substituting in the facts of the problem, we can solve for ρ, the cost of equity for the unlevered firm.

$$10(50) + 1,000 = \frac{100(1-.5)}{\rho} + .5\left[\frac{.08(1,000)}{.08}\right]$$

$$\rho = \frac{50}{1,000} = 5\%$$

Using this fact, we can determine the value of the levered firm after the swap.

$$V^{l} = \frac{100(1-.5)}{.05} + .5\left[\frac{.08(500)}{.08}\right] = 1,250$$

Therefore, the value of the firm has fallen to $1,250. The per share price after the swap will be

$$\frac{V^{l} - B}{n} = \frac{S}{n}, \qquad \text{where n = number of shares outstanding}$$

$$\frac{1,250 - 500}{20} = \frac{750}{20} = \$37.50$$

Therefore, the price/share will fall from $50 to $37.50. The new price-earnings ratio will be

$$\frac{37.50}{1.50} = 25$$

10. Since the new branch is an extension of Community Bank's business, and thus is in the same risk class, the appropriate discount rate is the weighted average cost of capital. The correct weights of debt and equity to use in the WACC formula are from the target debt/equity ratio:

$$\frac{B}{B + S} = .9$$

Then,

$$\text{WACC} = k_s \left(\frac{S}{B+S}\right) + k_b \left(\frac{B}{B+S}\right)$$

$$= .11\,(.1) + .0468\,(.9)$$

$$= .05312 \sim 5\%$$

where k_b is the total *marginal* cost of debt financing,

$$k_b = (.0625 + .0275)\,(1 - \tau_c)$$

$$= (.09)\,(1 - .48)$$

$$= .0468$$

The net present value of the project is the sum of the NPV of the cash flows:

Year	PVIF at 5%	CF	NPV
0	1.000	−500,000	−500,000
1	.952	25,000	23,800
2	.907	35,000	31,745
3	.864	45,000	38,880
4	.823	45,000	37,035
5	.784	50,000	39,200

For the years after 5, use the perpetuity formula.

$$\frac{CF}{r} = \frac{50,000}{.05} = 1,000,000$$

and discount five years to the present:

$$1,000,000 \ (.784) = 784,000$$

The NPV of the branch is

$$-500,000 + 23,800 + 31,745 + 38,880 + 37,035 + 39,200 + 784,000 = 454,660$$

Because the NPV > 0, the branch should be opened.

    The answer implicitly assumes that the firm does not change its leverage, yet the project is 100% equity financed. This assumption is valid if the bank intends to maintain its long-term capital structure at a target of 90% debt.

11. This question focuses on the fact that the firm's cost of capital is an opportunity cost appropriate for the riskiness of the firm's assets. In a world without taxes, the systematic risk of the firm's portfolio of assets must equal the systematic risk of its portfolio of liabilities.

Assets		Liabilities	
liquid assets	β_{a1}	debt	β_B
property, plant and equipment	β_{a2}	equity	β_S

Let W_{ai} = the percent in asset i, and W_j = the percent in liability j. Then we have

$$W_{a1}\beta_{a1} + W_{a2}\beta_{a2} = W_B\beta_B + W_S\beta_S$$

The cost of capital can be determined using the CAPM for the assets side of the balance sheet, even though a not-for-profit organization has no debt or equity.

$$WACC = R_f + [E\ (R_m) - R_f]\ (w_{a1}\beta_{a1} + W_{a2}\beta_{a2})$$

Once taxes are introduced into our set of assumptions, the correct answer is difficult to determine. The current IRS code allows individuals to deduct donations to not-for-profit organizations from their gross income before arriving at taxable income. Presumably, this lowers the after-tax opportunity cost of capital to such individuals.

12. From the option pricing model we know that the greater diversification created by the new investment will lower the rate of return variance of the firm's assets. If the firm is not levered the project will be accepted because it increases shareholders' wealth (although marginally), which is identical to the value of the all-equity firm. The project has positive NPV. However, with a levered firm, shareholders' equity may be thought of as a call option on the value of the firm. Consequently, the lower variance of return on the assets of the firm will decrease the value of the call. If the decrease is large enough to offset the small positive NPV of the project, it will be rejected by shareholders of the levered firm.

13. Figures S15.3 and S15.4 depict the high-variance and low-variance probability distributions of two firms' future value. Firm A in Figure S15.3 is a low-leverage firm, with face-value debt = D_A. S15.4 shows a highly leveraged firm. Obviously, the probability that future earnings will cover the face-value of debt (avoidance of bankruptcy) is higher for firm A than for firm B.

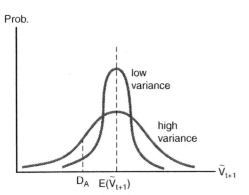

Figure 15.3   Probability Density Functions for Future Earnings of Firm A (Low Leverage)

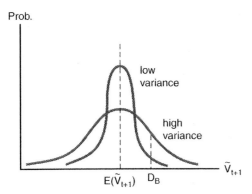

Figure 15.4   Probability Density Functions for Future Earnings of Firm B (High Leverage)

Regarding the stock as an option on $\tilde{V}_{t+1}$, with exercise price equal to the face value of the debt, shareholders benefit if the value of the underlying asset exceeds the exercise price, i.e.,

$$\tilde{V}_{t+1} > D$$

An increase of variance for Firm A assigns more probability to the outcome $\tilde{V}_{t+1} < D$, and hence is detrimental to shareholders. For Firm B, an increase in variance results in a higher probability that $\tilde{V}_{t+1} > D$, and is beneficial to shareholders. Thus, a 20 percent increase in variance is more apt to benefit the shareholders of a highly leveraged firm.

14. If we live in a world where markets are perfect, then two-fund separation implies (among their things) that everyone holds the market portfolio of risky assets. The market portfolio is composed of proportions of every asset held according to its market value weight. Therefore, every individual holds the market value fractions of the debt and equity of every firm. Any action which leaves the market value of the firm unchanged will not affect the value of the market portfolio. Therefore, even if the value of equity increases at the expense of an equal and offsetting decrease in the value of debt, every individual in the economy will be indifferent because his wealth is unaffected.

15. (a) We can use the Black-Scholes option pricing model and the facts of the problem to solve for the market value of the firm's equity. There are, however, two implicit assumptions: 1) we are dealing in a world without taxes (or in a world where there is not tax effect to leverage) and 2) the firm makes no disbursements of capital, such as dividend payments, during the year. The Black-Scholes formula applied to the pricing of corporate equity is

$$S = VN(d_1) - D\,e^{-r_f T} N\,(d_2)$$

where

$$d_1 = \frac{\ln\,(V/D) + r_f T}{\sigma\sqrt{T}} + (1/2)\,\sigma\sqrt{T}$$

$$d_2 = d_1 - \sigma\sqrt{T}$$

Substituting in the facts of the problem, we have

$$d_1 = \frac{\ln\,(25/10) + (.06)\,1}{(1.3)\sqrt{1}} + (.5)(1.3)\sqrt{1}$$

$$= \frac{.91629 + .06}{1.3} + .65 = 1.4$$

$$d_2 = 1.4 - 1.3\sqrt{1} = .1$$

From the Table of Normal Areas, we have

$$N(d_1) = .5 + .419 = .919$$

$$N(d_2) = .5 + .040 = .540$$

and substituting into the option pricing formula, we have

$$S = (25)\,(.919) - 10e^{-(.06)\,(1)}\,(.54)$$

$$= 22.975 - 5.086 = 17.89$$

Therefore, the market value of equity is $17.89 million and the market value of debt is $7.11 million.

$$B = V - S$$

$$= \$25 - 17.89 = \$7.11$$

(b) In order to determine the cost of debt and equity we can use the CAPM. From equations 15.42 and 15.49 we have the systematic risk of equity and debt respectively:

$$\beta_S = \frac{\partial S}{\partial V} \frac{V}{S} \beta_V, \qquad \beta_B = \frac{\partial B}{\partial V} \frac{V}{B} \beta_V$$

where

$$\frac{\partial S}{\partial V} = N(d_1)$$

$$\frac{\partial B}{\partial V} = 1 - N(d_1)$$

Using the facts of the problem, we have

$$\beta_S = (.919) \left[\frac{25}{17.89} \right] (1.5) = 1.93$$

$$\beta_B = (1 - .919) \left[\frac{25}{7.11} \right] (1.5) = .43$$

And finally, we can use the CAPM to determine the cost of equity and debt. The CAPM applies to any risky asset.

$$E(R_j) = R_f + [E(R_m) - R_f] \beta_j$$

For equity, we have

$$k_s = .06 + [.12 - .06](1.93) = .1758$$

and for debt we have

$$k_b = .06 + [.12 - .06](.43) = .0858$$

16. (a) True. If we assume an all-equity firm, then $N(d_1) = 1$ in the OPM, because the probability that the value of the option (here, the equity) will equal the value of the underlying asset (here, the firm) is a virtual certainty. The second term of the option pricing model drops out since the exercise price (here, face value of the debt) is zero. Thus

$$S = V N(d_1) - D e - r_f T N(d_2)$$

becomes

$$S = V$$

The OPM was used to obtain equation 15.48 for the cost of equity capital,

$$k_s = R_f + N(d_1)(R_v - R_f) \frac{V}{S}$$

substituting $N(d_1) = 1$,

$$k_s = R_f + (R_v - R_f)\frac{V}{S}$$

$$= R_f + (R_v - R_f)\frac{B}{S} + (R_v - R_f)\frac{S}{S}$$

$$= R_v + (R_v - R_f)\frac{B}{S}$$

which is the Modigliani-Miller definition of the cost of equity capital in a world without taxes. For an all-equity firm, this reduces to

$$k_s = R_v + (R_v - R_f)(0)$$

$$k_s = R_v$$

(b) If $N(d_1) = 1$ in the OPM, then $S = V$ as shown in (a) above. Thus $\dfrac{\partial S}{\partial V} = 1$, and the firm's capital structure is, by definition, 100 percent equity.

17. Given the Black-Scholes option pricing model, we have

$$S = V\,N(d_1) - e - r_f T\,D\,N(d_2)$$

where

$$d_1 = \frac{\ln(V/D) + r_f T}{\sigma\sqrt{T}} + (1/2)\sigma\sqrt{T}$$

$$d_2 = d_1 - \sigma\sqrt{T}$$

Substituting in the parameters of the question, we have

$$d_1 = \frac{\ln(2,000/1,000) + (.06)(4)}{(.2)\sqrt{4}} + (.5)(.2)\sqrt{4}$$

$$d_1 = \frac{.693147 + .24}{.4} + .2 = 2.533$$

$$d_2 = 2.533 - (.2)\sqrt{2} = 2.133$$

Using the Table of Normal Areas,

$$N(d_1) = .5 + .49434 = .99434$$

$$N(d_2) = .5 + .48352 = .98352$$

Substituting these values into the call formula gives us the market value of equity, since equity is a call option written on the value of the firm.

$$S = (2,000)(.99434) - e^{-(.06)(4)}(1,000)(.98352)$$

$$S = 1988.68 - (.786628)(983.52)$$

$$S = 1988.68 - 773.66437 = \$1,215.02$$

The market value of debt is

$$B = V - S$$

$$= 2,000 - 1215.02 = \$784.98$$

18. We can apply the Black-Scholes formula.

$$d_1 = \frac{\ln(2,000/1,000) + (.06)(4)}{(.3)\sqrt{4}} + (1/2)(.3)\sqrt{4}$$

$$d_1 = \frac{.693147 + .24}{(.3)(2)} + .3 = 1.85525$$

$$N(d_1) = .5 + .468 = .968$$

$$d_2 = 1.85525 - (.3)\sqrt{4} = 1.25525$$

$$N(d_2) = .5 + .395 = .895$$

$$S = (2,000)(.968) - e^{-(.06)(4)}(1,000)(.895)$$

$$S = 1,936 - 704 = \$1,232$$

Therefore, the market value of equity has increased and the market value of debt has decreased. The new debt-equity ratio is

$$\frac{768}{1232} = .62$$

The old debt/equity ratio was

$$\frac{785}{1215} = .65$$

19. The main empirical problem is that firms typically change their capital structure at the same time that they change their portfolio of assets by taking on new investment. Consequently, the effects are indistinguishable. Changes in the value of the firm may be attributed to investment policy, financial policy, or both.

   In addition to this fundamental problem, there are problems of measurement error. For example, how can one measure future growth in the firm, or expected rates of return, or differences in risk? Finally, the empirical work frequently uses cross-section regressions which are likely to have highly correlated residuals. This weakens the power of the statistical significance tests.

20. Each of the three reasons given by the president may be criticized.

   (a) If we assume that there really is a gain from leverage, then the value of the firm will increase by taking on more debt, at least to the point where the marginal gain from debt is offset by the marginal loss from potential bankruptcy. If the firm is already at its optimal capital structure, the project should be financed with approximately 75 percent debt (since B/(B + S) .75). If the firm is above its optimal amount of debt, then the project should be financed with a higher percentage of equity.

   (b) The earnings per share ratio has nothing to do with the economic value of the firm. Only the after-tax operating cash flows provided by the project are relevant. As given in the problem, these cash flows, when discounted at the appropriate risk-adjusted rate, will increase the value of the firm by $100 (NPV = $100). Therefore, the project should be accepted.

(c) If the project requires equity financing in order to bring the firm's capital structure back to its target leverage ratio, then equity should be issued to finance investments. The statement that "equity markets are currently depressed" has no meaning. If anyone *knew* that equities were undervalued in the market, then that individual would take advantage of his nonpublic information by placing his wealth in equity securities while prices were artificially low. Unless the firm's president has all of his wealth in the common stock of the firm, he probably does not really believe that the equity of the firm is undervalued.

21. Because Southwestern will finance the new project with 50 percent debt, the before-tax cost of debt is

$$k_b = R_f = \frac{7.5}{125} = 6\%$$

Since corporate debt is assumed to be risk-free, the market equilibrium risk-free rate is also 6 percent. It is important to recognize that the market equilibrium rate should not be adjusted by the tax rate.

Knowledge of the risk-free rate, the expected return on the market, and the market beta allows us to determine the market price of risk (the slope of the security market line).

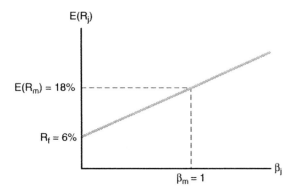

$$E(R_m) - R_f = \text{slope} = \frac{18\% - 6\%}{1.0} = 12\%$$

The firm has a $\dfrac{D}{D+E}$ ratio of 50 percent and a beta of .5.

(a) *Project 1.* The cash flows are operating cash flows and are, therefore, unlevered. First, we find ρ for project 1, then we solve for the appropriate discount rate assuming it has the same leverage as the firm.

$$\beta_j^U \text{ (the levered } \beta) \text{ is .4375}$$

$$\rho = E(R_j) = R_f + [E(R_m) - R_f]\beta_j$$

$$= .06 + [.18 - .06].4375$$

$$= .06 + .0525 = 11.25\%$$

The required rate of return on equity invested in the project assuming it has the same leverage as the firm is:

$$k_s = \rho + (\rho - R_f)(1 - \tau_c)\frac{B}{S} \qquad (15.18)$$

$$= .1125 + (.1125 - .06)(1 - .4)1$$

$$= .1125 + .0315 = 14.4\%$$

The correct discount rate on the project is its after-tax weighted average cost of capital.

$$WACC = k_b(1 - \tau_c) \frac{B}{B+S} + k_s \frac{S}{B+S}$$

$$= .06\,(1 - .4)\,(.5) + .144\,(.5)$$

$$= .018 + .072 = 9\%$$

Repeat the same procedure for project 2, which has an unlevered $\beta_j^U = .75$.

$$\rho = R_f + [E\,(R_m) - R_f]\,\beta_j$$

$$= .06 + (.18 - .06)\,.75$$

$$= .06 + .09 = 15\%$$

Now find the required rate of return on equity if the project has the same leverage as the firm as a whole.

$$k_s = E\,(R_j) = \rho + (\rho - R_f)\,(1 - \tau_c)\,\frac{B}{S}$$

$$= .15 + (.15 - .06)\,(1 - .4)\,1$$

$$= .15 + .054 = 20.4\%$$

The correct discount rate is

$$WACC = k_b(1 - \tau_c)\,\frac{B}{B+S} + k_s\,\frac{S}{B+S}$$

$$= .06\,(1 - .4)\,(.5) + .204\,(.5)$$

$$= .018 + .102 = 12\%$$

Since the projects are of equal size, the required rate of return is simply their weighted average.

$$WACC\,(joint\ project) = .5\,(.09) + .5\,(.12)$$

$$= 10.5\%$$

(b) The security market line gives us the required rate of return on the equity of the firm.

$$k_s = E\,(R_j) = R_f + [E\,(R_m) - R_f]\beta_j$$

$$= .06 + [.18 - .06]\,(.5)$$

$$= .06 + (.12)\,(.5)$$

$$k_s = 12\%$$

Therefore, the weighted average cost of capital for the levered firm is

$$WACC = k_b(1 - \tau_c)\left[\frac{B}{B+S}\right] + k_s\left[\frac{S}{B+S}\right]$$

$$= .06\,(1 - .4)\,(.5) + .12\,(.5)$$

$$= .018 + .06 = 7.8\%$$

(c) In order to determine the acceptability of the joint project, discount the joint cash flows at 10.5 percent. Interest expenses should not be included as part of the outflows because the discount rate already includes the interest factor.

Year	Outflow	Factor	NPV	Inflow	NPV
1	250	.9050	226.25	10	9.05
2	250	.8190	204.75	20	16.38
3	250	.7412	185.30	25	18.53
4	250	.6707	167.69	60	40.24
			783.99		84.20

Years 5–30

$$PV_5 = 110 \left[\frac{1-(1+r)^{-n}}{r} \right]$$

$$= 110 \left[\frac{1-(1.105)^{-26}}{.105} \right]$$

$$= 110 \,(8.814) = 969.50$$

Years 31–40

$$PV_{31} = 80 \left[\frac{1-(1.105)^{-10}}{.105} \right]$$

$$= 80 \,(6.015) = 481.18$$

Year 41

$$PV_0 = F\,(1+r)^{-n}$$

$$= 40\,(1.105)^{-41}$$

$$= 40\,(.0167) = .67$$

Finally, discount PV_5 and PV_{31} to the present:

$$PV_0 = PV_5\,(1.105)^{-4}$$

Note that you discount for four years because the annuity formula, which discounts payments at the end of each year from years 5 to 30 inclusive, will give you a present value which is at the *beginning* of year 5. This is the same as the end of year 4; therefore, you discount PV_5 for four years.

$$PV_0 = 969.50(1.105)^{-4}$$

$$= 969.50(.6707) = 650.28$$

$$PV_0 = PV_{31}(1.105)^{-30}$$

$$= 481.18(.0500) = 24.07$$

Add all of the present values to obtain the final NPV:

$$NPV = -783.99 + 84.20 + .67 + 650.28 + 24.07$$

$$= -24.77$$

Therefore, do *not* accept the joint project.

(d) Discount project 1 at 9 percent. Since both projects are of equal size, the cash inflows and outflows of the joint project can be divided by 1/2.

Project 1

Year	Cash Flow	PVIF	PV	
1	−120.0	.9174	−110.09	
2	−115.0	.8417	−96.80	
3	−112.5	.7722	−86.87	
4	−95.0	.7084	−67.30	
5–30	55.0	(9.9290) (.7084)	386.85	
31–40	40.0	(6.4177) (.0754)	19.36	
41	20.0	(.0292)	.58	
			45.73	NPV of project 1

Therefore, if it can be considered separately, project 1 would be accepted.

The NPV of project 2 is obtained by discounting its cash flows at 12 percent.

Project 2

Year	Cash Flow	PVIF	PV	
1	−120.0	.8929	−107.15	
2	−115.0	.7972	−91.68	
3	−112.5	.7118	−80.08	
4	−95.0	.6355	−60.37	
5–30	55.0	(7.8957) (.6355)	275.97	
31–40	40.0	(5.6502) (.0334)	7.55	
41	20.0	(.0096)	.19	
			−55.57	NPV of project 2

Therefore, if project 2 (the riskier project) can be considered separately, it should be rejected.

(e) If the joint project is accepted, the firm's equity beta is the weighted average of the original β and the project's β, since β's are additive.

$$\beta = .90 \, (\beta_f^L) + .10 \, (\beta_p^L)$$

where β_p^L is the levered β of the joint project.

The unlevered β of the joint project is

$$\beta^U = \frac{1}{2}(.75) + \frac{1}{2}(.4375) = .59375$$

We know by equation 12.45:

$$\beta^L = \beta^U \left(1 + (1 - \tau_c)\frac{B}{S} \right)$$

$$= .59375 \, (1 + .6 \, (1))$$

$$= .95$$

Therefore, the new risk level of the firm's equity is

$$\beta = .9 \, (.5) + .10 \, (.95) = .45 + .095 = .545$$

Chapter 16
Dividend Policy: Theory and Empirical Evidence

1. First, one must be careful to distinguish between the value of the firm and the value of equity. We are interested in a condition which might affect the value of the firm.

   If managers allow dividend policy to affect the investment decision, then the value of the firm will be affected, not because of dividend policy per se, but because improper use of dividend policy causes the firm to alter its investment decisions. For example, if a fixed dividend payout preempted the effort to invest in positive NPV projects, the value of the firm would be adversely affected.

2. If all market participants were corporations, the appropriate arbitrage condition would be that prices must adjust in a way which precludes any arbitrage profit from buying a security the day before it goes ex-dividend and selling it the day afterward. The potential arbitrage profit is

$$\pi = -P_B + D - \tau_c \ (.2D) + P_A + \tau_c \ (P_B - P_A)$$

   where

   π = the arbitrage profit

   P_B = the price before the stock goes ex-dividend

   P_A = the ex-dividend price

   τ_c = the corporate tax rate (for both capital gains and ordinary income)

   = 50 percent

   D = the dollar amount of the dividend payment

   In order for the arbitrage profit to be zero in equilibrium, we must have

$$P_B = .9D + .5P_A + .5P_B$$

$$P_B - P_A = \frac{.9}{.5}D$$

$$= 1.8D$$

   This implies that the decline in price on the ex-dividend date must be 180 percent of the dividend payment.

3. Even if a change in the firm's dividend policy results in a change in the average risk aversion of its clientele, this will have no effect on the value of the firm. As shown in Chapter 6, the market required rate of return depends on the market price of risk and the firm's covariance risk. It does not depend on the risk aversion of shareholders. Therefore, at most, all that will happen is that a change in dividend policy will result in a change in clientele. Old shareholders will be replaced by new shareholders without a change in the value of the firm.

4. The example income statement and balance sheets used to support the Miller-Scholes argument are replicated below:

Opening

Assets		Liabilities	
2,500 shares @ $10	25,000	Loan	16,667
Insurance	16,667	Net worth	25,000
	41,667		41,667

Closing

Assets		Liabilities	
2,500 shares @ $10.60	26,500	Loan	16,667
Accrued dividends	1,000	Accrued interest	1,000
Insurance	16,667	Net worth	26,500
	44,167		44,167

Ordinary Income		Capital Gains	
Dividends received	$1,000	Sale of 2,500 shares	
Less interest expense	1,000	@ $10.60	26,500
Taxable income	0	Less original basis	25,000
Nontaxable income	1,000		1,500
	$1,000		

It is possible to shelter any income, not just dividend income, by borrowing enough so that the interest payments reduce your taxable income to zero. Nontaxable income is provided by putting the borrowed funds into insurance, Keough plans, or some other similar tax shelter. The problem is that the nontaxable income from these shelters remains tax free only until it is consumed. Any portion of income which is consumed will also be taxed. This has the effect of converting the income tax into a consumption tax. People do pay taxes, but one might argue that they pay taxes only on that portion of income which they consume.

5. If the price of common stock increases when a dividend increase is announced, it is because the higher dividend payout is interpreted as an unambiguous message that future cash flows from investment are expected by management to be permanently higher. The dividend per se has no effect no shareholders' wealth.

6. (a) See the solution to Problem 15.17
   (b) Once again we use the OPM to determine the market value of equity. The relevant parameters on the ex-dividend data are:

$$V = \$1,500 \qquad \sigma = .25 \qquad r_l = 6\%$$

$$D = \$1,000 \qquad T = 4 \text{ years}$$

The value of d_1 will be

$$d_1 = \frac{\ln(V/D) + r_f T}{\sigma\sqrt{T}} + (1/2)\sigma\sqrt{T}$$

$$= \frac{\ln(1,500/1,000) + (.06)(4)}{(.25)\sqrt{4}} + (.5)(.25)\sqrt{4}$$

$$= \frac{.405465 + .24}{.5} + .25 = 1.54$$

and the value of d_2 is

$$d_2 = d_1 - \sigma\sqrt{T}$$

$$= 1.54 - (.25)(2) = 1.04$$

From the Table of Normal Areas, we have

$$N(d_1) = .5 + .4382 = .9382$$

$$N(d_2) = .5 + .3508 = .8508$$

Substituting into the OPM, we have

$$S = V\,N(d_1) - De - r_f T\,N(d_2)$$

$$= (1,500)(.9382) - (1,000)e^{-(.06)(4)}(.8508)$$

$$= 1407.30 - 669.26 = 738.04$$

From the solution to Problem 15.17, we determined that the market value of equity was $1,215. After receiving $500 in dividends, the market value of equity is $738. The ex-dividend wealth of shareholders is $500 + $738 = $1,238. This is an increase of $23 over their original wealth position. It results from both the increased leverage and increased instantaneous variance after the dividend payout.

7. Theoretically, the new dividend policy is irrelevant. The important fact is that the firm will continue to accept all profitable projects, i.e., dividend decisions will not affect the stream of expected future investments. Whenever dividend payout is "too low" from the point of view of an individual shareholder, he can always sell a portion of his share holdings in order to consume. The opposite is true if dividends are "too high." The shareholder can reinvest his dividends in shares of the firm. Finally, the increased variability of dividend payout is irrelevant. What counts is the riskiness of the anticipated cash flows from future investment and it will remain unchanged.

8. Since the rate of return on investment is assumed to remain constant forever, we can use the Gordon growth model, equation 14.17b, to value the firm's shares. First we need the expected end-of-year $\text{EBIT}_1(1 - T)$.

$$\text{EBIT}_1(1 - T) = \text{EBIT}_0(1 - T)(1 + g)$$

$$g = Kr = (.5)(.20) = .1$$

$$\text{EBIT}_1(1 - T) = (3.00)(1 + .1) = \$3.30$$

Applying these results to the formula, we have

$$V_0 = \frac{EBIT_1 \ (1-T)(1-K)}{\rho - Kr} = \frac{D_1}{\rho - g}$$

$$V_0 = \frac{3.30(1-.5)}{.15-.10} = \frac{1.65}{.05} = \$33.00$$

9. (i) If the firm decides to pay a cash dividend

   (a) The systematic risk of its portfolio of assets will increase because a low risk asset (i.e., the $2,000 of cash) will be "spun off" to shareholders.

   (b) The market value of bondholders' wealth will decline relative to the market value of equity because the debt-holders expect to have claim on fewer and riskier assets.

   (c) The debt to equity ratio will increase on the ex-dividend date. The ex-dividend balance sheet is shown below.

Cash	0	Debt	5,000
Inventory	2,000	Equity	3,000
P, P & E	6,000	Total liabilities	8,000
Total Assets	8,000		

$$\text{Predividend} \frac{D}{D+E} = \frac{5,000}{10,000} = .5$$

$$\text{Ex-dividend} \frac{D}{D+E} = \frac{5,000}{8,000} = .625$$

   (d) Prior to the ex-dividend date the market value of the firm will be unchanged in a world without taxes. After the ex-dividend date it will fall by $2,000, the amount of the dividend payment.

   (ii) If the firm decides to issue $1,000 of new debt and an equal amount of new equity in order to finance the dividend payment, the ex-dividend balance sheet will look like that below.

Cash	2,000	Debt	6,000
Inventory	2,000	Equity	4,000
P, P & E	6,000	Total liabilities	10,000
Total assets	10,000		

In anticipation of these changes the various impacts will be:

   (a) The systematic risk of the portfolio of assets will remain unchanged since the cash payment is raised from external funds, thereby leaving the assets side of the balance sheet unchanged.

   (b) If new debt is not subordinate to old debt, then the market value of the outstanding bonds will decline because their claim on the assets of the firm must be shared with new bondholders.

(c) The debt-equity ratio will obviously increase:

$$\frac{D}{D+E} = \frac{6{,}000}{10{,}000} = .6$$

(d) Prior to the ex-dividend date the market value of the firm will increase by \$2,000, the value of the new debt and equity. However, when the \$2,000 is paid out the value of the firm returns to its original level.

(iii) If the firm issues \$2,000 in new equity, then pays out an equal amount in dividends, the ex-dividend balance sheet will be exactly the same as the pre-dividend balance sheet. There will be no changes in

(a) the systematic risk of the firm's portfolio of assets,

(b) the wealth of original bondholders,

(c) the debt to equity ratio, or

(d) the market value of the firm.

(iv) Using cash to repurchase equity has the same effects (in a world without taxes) as paying a cash dividend to shareholders. Therefore, the same answer used in i) applies here.

10. From equation 15.6 the Modigliani-Miller valuation equation for a levered firm with no growth, we have

$$V^L = V^U + T_c B$$

We also know, from equation 15.13, the weighted average cost of capital, $k_0 = WACC$, is

$$k_0 = \rho \left(1 - T_c \frac{B}{V^L} \right) = WACC$$

Solving, for ρ, we have

$$\rho = \frac{V^L \cdot WACC}{V^L - T_c B}$$

$$\rho = \frac{V^L \cdot WACC}{V^U}, \qquad \text{since } V^L - T_c B = V^U$$

We also know that the value of the unlevered firm is

$$V^U = \frac{E\,(EBIT_1)(1-T)}{\rho}$$

Therefore

$$\rho = \frac{\dfrac{V^L \cdot WACC}{EEBIT_1 (1-T)}}{\rho}$$

Solving for V^L, we have

$$V^L = \frac{E(EBIT_1)(1-T_c)}{WACC}.$$ \hfill Q.E.D.

11. An increase in the retention rate does not necessarily affect the anticipated stream of investments at all. Referring back to the sources and uses of funds equation (for an all-equity firm), we know that

$$EBIT + mP = I + D \qquad (16.3)$$

Retention is simply the difference between earnings and dividends, (EBIT – D). The firm can retain any percentage of earnings it desires without affecting planned investment if it balances the sources and uses of funds by either selling new shares (if extra funds are needed for investment) or repurchasing shares (if excess funds remain after investment and dividends). If the firm does not make use of external funding (i.e., mP = 0), then a higher retention rate will imply more investment. This may lead to improper use of funds in projects with low rates of return.

12. If the firm pays a cash dividend the market value of the firm goes down, ceteris paribus, and the riskiness of the firm's assets increases. These results follow from the fact that the cash paid out is a relatively low risk asset. Not only does the cash payout diminish the assets which the firm holds, but it also increases the systematic risk of the firm's portfolio of assets. From the point of view of bond-holders, this is an undesirable effect for two reasons: First, the diminished asset base implies that bondholders have claim on less collateral in the event of bankruptcy. Second, the greater risk of the firm's portfolio of assets implies that the market value of equity increases if we think of equity as an option on the value of the firm. If the market value of equity increases, the market value of debt decreases.

   The option pricing model leads to the conclusion that, ceteris paribus, the market value of debt should fall when dividends are paid from cash. However, the ceteris paribus assumption is important. If bondholders believe that higher dividend payout also implies greater future cash flows from investment, the market value of their collateral may actually increase in spite of the dividend payout. This would leave them better off. However, if dividend payout carries no implications about cash flows from investment, then we should observe the OPM implication—namely, a decline in the market value of debt.

Chapter 17
Applied Issues in Corporate Finance

1. Equation 17.4 shows the NPV of lease financing from the lessee's point of view, but it assumes that lease payments are made at the end of each year. If lease payments are made at the beginning of each year, the formula must be modified as follows:

$$\text{NPV (to lessee)} = I_0 - L\,(1-\tau_c) - \sum_{t=1}^{N-1} \frac{L_t\,(1-\tau_c)}{[1+(1-\tau_c)\,k_b]^t}$$

$$-\sum_{t=1}^{N} \frac{\tau_c\,\text{dep}_t}{[1+(1-\tau_c)k_b]^t}$$

Note that the information about the firm's capital structure (50% debt to total assets) is irrelevant because leasing is a perfect substitute for debt. Substituting the facts of the problem into the above equation, we have:

$$\text{NPV (to lessee)} = 100,000 - 32,000\,(1-.3) - 32,000\,(1-.3)$$

$$\text{PVIF}_a\,(4 \text{ yrs., } 7\%) - .3\,(20,000)\,\text{PVIF}_a\,(5 \text{ yrs., } 7\%)$$

$$= 100,000 - 22,400 - 22,400\,(3.3872)$$

$$- 6,000\,(4.1002)$$

$$= -22,874$$

The negative net present value of the lease contract clearly indicates that debt financing (i.e., owning) is preferred to leasing for this project.

2. (a) The NPV to the lessor is determined by using the following formula

$$\text{NPV (to lessor)} = -I + \sum_{t=1}^{N} \frac{L_t\,(1-\tau_c) + \tau_c\text{dep}_t}{(1+\text{WACC}_B)^t}$$

The weighted average cost of capital to the lessor is assumed to be the after-tax rate of return on the lease

$$\text{WACC}_B = k_b\,(1-\tau_c)$$

$$\text{WACC}_B = .15\,(1-.4) = 9\%$$

Substituting the facts of the problem into the formula we have

$$\text{NPV (to lessor)} = -500,000 + \sum_{t=1}^{5} \frac{147,577(1 - .4) + .4(100,000)}{(1 + .09)^t}$$

$$= -500,000 + (147,577)(.6) + 40,000)$$

$$(\text{PVIF}_a(5\text{yrs.,}9\%))$$

$$= -500,000 + (88,546.2 + 40,000)(3.889651)$$

$$= -500,000 + 500,000$$

$$\text{NPV (to lessor)} = 0$$

Thus, the lessor is charging a competitive lease rate. The NPV of the lease for Reddi Roller Leasing is zero. If the lease payments were larger, then the lessor would have a positive NPV.

(b) The formula for the NPV of the lease to the lessee is rewritten below.

$$\text{NPV (to lessee)} = I - \sum_{t=1}^{N} \frac{L_t (1 - \tau_c) + \tau_c dep_t}{[1 + (1 - \tau_c) k_b]^t}$$

Substituting in the numbers from the problem, we have

$$\text{NPV (to lessee)} = -500,000 + \sum_{t=1}^{5} \frac{147,577}{(1 + .15)^t}$$

$$= 500,000 - 147,577 (\text{PVIF}_a (5 \text{ yrs., } 15\%))$$

$$= 500,000 - 147,577 (3.352155)$$

$$= 500,000 - 494,701$$

$$\text{NPV (to lessee)} = 5,299$$

(c) It is usually the case that if the lessor is charging a competitive rate (i.e., if he earns his weighted average cost of capital) and if the lessor has a higher rate than the lessee (which is always true when the lessee is a tax-free institution) then leasing is better than borrowing from the lessee's point of view.

3.   (a) To answer this problem, given the complex pattern of cash flows, it is useful to construct a table similar to Table S17.1.

Table S17.1   Cash Outflows From The Lessee's Point of View

(1)	(2)	(3)	(4)	(5)	(6)	(7)	(8)	(9)	(10)
							After-tax		
Year	τ_c	dep	$(1-\tau_c)L_t$	D_{t-1}	$\Delta k_b D_{t-1}$	ΔD_t	Salvage Value	CF_t	$(1+k_b)^{-t}$
0	—	—	L	—	—	—	—	L	1.0000
1	0	40,000	L	100,000	17,000	14,256	0	L	.8547
2	0	30,000	L	85,744	14,576	16,680	0	L	.7305
3	.48	20,000	.52L	69,064	11,741	19,516	0	15,236 + .52L	.6244
4	.48	10,000	.52L	49,548	8,423	22,833	0	8,843 + .52L	.5337
5	.48	0	0	26,715	4,542	26,715	(7,600)	(8,969)	.4561

Obviously, an explanation of the cash flow column (column 9) is in order. It is the sum of:

* τ_c dep, the depreciation tax shield (column 2 times column 3),

* $(1-\tau_c)L_t$, the after-tax lease payments (from column 4). Note that the lease payments are made at the beginning of each year, hence there is an immediate payment (in year 0) but no payment at the end of year 5.

*   The opportunity cost of displaced debt. The amount of displaced debt is initially $100,000, but it is reduced each year because annual (end-of-year) amortization payments are $31,256. Column 6 shows the portion of each amortization payment which is interest and column 7 shows the reduction of principal. Columns 6 plus 7 always add to equal $31,256. The actual interest tax shield which is displaced by leasing (and which is added to cash flows in column 9) is equal to column 6 times column 2,

*   The after-tax salvage value is assumed to be received by the lessee (for a price of $1). To keep things simple we assumed the lessee reports a capital gain of ($10,000 – $1) and pays capital gains taxes immediately. Future depreciation of the $10,000 salvage value (using sum-of-years' digits over 4 years) has a present value (at 17%) of $7393 which amounts to a tax shield of $3549. This is a tax shield received by the lessee, i.e., a positive cash inflow. Column 9, row 5 is the sum of: the displaced interest tax shield, $2180, the after-tax salvage value ($7600) and the present value of the depreciation tax shield, ($3549). The sum is ($8969). Note that the problem discounts the salvage value as if it had the same risk as the other cash flows, i.e., using a 17% discount rate. This is an unreasonable assumption because the salvage value usually has greater uncertainty than the leasing (debt) cash flows; and should be discounted at a higher rate. Nevertheless, we used 17% for convenience.

The cash flows in column 9 are all outflows, with the exception of the after-tax salvage value which is an inflow. If we add the $100,000 investment outlay, which is saved by leasing, the NPV for the lessee is

$$\text{NPV (lessee)} = 100,000 - L - .8547L - .7305L - .6244\,(15,236$$
$$+ .52L) - .5337\,(8,843 + .52L) + .456\,(8,969)$$

If we set the NPV (lessee) equal to zero, and solve for L, the result will be the maximum lease fee which the lessee can afford to offer in negotiations

$$\text{NPV (lessee)} = 0 = 89,857 - 3.187412L$$

$$L = \$28,191$$

(b) Next, we need to analyze the same contract from the lessor's point of view. Table S17.2 shows the cash flows for the lessor.

Table S17.2 Cash Inflows From the Lessor's Point of View

(1)	(2)	(3)	(4)	(5)	(6)
Year	τ_c	dep	$(1 - \tau_c)L_t$	CF_t	$(1 + WACC_B)^{-t}$
0	—	—	.52L	.52L	1.0000
1	.48	40,000	.52L	19,200 + .52L	.9188
2	.48	30,000	.52L	14,400 + .52L	.8442
3	.48	20,000	.52L	9,600 + .52L	.7756
4	.48	10,000	.52L	4,800 + .52L	.7126
5	.48	0	0	0	.6547

Cash flows for the lessor are the sum of:

- τ_c dep, the depreciation tax shield received, column 2 times column 3, and
- $(1 - \tau_c)L_t$, the after-tax lease receipts, column 4.

The weighted average cost of capital for the lessor is

$$WACC_B = k_b (1 - \tau_c) = .17 (1 - .48) = .0884$$

Therefore, the discount factors in column 6 are based on a 8.84% interest rate. Note that no capital gains are received by the lessor when the asset is sold because the sale price, $1, and the book value, $0, are essentially the same. The lessor spends $100,000 to acquire the asset and receives the cash flows in column 6, therefore the NPV to the lessor is

$$NPV \text{ (lessor)} = -100,000 + .52L + .9188(19,200 + .52L)$$

$$+ .8442 (14,400 + .52L) + .7756 (9,600 + .52L)$$

$$+ .7126 (4,800 + .52L)$$

Setting this equal to zero and solving for L, the lessor's minimum acceptable lease payment, we have

$$NPV \text{ (lessor)} = 0 = 2.2106L - 59,336$$

$$L = \$26,842$$

The results show that the lessor requires at least $26,842 per payment while the lessee is willing to offer up to $28,191, therefore there is room to bargain. Any lease fee between these limits will provide a positive NPV to both parties.

4. If we assume the Modigliani-Miller framework for our analysis, then our cost of equity may be computed from the following formula (see Chapter 15, Eq. 15.18)

$$k_s = \rho + (\rho - k_b)(1 - \tau_c)\frac{B}{S}$$

The information in the problem indicates that your tax rate is 40%, B/S = 9, and k_b = 14%. All you need to estimate is the before-tax rate of return on equity, ρ. The weighted average cost of capital for the lessor is

$$WACC_B = k_b (1 - \tau_c)$$

The rate paid on the lease contract is 18% and the lessor's tax rate is 48%, therefore

$$WACC_B = .18 (1 - .48) = 9.36\%.$$

Using the Modigliani-Miller definition of the weighted average cost of capital (Chapter 15, Eq. 15.12) we have

$$WACC = \rho \left(1 - \tau_c \frac{B}{B+S} \right)$$

$$.0936 = \rho \, (1 - .48 \, (.9))$$

$$\rho = \frac{.0936}{1 - .48(.9)} = 16.4789\%$$

Substituting this back into the cost of equity formula, we have

$$k_s = .164789 + (.164789 - .14) (1 - .4) 9$$

$$k_s = 29.86\%$$

This is the required rate of return on equity for your firm.

5. (a) First, compute the NPV of the project to Mortar Bored Company using the usual NPV formula

$$NPV = -I + \sum_{t=1}^{N} \frac{E \, (\Delta EBIT_t) \, (1 - \tau_c) + \tau_c \Delta dep_t}{(1 + WACC)^t}$$

The WACC is computed as follows

$$WACC = k_b (1 - \tau_c) \frac{B}{B+S} + k_s \frac{S}{B+S}$$

$$WACC = .15 \, (1 - .4) \, (.5) + .25 \, (.5) = 17\%$$

Substituting in the information from the problem we have

$$NPV = -100,000 + \sum_{t=1}^{8} \frac{31,000 \, (1 - .4) + .4 \, (12,500)}{(1.17)^t}$$

$$= -100,000 + (18,600 + 5,000) \, [PVIF_a \, (17\%, 8 \text{ yrs.})]$$

$$= -100,000 + (23,600) \, (4.207163)$$

$$= -100,000 + 99,289$$

$$NPV = -711$$

Therefore, if the company buys the project and finances it with debt, the NPV is negative and the project should be rejected.

(b) The NPV of the lease is computed by using Eq. 17.5.

$$\text{NPV (lessee)} = I - \sum_{t=1}^{N} \frac{L_t \, (1 - \tau_c) + \tau_c \text{dep}_t}{[1 + (1 - \tau_c)k_b]^t}$$

Substituting in the data from the problem we have

$$\text{NPV (lessee)} = 100,000 - \sum_{t=1}^{8} \frac{21,400 \, (1 - .4) + .4 \, (12,500)}{[1 - (1 - .4).15]^t}$$

$$= 100,000 - (21,400(.6) + 5,000)$$

$$[\text{PVIF}_a \, (9\%, 8\text{yrs.})]$$

$$= 100,000 - (17,840) \, (5.534819)$$

$$= 100,000 - 98,741$$

$$\text{NPV (lessee)} = 1,259$$

Consequently, the NPV of the lease contract is $1,259.

(c) If the project is leased, the positive NPV of the lease contract will offset the negative NPV of the project. Hence, the project is acceptable if leased.

Chapter 18
Acquisitions, Divestitures, Restructuring, and Corporate Governance

1. (a)

Solution to Table S18.5   Model of Differential P/E Ratios

	Acquirer (A)	Target (T)	Combined
1. Net Income	$100	$100	$200
2. Number of Shares	100	100	140
3. EPS (old)	$1	$1	$1.43
4. P/E Ratio	50x	10x	50x
5. Price/Share	$50	$10	$71.50 (new)
6. Total Market Value (old)	$5,000	$1,000	$6,000
7. Proportions (old)	83.3%	16.7%	
8. Terms Paid (A for T)	0.4A/1	$20	
9. Premium to T		100%	
10. EPS (new)	$1.43	0.4(1.43) = $0.572	
11. EPS (% change)	+43%	−43%	
12. Total Market Values (new)	100($71.50) = $7,150	0.4(100)($71.50) = $2,860	140($71.50) = $10,010
13. Market Values (% change)	(7,150/5,000)−1 = 43%	(2,860/1,000)−1 = 186%	
14. Proportions (new)	(7,150/10,010) = 71.43%	(2,860/10,010) = 28.57%	

(b) The basic generalization is that when a buying company has a higher P/E ratio than the target, the buyer will achieve accretion in earning per share while the target will suffer dilution in earnings per share. The relative P/E ratio is the one reflected in the deal terms. The target may end up with a higher market value per share received if the buyer has a really high P/E ratio as in the example.

For the buyer as its EPS grows, its P/E may actually increase. This facilitates doing other acquisitions with its growing P/E ratio.

The basic fallacy in this process is that the higher P/E ratio company has either higher growth and/or lower risk than the low P/E ratio company. So as more low P/E companies are bought, the weighted average growth will drop and/or risk of the buyer will increase. A second problem is that when low P/E ratios companies are not available, the buyer will not have this artificial growth stimulus any more. Its EPS growth and P/E ratio are likely to collapse. Also this works great in a booming stock market. In a weak stock market, the P/E ratio of the buyer may drop considerably. The problem was aggravated at Tyco because as the company seemed to prosper, top executives received loans which were later forgiven. Some executives have been charged with stealing from the company. These practices, of course, are not inherent in playing the differential P/E game. However, the manipulative atmosphere of the activity may provide a fertile soil for such behavior.

2. We can apply the Black-Scholes option pricing formula, using the parameters for the merged firm.

$$V = 4{,}000 \qquad r_f = .06 \qquad \sigma = .179$$
$$D = 2{,}000 \qquad T = 4$$

Substituting into the formula, we have

$$d_1 = \frac{\ln(4{,}000/2{,}000) + (.06)(4)}{(.179)\sqrt{4}} + (1/2)(.179)\sqrt{4}$$

$$d_1 = \frac{.693147 + .24}{.358} + .179 = 2.7856$$

$$d_2 = 2.7856 - (.179)\sqrt{4} = 2.428$$

Referring to the Table of Normal Areas, we have

$$N(d_1) = .5 + .49733 = .99733$$

$$N(d_2) = .5 + .49240 = .99240$$

and substituting into the Black-Scholes formula yields

$$S = (4{,}000)(.99733) - e^{-(.06)(4)}(2{,}000)(.9924)$$

$$S = 3989.32 - 1561.30 = \$2{,}428.02$$

Prior to merger the value of equity in each firm was $1,215.02. Doubling it, we have $2,430.04. This is more (albeit, only slightly more) than the value of equity after merger. Therefore, shareholders would oppose the merger if there were no other merger effects.

3. From problem 18.2, the market value of equity in the merged firm was $2,428.02. With 1,000 shares outstanding, this amounts to $2.43 per share. By taking on an additional $1,000 in debt, the face value of debt in the merged firm increases to $3,000 and the market value of the firm to $5,000. We can use the OPM to determine the market value of equity.

$$S = V\, N(d_1) - D\, e^{-r_f T} N(d_2)$$

where

$$d_1 = \frac{\ln(V/D) + r_f T}{\sigma\sqrt{T}} + (1/2)\sigma\sqrt{T}$$

$$= \frac{\ln(5{,}000/3{,}000) + (.06)(4)}{(.179)\sqrt{4}} + (.5)(.179)\sqrt{4}$$

$$= \frac{.510825 + .24}{.358} + .179 = 2.276$$

$$d_2 = d_1 - \sigma\sqrt{T}$$

$$= 2.276 - (.179)(2) = 1.918$$

From the Table of Normal Areas, we have

$$N(d_1) = .5 + .4886 = .9886$$

$$N(d_2) = .5 + .4724 = .9724$$

Substituting these values into the OPM, we have

$$S = (5,000)(.9886) - (3,000)e^{-(.06)(4)}(.9724)$$

$$= 4,943 - 2294.75 = 2648.25$$

Price per share = 2648.25/1,000 = \$2.65
Therefore, the price per share increases by 22 cents.

4. (a) If we regard the stock as a call option on the firm, with an exercise price equal to the face value of
        the debt outstanding, then the value of the stock is given by

$$S = VN(d_1) - De^{-r_f T}N(d_2)$$

where

$$d_1 = \frac{\ln(V/D) + r_f T}{\sigma\sqrt{T}} + (1/2)\sigma\sqrt{T}$$

and

$$d_2 = d_1 - \sigma\sqrt{T}.$$

Substituting into d_1, we have

$$d_1 = \frac{\ln\left[\frac{1,000}{500}\right] + (.08)(5)}{\sqrt{.10}\sqrt{5}} + (1/2)\sqrt{.10}\sqrt{.5}$$

$$= \frac{\ln 2 + (.08)(5)}{(.31623)(2.236)} + (.5)(.31623)(2.236)$$

$$= \frac{.693 + .4}{.70709} + .353545 = \frac{1.093}{.70709} + .353545$$

$$= 1.546 + .353545 = 1.899545 = 1.9$$

Using the Table of Normal Areas,

$$N(d_1) = .971$$

$$d_2 = d_1 - \sigma\sqrt{T}$$

$$= 1.9 - .70709 = 1.19291$$

$$N(d_2) = .883$$

Therefore,

$$S = 1{,}000\,(.971) - e^{-(.08)(5)}\,500\,(.883)$$

$$= 971 - 500\,(.883)\,(.6703)$$

$$= 971 - (441.5)\,(.6703)$$

$$= 971 - 296$$

$$= \$675$$

The value of the debt, B, for each firm is $325.

$$V = S + B$$

$$1000 = 675 + B$$

$$B = 325$$

The combined equities of Firms A and B are worth $1,350.

$$S_A + S_B = 675 + 675$$

$$= \$1350$$

To calculate B and S for the merged firm, first calculate the new variance of returns, setting the covariance term equal to zero.

$$\sigma^2 = w^2\sigma_A^2 + (1-w)^2\sigma_B^2 = (.25)(.1) + (.25)(.1) = .05$$

$$\sigma = .2236$$

Using the Black-Scholes formula once more,

$$d_1 = \frac{\ln 2 + (.08)\,(5)}{(.2236)(2.236)} + (.5)(.2236)(2.236)$$

$$= \frac{1.093}{.5} + .25 = 2.186 + .25 = 2.436$$

$$N\,(d_1) = .9926$$

$$d_2 = 2.436 - .5 = 1.936$$

$$N\,(d_2) = .9735$$

Therefore, the value of the equity for the merged firm is

$$S = 2{,}000\,(.9926) - e^{-(.08)\,(5)}\,1{,}000\,(.9735)$$

$$= 1985.2 - 1{,}000\,(.9735)\,(.6703)$$

$$= 1985.2 - (973.5)\,(.6703)$$

$$= 1985.2 - 652.54$$

$$= 1{,}332.66$$

$$= 1{,}333$$

$$B = 2{,}000 - 1{,}333 = \$667$$

Shareholders lose $17:

$$\$1350 - 1,333 = \$17$$

The bondholders gain $17:

$$B_A + B_B = 2\,(325)$$
$$= 650$$
$$667 - 650 = \$17$$

(b) In order to restore the equity holders to their original position, the merged firm increases the face value of debt D'_{AB}. The funds raised with the new debt are used to retire a portion of the equity (so that the value of the firm remains at $2,000). Let L = the loss to the equityholders as a result of the merger:

$$L = S_{AB} - (S_A + S_B) = 1,333 - 1,350 = -17$$

So the merger transfers wealth from the equityholders to bond-holders. We can increase the face value of the debt to D'_{AB} to reverse and neutralize the effect of the merger such that;

$$B'_{AB}(D_{AB}/D'_{AB}) - B_{AB} = L$$

For the facts of this case, Company AB should issue new debt with a face value of $560. The resulting market values of debt and equity are calculated below:

$$V_{AB} = 2,000$$
$$D'_{AB} = 1,560$$

$$d_1 = \frac{\ln(2,000)/1,560 + (.08)(5)}{(.2236)(2.236)} + (.5)(.2236)(2.236)$$

$$= \frac{.6485}{.5} + .25 = 1.547$$

$$N\,(d_1) = .5 + .4390 = .9390$$

$$d_2 = 1.547 - .5 = 1.047$$

$$N\,(d_2) = .5 + .3524 = .8524$$

$$S'_{AB} = 2,000(.9390) - 1,560(.6703)(.8524) = 1,878 - 891 = 987$$
$$B'_{AB} = 2,000 - 987 = 1,013$$

Test of results:

$$B'_{AB}(D_{AB}/D'_{AB}) - B_{AB} = L$$
$$1,013(1,000/1,560) - 667 = -18 \cong -17$$

Note that $B_A + B_B = 325 + 325 = 650$. This is equivalent to

$$B'_{AB}(D_{AB}/D'_{AB}) = 1,013(1,000/1,560) = 649.$$

The wealth of the equityholders is now composed of the current value of equity (987) *plus* the amount of cash they have received, which is equal to the market value of the new debt:

B'_{AB}	1,013	Market value of debt in merged firm
$B_A + B_B$	-650	Original market value of debt
Market value of net debt	363	Cash received by equityholders
S'_{AB}	$+987$	Market value of equity in merged firm
$S_A + S_B$	1,350	$= 2 \times 675 =$ Original market value of equity

5. Studies have shown that betas usually approach 1 if investors diversify randomly among 15 or more stocks. Since many conglomerates engaged in more than 15 mergers and still had betas well above 1 (and well above non-merging firms), this indicates that diversification as such was not the dominant motive for conglomerate mergers. A high percentage of the firms initiating merger activity in the early 60's were in narrow lines of business whose growth outlook was highly uncertain or unfavorable. They presumably sought a carry-over of some technical or general managerial abilities with the firms that they acquired.

6. Over a long period of time one would not expect the risk-adjusted performance of conglomerate firms to be significantly different from the risk-adjusted performance of a broad market index. If the firms' performance were better, it would imply that conglomerate firms were able to buy under-valued securities. This is inconsistent with efficient markets. One hypothesis of superior conglomerate performance is that synergy exists between the components of combining firms. However, unless this synergy is firm-to-firm specific, a competitive market among acquiring firms would cause any advantages to be priced according to their value. Similarly, one would not expect the performance of conglomerate firms to be significantly worse than a broad market index, because persistent evidence that conglomerate firms were making bad choices (or overpaying) would result in a reassessment of their market values. Hence both their risk measures and return measures would be changed, until the returns and risk of the conglomerate firms plotted on the security market line.

7. Non-owner managers of the firm may be motivated to act like bondholders, if there are costs to losing their jobs. The managers would prefer to prevent bankruptcy by decreasing the probability of default on debt. Thus, manager-agents may behave in a manner more risk-averse than stockholders would wish.

8. Alternative Strategies for Growth
   (a)

Solution to Table S18.8   Multiple Strategies for Growth*

	Internal	Merger	JV	Alliance	Licensing	Investment
Speed	L	**H**	M	M	**H**	M
Cost known	L	M	**H**	M	L	**H**
Add capabilities	L	**H**	**H**	M	L	**H**
Add products	L	**H**	M	L	L	L
Add markets	L	**H**	M	M	**H**	L
Avoid antitrust	**H**	L	**H**	**H**	**H**	M
Clarity	**H**	M	M	L	**H**	M

* L = low, M = medium, H = high

(b) Table S18.8 depicts multiple strategies for growth. The relative contributions and limitations of six major alternatives are depicted. The criteria in the first column reflect the important potential benefits of each alternative growth strategy. Compared with internal growth, mergers have the advantage of speed in adding capabilities, product, and markets. Joint ventures reduce antitrust problems, investment requirements, and risk. Alliances provide opportunities for gaining knowledge about new areas but the relationships have greater ambiguity. Licensing quickly adds revenues, but may create competitors. Investments in other companies may provide new knowledge, high returns, and lead to joint ventures and mergers.

9. Asset Restructuring
   (a)

   Solution to Table S18.9   Asset Restructuring

	Divestiture	Equity Carve-Out	Spin-Off	Tracking Stock
Raise funds	H	H	L	L
Improve efficiency by focus	M	M	H	H
Measure performance better	L	H	H	H
Tie compensation to performance	L	H	H	H
Parent focus on core business	H	H	H	M

(b) Table S18.9 illustrates alternative approaches to asset restructuring. The strength of divestitures is in raising funds and enabling the parent to focus on its core business. Equity carve-outs raise funds as an initial step toward a spin off. Spin offs may facilitate performance measurements and strengthen incentives. Tracking stocks achieve similar results but give the parent continuing control over the operations.

10. Changes in Ownership Structure
    (a)

    Table S18.10   Changes in Ownership Structure (Financial Engineering)

	Leveraged Recap	LBO or MBO	Dual-Class Recap	Share Repurchase	Proxy Contest
Infusion of new capital	H	H	M	L	L
Achieve a turnaround	M	H	M	L	M
Tax benefits	H	H	L	L	L
Takeover defense	H	H	H	M	H
Leverage is increased	H	H	L	H	L
Maintain control	H	H	H	M	L
Management incentives	M	H	L	L	M

(b) In Table S18.10, financial engineering and changes in financial structure are evaluated by a different set of criteria. A leveraged recap maintains control by a capital infusion to pay a large dividend to existing shareholders; management is compensated by additional shares of stock which increase their ownership percentage. Dual class recapitalizations enable management, often a founding group, to trade higher income to other shareholders in return for a class of stock with higher voting power. Share repurchases provide flexibility in returning cash to shareholders in a tax advantaged form, and also offset dilution from the exercise of stock options. A proxy contest represents an effort to change the management control group in a company.

11. (a)

Assets ($ millions)		Claims on Assets ($ millions)	
WATRO		Debt	$50
		Equity	50
Total assets	$100	Total claims	$100
ALBER		Debt	$20
		Equity	20
Total assets	$40	Total claims	$40
SABEN		Debt	$20
		Equity	20
Total assets	$40	Total claims	$40

(b)

	Watro	Alber	Saben
After-tax r	.09	.18	.15
Before-tax r = r/(1−T_c)	.15	.30	.25
EBIT = before-tax r (TA)	$15.00	$12.00	$10.00

(c) Using a form of Equation (14.21) for a levered firm, the value of the levered firm is:

$$V_L = \frac{EBIT_1(1-T_c)}{WACC} + K[EBIT_1(1-T_c)]N\left[\frac{r-WACC}{WACC(1+WACC)}\right] \quad (14.21)$$

Value of Watro:

$$V_W^L = \frac{(15)(1-.4)}{.09} + 1(15)(1-.4)(10)\left[\frac{.09-.09}{.09(1.09)}\right]$$

$$= \$100 + 0$$

$$= \$100$$

Value of Alber:

$$V_A^L = \frac{12(1-.4)}{.11} + 1(12)(1-.4)(10)\left[\frac{.18-.11}{.11(1.11)}\right]$$

$$= \$65.45 + 72(.5733)$$

$$= \$65.45 + 41.28$$

$$= \$106.73$$

Value of Saben:

$$V_S^L = \frac{10(1-.4)}{.12} + 1.5(10)(1-.4)(10)\left[\frac{.15-.12}{.12(1.12)}\right]$$

$$= \$50 + 90(.2232)$$

$$= \$50 + 20.09$$

$$= \$70.09$$

(d) Value of Watro-Alber combination:

$$V_{WA}^L = \frac{30(1-.4)}{.11} + 1.1(30)(1-.4)(10)\left[\frac{.2009-.11}{.11(1.11)}\right]$$

$$= \$163.63 + 198\,(.7445)$$

$$= \$163.63 + 147.41$$

$$= \$311.04$$

Value of Watro-Saben combination:

$$V_{WS}^L = \frac{23(1-.4)}{.12} + 1(23)(1-.4)(10)\left[\frac{.16-.12}{.12(1.12)}\right]$$

$$= \$115 + 138\,(.2976)$$

$$= \$115 + 41.07$$

$$= \$156.07$$

Value of Watro-Alber =	$311 million
Less value of Alber =	107 million
	$204 million
Less initial value of Watro =	100 million
Increase in value	$104 million
Value of Watro-Saben =	$156 million
Less value of Saben =	70 million
	$86 million
Less initial value of Watro =	100 million
Increase (decrease) in value	($14) million

12. (a)

Accounting Balance Sheets (millions of dollars)

	Jordan	Konrad	Loomis
Debt	$80	$40	$40
Equity	80	40	40
Total Assets	160	80	80

(b)

After tax r	6%	12%	15%
Before tax r = r/(1 − T_c) = r/.6	10%	20%	25%
EBIT = (before tax r) (TA)	$16	$16	$20

(c)

EBIT	$16	$16	$20
Less Interest (10% × debt)	−8	−4	−4
Income before taxes	8	12	16
Taxes @ 40%	−3.2	−4.8	−6.4
Net Income	4.8	7.2	9.6
EPS (earnings/shares) (in dollars)	$1.20	$3.60	$4.80
P/E	6X	15X	12X
Price = EPS (P/E) (in dollars)	$7.20	$54.00	$57.60
Total market value of equity (S)	28.8	108	115.2

(d) **Jordan Merges With**

	Konrad or	Loomis
1. $\dfrac{\text{share price of K or L}}{\text{share price of J}}$	7.5X	8X
2. number of acquired firm shares (millions)	2	2
3. number of new shares	15	16
4. number of old J shares	4	4
5. Total shares	19	20
6. Net income of J + net income of K or L	12	14.4
7. New EPS (in dollars per share)	$.632	$.72
8. J's original EPS (in dollars per share)	1.20	1.20
9. Dilution $\left(\left(\dfrac{\text{row 8} - \text{row 7}}{\text{row 8}}\right)100\right)$	47%	40%

(e) Because β's are additive, we simply weight the β of each firm according to the market value of its equity, as calculated in part (c). The total market value of equity for the proposed merged firm would be

JK: $136.8 million = (28.8 + 108)

JL: $144 million = (28.8 + 115.2)

$$\beta_{JK} = \frac{28.8}{136.8}(1.4) + \frac{108}{136.8}(1.2)$$
$$= .2947 + .9474$$
$$= 1.24$$

$$\beta_{JL} = \frac{28.8}{144}(1.4) + \frac{115.2}{144}(1.5)$$
$$= .28 + 1.2$$
$$= 1.48$$

The required return for equity of the proposed mergers can be found from the security market line:

$$E(R_j) = R_f + (E(R_m) - R_f)\beta_j$$

$$k_s(JK) = .06 + (.11 - .06)(1.24)$$

$$= 122 = 12.2\%$$

$$k_s(JL) = .06 + (.11 - .06)(1.48)$$

$$= 134 = 13.4\%$$

(f) Use the proposed merged firms' market values of debt and equity to determine the weights for the cost-of-capital formula. In this instance, the market value of the debt is assumed to be equal to its book value.

(in millions of dollars)	JK	JL
Debt (D = B)	$120	$120
Equity (S)	136.8	144
Value (V)	$256.8	$264

$$WACC = k_b (1 - T_c) (B/V) + k_s (S/V)$$

$$WACC_{JK} = (.10)(1 - .4)\left(\frac{120}{256.8}\right) + \frac{136.8}{256.8}(.122)$$

$$= .028 + .065$$

$$= .093 = 9.3\%$$

$$WACC_{JL} = (.10)(1 - .4)\left(\frac{120}{264}\right) + \frac{144}{264}(.134)$$

$$= .027 + .073$$

$$= .10 = 10\%$$

(g) Using the Modigliani-Miller valuation equation (equation 14.21) we have

$$V_0^L = \frac{EBIT_1(1 - T_c)}{k_u} + T_c B + K(EBIT_1)(1 - T_c)N\left[\frac{r - WACC}{WACC(1 + WACC)}\right]$$

where: $EBIT_1 (1 - T_c) = EBIT_0 (1 + g) (1 - T_c) =$ the after tax end-of-period cash flows from operations

$$WACC = k_u\left(1 - T_c\frac{B}{B + S}\right) = \text{the weighted average cost of capital}$$

$(1 + g) = (1 + Kr) =$ the growth rate of the firm

   $K =$ the investment rate (sometimes called the retention ratio)

   $B =$ the market value of debt

   $k_u =$ the cost of capital for an all equity firm

   $T_c =$ the marginal corporate tax rate

   $N =$ the number of years of supernormal growth where $r > WACC$

   $r =$ the rate of return anticipated on new investment

Note that:

$$V_L = \frac{EBIT_1(1 - T_c)}{WACC} = \frac{EBIT_1(1 - T_c)}{k_u} + T_c B$$

Using this fact and the parameters of the problem we have

$$V(JK) = \frac{32(1 - .4)}{.093} + (1)(32)(1 - .4)(10)\left[\frac{.16 - .093}{.093(1 + .093)}\right]$$

$$= 206.45 + 126.5$$

$$= \$333.00 \text{ million}$$

For JL, we have

$$V(JL) = \frac{36(1 - .4)}{.10} + (1)(36)(1 - .4)(10)\left[\frac{.13 - .10}{.10(1 + .10)}\right]$$

$$= 216 + 58.91$$

$$= \$274.91 \text{ million}$$

figures in millions of dollars	JK	JL
Post-merger value (V)	$333.00	$274.91
Less: amount of debt (B)	120.00	120.00
Value of equity (S)	213.00	154.91
Less: J's pre-merger market value of equity	28.8	28.8
Gain in equity value	184.2	126.11
Cost if acquired at market (market value of equity for K or L)	108.0	115.20
Gain in value (loss)	$76.2	$10.91

If Jordan merges with Konrad, the indicated net increase in value is $76.2 million. A merger with Loomis results in a gain of $10.91 million in value. The merger with Konrad is preferred and it also meets the capital budgeting requirement of having a substantial positive net value. Jordan could pay a premium to Konrad shareholders and still have a positive NPV.

Chapter 19
International Financial Management

1 Interest Rate Parity for FC/$:

In the text example of covered interest arbitrage the foreign exchange rate was expressed as dollars per euros. It is also useful to analyze the adjustment processes for departures from IRP when the foreign exchange rate is expressed as Mexican pesos (foreign currency) per dollars.

(a) Parity relationships are illustrated in Table S19.1a. One hundred dollars invested in a dollar security gives an end of year return of $105. Alternatively, we could convert the $100 dollars into pesos at the spot rate of 10p/$. Simultaneously we enter into a forward contract in which pesos are exchanged for dollars at an exchange rate 10.38p/$. The 1000p invested in the Mexican security carrying a 9% rate has an end of year value of 1090p. This amount is exchanged at the forward rate shown in Table S19.1a to obtain $105. The premium on the dollar is matched by the differential interest rate paid on the peso denominated security, so IRP obtains.

Table S19.1a   Example of Interest Rate Parity
(A) Equilibrium Mexican Peso and U.S. Dollar, $F_{p/\$,0} = 10.381p/\$$

$S_{p/\$,0} = 10p/\$$

$F_{p/\$,0} = 10.381p/\$$

$R_{\$,0} = 5\%$ per annum

$R_{p,0} = 9\%$ per annum

	Year 0	Year 1
Dollar	$100	$\$100 \times (1 + R_{\$,0}) = \$100 \times 1.05$ $= \$105.0$
Peso	$\$100 \times S_{p/\$,0}$ $= \$100 \times 10p/\$$ $= 1000p$	in pesos: $1000p \times (1 + R_{p,0})$ $= 1000p \times 1.09$ $= 1090p$ in $: $1090p \times (1/F_{p/\$,0})$ $= 1090p \times (\$1/10.381p)$ $= \$105.0$

$$\frac{F_{p/\$,0} - S_{p/\$,0}}{S_{p/\$,0}} = \frac{R_{p,0} - R_{\$,0}}{1 + R_{\$,0}}$$

$$\frac{10.381 - 10}{10} = \frac{0.09 - 0.05}{1.05}$$

$$\frac{0.381}{10} = \frac{0.04}{1.05}$$

$$0.03810 = 0.03810$$

(b) Case B, Table S19.1b reflects the condition that the forward rate for the peso is higher than the IRP rate holding everything else the same. The forward premium on the dollar is increased to 5%. Hence, capital will flow from pesos to dollars. The analysis will show that the return from investing in a dollar security will be higher than investing in a peso security. An investment is made in pesos to provide a comparison return. Alternatively, the pesos borrowed are converted into dollars at the spot exchange rate to obtain $100. The $100 is invested in the dollar denominated security to yield $105 at the end of the period. A forward contract has been entered into in which at the end of the year dollars are converted into pesos at the forward rate of 10.5p/$. This yields 1102.5p, representing a gain on the roundtrip of 12.5p, discounted at the U.S. rate, its present value is 11.905p which is equal to the forward premium of the dollar less the premium of the interest rate on the peso security over the interest rate of the dollar security.

Table S19.1b   Example Covered Interest Rate Arbitrage
(B) Mexican Peso to U.S. Dollar, $F_{p/\$,0} = 10.5p/\$$

$S_{p/\$,0} = 10p/\$$

$F_{p/\$,0} = 10.5p/\$$

$R_{\$,0} = 5\%$ per annum

$R_{p,0} = 9\%$ per annum

	Year 0	Year 1
Borrow (short) pesos. Repay at $R_{p,0}$	$-1000p$	$-1000p \times (1 + R_{p,0})$ $= -1000p \times 1.09$ $= -1090p$
Sell pesos spot. Invest (long) dollars at $R_{\$,0}$. Buy peso forward.	$1000p \times (1/S_{p/\$,0})$ $= 1000p \times (\$1/10p)$ $= \$100$	in \$: $\$100 \times (1 + R_{p,0})$ $= \$100 \times 1.05$ $= \$105.0$ in pesos: $\$105.0 \times F_{p/\$,0}$ $= \$105.0 \times 10.5p/\$$ $= 1102.5p$
Net peso position	0p	$-1090p + 1102.5p$ $= 12.5p$
PV net peso position at $R_{\$,0}$	0p	$12.5p/(1.05)$ $= 11.905p$

$$d = \frac{F_{p/\$,0} - S_{p/\$,0}}{S_{p/\$,0}} - \frac{R_{p,0} - R_{\$,0}}{1 + R_{\$,0}}$$

$$= \frac{10.5 - 10}{10} - \frac{0.09 - 0.05}{1.05}$$

$$= \frac{0.5}{10} - \frac{0.04}{1.05}$$

$$= 0.05 - 0.03810$$

$$= 0.01190$$

(c) In Case C, Table S19.1c, the dollar is at a discount in the forward market, so outflows take place from dollars to pesos. The reference investment will be to sell a dollar security short. At the end of the year, the investor owes $105. Alternatively, we convert the $100 into pesos at the spot exchange rate of 10p/$, simultaneously entering a forward contract in which pesos will be converted into dollars at the current forward rate of 9.8p/$. The amount of dollars received is $111.225. The investor can close his short position with a gain of $6.225. This amount converted into pesos at the forward rate and discounted at the U.S. interest rate gives 58.095p which is equal to the algebraic difference between the forward discount of the dollar and the discount on the dollar interest rate.

Table S19.1c   Example of Covered Interest Arbitrage
(C) U.S. Dollar to Mexican Peso, $F_{p/\$,0}$ = 9.8p/$

$S_{p/\$,0}$ = 10p/$

$F_{p/\$,0}$ = 9.8p/$

$R_{\$,0}$ = 5% per annum

$R_{p,0}$ = 9% per annum

	Year 0	Year 1
Borrow (short) $100. Repay at $R_{\$,0}$	−$100	−$100 × (1 + $R_{\$,0}$) = −$100 × 1.05 = −$105.0
Buy peso spot. Invest (long) peso at $R_{p,0}$. Sell peso forward.	$100 × $S_{p/\$,0}$ =$100 × 10p/$ = 1000p	in pesos: 1000p × (1 + $R_{p,0}$) = 1000p × 1.09 = 1090p in $: 1090p × (1/$F_{p/\$,0}$) = 1090p × ($1/9.8p) = $111.225
Net dollar position	$0	−$105.0 + $111.225 = $6.225
Net peso position	0p	$6.225 × $F_{p/\$,0}$ = $6.225 × 9.8p/$ = 61.0p
PV net peso position at $R_{\$,0}$	0p	61.0p/(1.05) = 58.095p

$$d = \frac{F_{p/\$,0} - S_{p/\$,0}}{S_{p/\$,0}} - \frac{R_{p,0} - R_{\$,0}}{1 + R_{\$,0}}$$

$$= \frac{9.8 - 10}{10} - \frac{0.09 - 0.05}{1.05}$$

$$= \frac{-0.2}{10} - \frac{0.04}{1.05}$$

$$= -0.02 - 0.03810$$

$$= -0.05810$$

(d) In Figure S19.1, the IRP (Table S19.1a) is plotted as point A in the first quadrant with coordinates of 0.0381. Point B calculated from the data in Table S19.1b plots as 0.05 on the dollar premium axis and 0.0381 on the interest differential axis. Note also that it plots above the IRP line in the area where capital inflows take place from the peso to the dollar. Point C calculated from the data in Table S19.1c plots below the IRP line in the area of capital outflows with coordinates (−0.0381, −0.02). The adjustment processes move toward decreasing the dollar discount in the forward market and/or decreasing the interest rate differential of a dollar security versus a peso security.

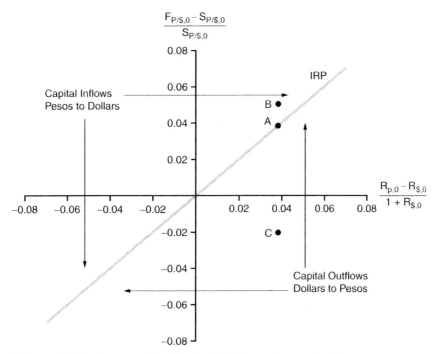

Figure S19.1 Interest Rate Parity Relations Pesos, Dollars

2. (a) Two possible explanations for the bias are common in the literature. One is that $\beta < 1$ is evidence of a risk premium on foreign exchange. If investors are risk averse and foreign exchange risk is not fully diversifiable, the interest differential or the forward rate discount is no longer a pure estimate of the expected change in future exchange rates, but the sum of the expected change in the exchange rate plus a risk premium. When the dollar interest rate rises, investments in dollar assets become more risky. Another explanation is that the bias is evidence of expectational errors. An example of expectational errors could be a counter monetary, fiscal shock, or real economy shock. Specifically, in the country with higher interest rates, unexpected major improvements in economic activity could raise real interest rates. Hence, the higher nominal rates could represent lower future inflation rates since the higher real rates deducted from the nominal rates would represent lower inflation rates.

(b) Investment banks had sought to develop models forecasting foreign exchange rates based on movements from short run departures, but long run movements toward parity relationships. The Deutsche Bank explains the forward rate bias as resulting from investors risk aversion to short term losses that can be substantial (Deutsche Bank, *FX Weekly*, January 24, 2003, p. 4–7). Hence, currencies trading at a forward discount (premium), on average, tend to weaken (rise) less than what is implied by the forward discount (premium). Thus currencies trading at a forward discount tend to outperform those trading at a forward premium. This bias could be exploited by taking long positions in currencies that trade at a forward discount and short currencies that trade at a forward premium. In theory, in the long run, this arbitrage opportunity will disappear as investors make such trades. But because of risk aversion, the forward rate bias persists.

The Deutsche Bank investment strategy is to go long in the three highest-yielding (highest forward discount) currencies and going short in the three lowest-yielding (highest forward premium) currencies. This is called going long in the forward-rate bias trades. This strategy is combined with a daily optimized technical moving-average model that yields a trading rule on when to move in and out of the forward-rate bias trades, i.e., whether to go long in the forward-rate bias trade or to close the position and do nothing.

3. (a) Exchange rate uncertainties may be reduced by offsetting economic developments within the larger area.

    Transaction costs of exchanging one currency for another are avoided.

    The fixed exchange relationships within the union avoid speculative attacks.

    (b) A country loses monetary and fiscal independence.

    A country loses the use of the exchange rate as a mechanism to facilitate adjustments to shocks among the nations within the union.

    (c) Benefits are greater than costs if the underlying economies are highly integrated which implies a high level in trade in goods. Labor mobility between countries in the union is high. Monetary and fiscal integration are successfully integrated.

4. The parity conditions are equilibrium relationships. They represent strong forces toward which foreign exchange rates will move. The parity conditions therefore represent a useful framework for guiding economic policies. In addition, forecasters are guided by the parity conditions as relationships toward which exchange rates will move.

5. If country A imports X, the price is $FC12 \times (\$1/FC5) = \$2.40$.

    If country B imports X, the price is $\$3 \times (FC5/\$1) = FC15$.

    Other prices can be calculated the same way. Results are summarized in Table S19.5

Table S19.5   Domestic and Import Prices When FC5 = $1

Product X		
A imports $2.40	vs.	$3.00 domestic
B imports FC15	vs.	FC12 domestic

Product Y		
A imports $1.20	vs.	$1.00 domestic
B imports FC5	vs.	FC6 domestic

Hence country A would import X and export Y. Country B would export X and import Y. Equilibrium would require for B: For one unit of X exported B could import 6Z of Y.

$$12 = 6Z$$

$$Z = 2 = \text{number of units of imports of Y.}$$

For A: We have exports of 2Y and imports of 1X from B.

$$\text{So } FC12/W = 2(\$1), W = FC6/\$1 \text{ so } FC6 = \$1.$$

We then have:

$$\begin{array}{lll} \text{A imports } 1X = \$2 & \text{and} & \text{exports } 2Y = \$2. \\ \text{B exports } 1X = FC12 & \text{and} & \text{imports } 2Y = FC12. \end{array}$$

At FC6 = $1, each country's exports and imports are equal in total value measured in units of its own currency.

6. A formulation first set forth in the mid-eighteenth century is the price-gold-flow mechanism. Country A runs an export balance surplus, while Country B runs a deficit. Hence gold flows into Country A while it flows out of Country B. Domestic prices in Country A rise, the prices in Country B fall. Country A is an attractive market in which to increase sales from other countries and A's imports increase. A's goods are more expensive in other countries so its export sales decrease. A's export surplus will be reduced or reversed until equilibrium between relative price relationships of the countries is restored. The flows of gold operate through prices to function as an adjustment mechanism for international balances of trade and payments as well as to regulate the price change relationships between countries.

    Income and employment effects may also enter into the adjustment process as well as price changes. IF the surplus country was not functioning at full employment, the export surplus increases its income and employment. The export deficit decreases income and employment in the deficit country. Also, in the adjustment process, employment may decline in A and increase in B.

7. The A currency has four times as much gold content. Hence 1A will be equal to 4B. Or 1B is worth 0.25A.

8. To illustrate the operation of the adjustment process let us assume an initial relationship of $1 to 4 FC: $1 = FC4.

    Let us now assume that the volume of imports in the United States exceeds its exports in relationship to countries whose currency is the FC. The demand for FC relative to dollars increases. The value of the dollar falls. Let us assume, for purposes of illustration, that the new relationship is now: $1 = FC2.

    At the new exchange rate, the prices of the U.S. imports and exports in dollars rise. For example, suppose that an auto sold in the United States for $2,000 when the exchange rate was $1 to FC4. A sale at $2,000 provided the auto exporter with FC8,000. At the new exchange rate the auto exporter still seeks to receive FC8,000. But to do so at the new exchange rates, he must receive $4,000 for the auto.

    Similarly, at the old exchange rate, the U.S. sold wheat at $4 per bushel, receiving FC16. At the new exchange rates, in order to receive $4 per bushel, the wheat can be sold at FC8. Thus the prices of imports in dollars would rise substantially at the new exchange rates. Conversely, the prices of exports in the foreign currency have fallen. The dollar price for exports could be increased and still represent substantially lower prices in the foreign currency.

    In the U.S., import purchases would have to be made at higher prices and export sales could be made under more favorable conditions than before. Conversely, in the foreign country, lower prices in FC for both their imports and exports would stimulate purchases from the U.S. and reduce sales to the U.S.

    Note the adjustment process. A higher rate of inflation in the U.S. results in higher relative prices. U.S. imports rise and its exports fall. Conversely for the foreign country, the increased relative demand for FC in relation to the $, causes the FC to rise in value relative to the $. But the higher value of the FC causes imports into the U.S. to be more expensive in $ and to represent a smaller number of FC to exporters at previous $ prices in the U.S. At higher $ prices in the U.S., the demand for foreign goods will decline. Conversely, the demand for U.S. goods in the foreign country will rise. The change in exchange rates in response to shifts in relative prices helps readjust the export–import imbalances.

An argument for the use of flexible exchange rates is that trade imbalances caused by changed relative prices of domestic and foreign goods are adjusted through shifts in exchange rates. The prices of internationally traded goods carry most of the adjustment process.

9.

a)	Plus 1.	$10,000	Minus 2.	$10,000
b)	Plus 2.	$5,000	Minus 1.	$5,000
c)	Plus 1.	$2,000	Minus 3.	$2,000
d)	Plus 2.	$1 million	Minus 3a.	$1 million
e)	Plus 2.	$3,000	Minus 1.	$3,000
f)	Plus 2.	$500	Minus 1.	$500

10. (a) The PPP:

$$\frac{X_1}{X_0} = \frac{P_{f1}/P_{f0}}{P_{d1}/P_{d0}}$$

In this example, the subscript d represents the U.S., and f represents foreign. $X_0 = 3/1$ is the beginning exchange ratio. So we solve for X_1:

$$\frac{X_1}{3} = \frac{1.05}{1.10}$$

$$1.1X_1 = 3.15$$

$$X_1 = 2.8636$$

The expected future spot rate is FC2.86 per $1.

(b) The Fisher Relation is

$$\frac{1+r}{1+R_n} = \frac{P_0}{P_1}$$

where r = the real interest rate and R_n is the nominal interest rate. We know that the U.S. inflation rate = 10%, and the foreign country inflation rate = 5%. The Fisher Relation may be written as

$$1 + R_n = (1 + r)(P_1/P_0)$$

Solving for the foreign country,
$1 + R_n = (1.04)(1.05) = 1.092 = 9.2\%$ nominal interest rate for the foreign country.
For the U.S.,
$1 + R_n = (1.040)(1.10) = 1.144 = 14.4\%$ nominal interest rate for the U.S.

(c) The Interest Rate Parity relation is:

$$\frac{X_f}{X_0} = \frac{1+R_{f0}}{1+R_{d0}}$$

where R_{f0} is the nominal interest rate in the foreign country, and R_{d0} is the nominal rate in the U.S. X_0 is the current exchange rate, and X_f is the forward rate. So we solve for X_f.

$$\frac{X_f}{3} = \frac{1.092}{1.144}$$

$$1.144 \, X_f = 3.276$$

$$X_f = 2.8636$$

(d) The estimates are the same.

(e) The Fisher relation for country f can be written

$$\frac{1+R_f}{1+r} = \frac{P_{f1}}{P_{f0}} \qquad (1)$$

and for country d,

$$\frac{1+R_d}{1+r} = \frac{P_{d1}}{P_{d0}} \qquad (2)$$

dividing (1) by (2) (and assuming the real rate of interest is equal across the two countries), we have

$$\frac{1+R_f}{1+R_d} = \frac{\dfrac{P_{f1}}{P_{f0}}}{\dfrac{P_{d1}}{P_{d0}}}$$

The left-hand side is IRP = $\dfrac{1+R_f}{1+R_d} = \dfrac{X_1}{X_0}$

The right-hand side is the PPP = $\dfrac{P_{f1}/P_{f0}}{P_{d1}/P_{d0}} = \dfrac{X_1}{X_0}$

The fundamental relations assumed are certainty, equal real rates of interest, and equilibrium.

11. (a)

Loan amount $1,000,000
Interest @ 10% $ 100,000

Amount received in pesos = $1,000,000 × 10 =   10,000,000 pesos
Amount repaid in pesos = $1,100,000 × 10.5 =   11,550,000 pesos
Effective interest paid in pesos   1,550,000 pesos

Interest rate = $\dfrac{\text{Interest paid in pesos}}{\text{Pesos received}} = \dfrac{1,550,000}{10,000,000} = 15.5\%$

(b) *Interest Rate Parity Theorem*

$$\frac{1+R_{f0}}{1+R_{d0}} = \frac{X_f}{X_d}$$

$X_f = 10.5$ pesos/$, $X_0 = 10$ pesos/$ and $R_{d0} = 10\%$

$$\frac{1+R_{f0}}{1.10} = \frac{10.5}{10}$$
$$1+R_{f0} = 1.05(1.10)$$
$$R_{f0} = 15.5\%$$

If the interest rate in Mexico were below 15.5%, it would have been cheaper to borrow in pesos than to borrow in dollars at 10%, which was an effective rate of 15.5%.

12. (a) The company goes long on FC futures. It buys FCs at the current forward rate for delivery in 180 days, to pay for the machinery at that time.

(b) Use Interest Rate Parity relation

$$\frac{X_f}{X_0} = \frac{1 + R_{f0}\left[\dfrac{n}{365}\right]}{1 + R_{d0}\left[\dfrac{n}{365}\right]}$$

Solving for the forward rate

$$\frac{X_f}{2.08} = \frac{1 + 0.08/2}{1 + 0.09/2}$$

$$= 2.08\left(\frac{1.040}{1.045}\right)$$

$$= 2.08(0.9952)$$

$$X_f = 2.07 \text{ FC/\$}$$

(c) FC are more expensive by the commission, so the net result is fewer FC/\$.

$$2.07/1.0025 = 2.0648379 \text{ FC/\$}$$

(d) The dollar price is FC 4.6 million divided by the 6 month forward rate of FC per dollar (including commission costs):

$$4,600,000 \text{ FC}/(2.0648379 \text{ FC/\$}) = \$2,227,778.$$

13. (a) It goes long on dollar futures. It buys dollars at the current forward rate for delivery in 180 days.

(b) By IRP,

$$\frac{E_0}{E_f} = \frac{1 + R_{f0}\left[\dfrac{n}{365}\right]}{1 + R_{d0}\left[\dfrac{n}{365}\right]}$$

$$\frac{\$0.49}{E_f} = \frac{(1 + 0.08/2)}{(1 + 0.09/2)}$$

$$= \$0.49(1.004807692)$$

$$E_f = \$0.492356/\text{FC}$$

(c) Dollars are more expensive; so commission decreases the dollar value of the FC.

$$0.492356/1.0025 = \$0.491128/\text{FC}$$

(d)

$$\$10,000,000/(\$0.491128/\text{FC}) = \text{FC } 20,361,291$$

14. (a) First calculate the amount borrowed now in FC currency that will yield FC 380,000 in 3 months. If the amount = X, then:

$$X[1 + R_n \, (n/365)(1 - \tau)] = FC \; 380{,}000$$

Substituting the correct numbers,

$$X[1 + (0.28/4) \, (1 - 0.4)] = FC \; 380{,}000$$

$$X(1.042) = 380{,}000$$

$$X = 364{,}683$$

This amount plus interest equals FC 380,000 in three months. Divide by the current exchange rate to convert this amount to dollars,

$$FC \; 364{,}683/1.90 = 191{,}939$$

Now compound the dollar amount for three months, at the U.S. nominal interest rate, to determine the final net payment in dollars.

$$191{,}939[1 + (0.08/4)(1 - 0.4)] = 191{,}939(1.012) = \$194{,}242$$

At the end of the three months, Globalcorp receives FC 380,000 which it uses to pay off the principal plus interest on the FC 384,683 loan. Globalcorp realizes $194,242.

(b) If the payment were made immediately, Globalcorp would receive

$$FC \; 380{,}000/(FC1.90/\$) = \$200{,}000$$

$$\$200{,}000 - 194{,}242 = \$5{,}758$$

This amount is equivalent to an "insurance premium" that Globalcorp is paying to limit the magnitude of unexpected foreign exchange rate losses during the next three months.

(c) To determine the equivalent (non-arbitrage) forward rate, use the relationship:

$$\frac{F_0}{X_f} + \left[\left(\frac{F_0}{X_0} - \frac{F_0}{X_f} \right) \tau_{US} \right] = 194{,}242$$

$$\underset{\substack{\text{amount} \\ \text{received}}}{} \qquad \underset{\substack{\text{tax shelter} \\ \text{on loss}}}{}$$

$$\frac{F_0}{X_f} + \frac{F_0}{X_0}(\tau_{US}) - \frac{F_0}{X_f}(\tau_{US}) = 194{,}242$$

$$\frac{380{,}000}{X_f} + \frac{380{,}000(0.4)}{1.90} - \frac{380{,}000(0.4)}{X_f} = 194{,}242$$

$$380{,}000 + 80{,}000 \, X_f - 152{,}000 = 194{,}242 \, X_f$$

$$114{,}242 \, X_f = 228{,}000$$

$$X_f = FC \; 2.00/\$$$

(d) Globalcorp would have sold FC forward short. When Globalcorp was paid in FC, they could have covered their short position. The speculator would go long in FC. If the speculator receives a risk premium for going long in FC, this means X_f (the forward exchange rate in FC/$) is lower (its value higher) than the expected future spot rate of FC/$.

15. (a) Let X be the amount of FC which, when invested, will equal FC 380,000 in 6 months. Then,

$$X[1 + (0.08/2)(1 - 0.4)] = FC\ 380,000$$

$$X(1.024) = FC\ 380,000$$

$$X = FC\ 371,093.75$$

If FC 371,094 is invested in the foreign country today, it will yield FC 380,000 in six months. The amount that must be borrowed in dollars today to convert to FC is

$$FC\ 371,094/(FC\ 2.00/\$) = \$185,547$$

The net cost (or opportunity lost) that results from this $185,547 investment is equal to the amount Transcorp could have earned if the dollars had been invested in the U.S.

$$X = [1 + (0.12/2)(1 - .04)](185,547)$$

$$= (1.036)(185,547)$$

$$= \$192,227 \text{ net cost}$$

(b) If payment were made immediately, Transcorp would pay

$$380,000/(FC\ 2.00/\$) = \$190,000$$

The difference between this amount and their actual cost, including opportunity loss, is $192,227 − 190,000 = \$2,227$. This represents an insurance premium against a rise in the FC rate while Transcorp delays six months in making the FC payment.

(c)

$$E_f F_0 + (E_f - E_0)\ F_0\ (\tau_{US}) = \$192,227$$

$$380,000\ E_f + (0.4)(380,000)\ E_f - (0.5)(380,000)(0.4) = \$192,227$$

$$380,000\ E_f + 152,000\ E_f - 76,000 = 192,227$$

$$532,000\ E_f = 268,227$$

$$E_f = \$0.5042/FC$$

Transcorp would go long in FC forward to hedge their position, and insure payment abroad in six months.

(d) The speculator would short the FC forward. If the speculator receives a premium for his short position then $E_f > E_1$, i.e., he sells at a higher forward value of FC relative to the future expected spot rate. E.g., $E_1 = 0.5042$, $E_f = 0.505$.